Ready for Air

Ready for Air

A Journey through Premature Motherhood

Kate Hopper

University of Minnesota Press
Minneapolis • London

"Relinquishment" is from *The Dead and the Living* by Sharon Olds, copyright 1987 by Sharon Olds. Reprinted by permission of Alfred A. Knopf, a division of Random House, Inc. Any third-party use of this material, outside of this publication, is prohibited. Interested parties must apply directly to Random House, Inc. for permission.

Published by the University of Minnesota Press
111 Third Avenue South, Suite 290
Minneapolis, MN 55401-2520
http://www.upress.umn.edu

Library of Congress Cataloging-in-Publication Data
Hopper, Kate.
Ready for air : a journey through premature motherhood / Kate Hopper.
ISBN 978-0-8166-8932-3 (pb : alk. paper)
1. Hopper, Kate—Health. 2. Premature infants—Biography. 3. Premature infants—Care. 4. Premature infants—Care—Psychological aspects. 5. Mother and infant—Psychological aspects. I. Title.
RJ250.H59 2013
618.92′011—dc23

2013014537

Printed in the United States of America on acid-free paper

The University of Minnesota is an equal-opportunity educator and employer.

20 19 18 17 16 15 14 13   10 9 8 7 6 5 4 3 2 1

For my family

As if no one had ever tried before,
try to say what you see
and feel and love and lose.

RAINER MARIA RILKE

1

IT'S MIDMORNING, BUT ALREADY THE AIR IS THICK and the streets are gummy. Heat rises in rippling waves from the asphalt, inflating me beyond what pregnancy seems to mandate. At seven months pregnant, the only shoes that still fit are plastic flip-flops, and as I make my way slowly into the heart of downtown, they slap against the concrete. I should have splurged on the parking ramp next to my obstetrician's office, but it's a luxury I can't afford.

I didn't expect pregnancy to be so unpleasant. My mother claims that she never felt better, that she was "full of energy," that she "glowed." She looks perplexed when I tell her how much I hate it. But it's not just the swelling and heaviness I dislike, or even having to eliminate alcohol, caffeine, and decongestant from my diet; it's the worrying and waiting that bother me most. Pregnancy has brought my neuroses bubbling to the surface, and I worry about everything: the six (or ten?) glasses of wine I downed in the days before I knew I was pregnant; the antidepressants I weaned myself from during those first weeks; the level of mercury in the fish I ate last month. I also worry about things like cell division, meiosis and mitosis, those hazy terms from high school biology that now have an immediate bearing on my life, on my child's life.

My mom says she didn't worry about any of those things when she was pregnant. "We didn't know enough to be worried," she says. I raise my eyebrows, skeptical. I'm convinced that her memory has rewritten the worry just as it has rewritten the discomfort of pregnancy: the swollen ankles, the bloating, the sluggishness.

To make matters worse, I've developed a horrible cough. It's a dry, hacking cough, and by the time I get to the center of downtown, my chest feels raw and heavy. I'm determined to get my doctor to prescribe something to quell it.

I'm drenched by the time I check in with the receptionist and make my way into the bathroom to leave a urine sample. I drink liters of water every day, but in the last few weeks, I haven't been peeing much at all. Today, as I twist the lid onto the container, I notice that I've captured less than two ounces. But I'm sweating so much in this heat, it's no wonder.

The nurse weighs me, and I cringe when the scale settles at 173 pounds. "Oh, my God," I say. "I've gained almost fifty pounds!" The nurse's only response is a tight smile, and I'm immediately embarrassed by my outrage. We are supposed to gain weight, after all. But fifty pounds seems excessive considering I still have two months until my due date. And a few weeks ago I even gave up my nightly bowl of chocolate ice cream, a sacrifice that apparently hasn't made a difference.

The nurse checks my blood pressure, then leaves me in the small exam room, where I lie on the table, coughing. Each time I cough, my belly tightens, and I wonder if it's possible to cough myself into early labor.

"What are you doing in there, sweetie?" I whisper. We know the baby is a girl. I had an ultrasound a few weeks ago to rule out placenta previa, a condition in which the placenta attaches to the uterine wall on or near the cervix. An earlier ultrasound had indicated this might be a problem, but in the follow-up my placenta looked fine. Donny wasn't able to make the appointment because he had just started his first teaching job, and although we were desperate to know the baby's gender, I didn't want to discover it without him. As the doctor wiped the cool gel from my belly, I asked her to write the baby's gender on a piece of paper and seal it in an envelope.

I carried it in my purse all day, periodically removing it to hold it in my hands, as if the weight of it alone would reveal the answer. The moment Donny walked through the door that afternoon, we tore it open. We both started to cry when we saw the doctor's writing: "It's a girl!"

I was relieved to be having a girl because I felt I understood girls. Clearly *I* was a girl, and I grew up with two sisters and no brothers. A boy represented challenges I didn't feel ready to meet. I worried about teaching him to respect women. What if he wasn't as kind and gentle as Donny?

There is a knock on the door, and Dr. Bradford steps into the room. "How are you feeling?" she asks, closing the door behind her. She's a no-nonsense doctor, and I like her.

"Awful," I say, pulling myself up to a sitting position. "I have a terrible cough." I'm convinced that if she sees how miserable I am, she'll give me a prescription for something strong—safe for the baby, of course, but strong enough to allow me to sleep at night.

Dr. Bradford looks down at my chart. Her dark hair is cut short around her face, and her glasses are stylish in a midfifties kind of way.

I begin to cough again, and Dr. Bradford furrows her brow.

"It feels even worse than it sounds," I manage. "And the semester just started." I teach creative writing at the University of Minnesota, where I'm also a graduate student, and yesterday I hacked my way through the first meeting of my intermediate nonfiction course. My students were, quite appropriately, disgusted.

Dr. Bradford looks down at my feet, dangling over the edge of the examination table. "Colds," she says slowly, "take time to pass through your system when you're pregnant."

That's it? You're not going to give me anything for this?

She points at my plastic flip-flops on the floor. "Is that what you're wearing?"

"Yeah," I say, sheepishly. "None of my other shoes fit anymore."

Dr. Bradford kneels and presses her fingers into the mottled skin of my ankles, leaving imprints of her thumbs in my flesh. When she stands up, she says, "I'm worried about a couple of things."

Ha! I knew the rattling in my chest was serious.

"You're leaking a little protein in your urine," she says, glancing at her clipboard.

"Oh," I say, not knowing what that means.

"You've also gained nine pounds in the last two weeks," she says.

"I know," I say, grimacing. "But I've been cutting back."

Dr. Bradford shakes her head. "It's not from eating. You're retaining water."

I cough hard and look down at my feet, which have begun to

throb. Tonight they will be so swollen and itchy that I'll have to sit on the edge of the bathtub and soak them in freezing water before bed or I won't be able to fall asleep. But it's not just my feet that are swollen; my collarbone has been enveloped by flesh, and when I look in the mirror I hardly recognize the chubby face staring back at me.

"Water retention is common during pregnancy," Dr. Bradford says, "but I'm concerned because you're also leaking protein." Her brown eyes are earnest. "Both of these are signs of pregnancy-induced hypertension."

There is something like a hiccup in my chest, and the room suddenly feels too cold. I shift on the exam table, and the paper sticks to my thighs and tears loudly. Dr. Bradford doesn't seem to notice.

"Have you heard of it?" she asks.

I cough into my shoulder and nod, searching my mind for the paragraph I read when I was looking for an explanation—other than the weather—for my swollen feet. I remember that one book said *extreme* swelling could be a sign of pregnancy-induced hypertension, or preeclampsia, but I didn't think I was extremely swollen. Was I? I mean, how do you know?

"The good thing," Dr. Bradford goes on, "is that your blood pressure is beautiful."

I never would have put "beautiful" and "blood pressure" together, and this suddenly seems very funny to me. I smile, spreading my hands over my huge belly.

Dr. Bradford tilts her head, looking perplexed, and I realize I'm not responding the way she expected. But how does one respond? I wish Donny were here. He would know what to say. Or he would help *me* know what to say, his light eyes somehow slicing through clutter to help me think more clearly. Finally, I ask whether pregnancy-induced hypertension is the same thing as preeclampsia.

"Yes," she says, "but we don't call it preeclampsia anymore."

"Oh," I say, wondering if that's a good thing.

"You don't have it yet, but you have signs of it, so I want to keep an eye on you." Dr. Bradford looks at me over the rims of her glasses. "I'm going to have you come back next week rather than waiting two weeks. In the meantime, you need to take it easy."

Ready for Air

"The semester just started," I say lamely, my to-do list suddenly lumbering awake in my mind, each bullet point clamoring for attention.

"You're teaching?"

"Yes."

"You might need to rethink that."

"Oh," I say. I don't tell Dr. Bradford that I can't stop teaching. I don't tell her that I had to fight for this class—my dream class. I don't tell her about the countless hours I spent this summer walking from one University building to another, filling out forms, submitting them and resubmitting them in order to receive a paid six-week maternity leave in November. I don't tell her that I *must* teach if I want the University to continue paying for my graduate classes and my health insurance.

"Do you have a scale at home?" Dr. Bradford asks.

I shake my head.

"Well, you should get one. I want you to weigh yourself before bed and then first thing in the morning. If you gain more than one pound overnight, call me." Dr. Bradford takes off her glasses and rubs the bridge of her nose. When she puts them back on, she looks at me. "The other things to watch for are severe headaches, pain in your shoulder or upper abdomen, blurry vision, and vomiting."

"Oh," I say, suddenly sober, trying to memorize these symptoms. *Headaches, pain in shoulder or abdomen, blurry vision, vomiting.*

"I'll see you next week," she says, opening the door. "And remember to take it easy."

"Okay," I say again, but I'm not sure how I can do less than what I am doing. I raise my hand in a half-wave as Dr. Bradford shuts the door behind her.

When I walk out of the office a few minutes later, I'm clutching an appointment card with one hand and my belly with the other. I concentrate on the heat of my skin as I step into the bustle of downtown. I don't notice the cars or the blaring of horns. I don't notice the sweat running down the backs of my legs. I walk the eight blocks back to my car, holding tight to my belly and trying to convince myself that everything will be fine.

2

As I DRIVE THE TEN MINUTES HOME TO OUR SMALL two-story house in South Minneapolis, I stare at my thick fingers on the steering wheel. A few weeks ago, I removed my engagement and wedding rings and tucked them into a corner of my jewelry box. This seemed a normal-enough ritual, something that many pregnant women do during their third trimester. But now that I know my swelling is *not* normal, I can't believe I ever thought it was. My wrists are as thick as ankles. And as I stare at my stretched skin, worry takes over. I have no idea what this means for the baby. What if something happens to her? But I remind myself what Dr. Bradford said—the swelling and protein are just signs, something to watch.

I pull up in front of our pale-green house, which we moved into three months ago. Donny and I have been married for almost four years, but this is our first house, and it's still difficult for me to believe that it's really ours. When I push open the door, I drop my purse on the sofa and pause, taking in the slant of sun across the maple floor. Even in the heat, the house feels light, airy, and this reassures me. The baby will be fine. Everything will be fine.

Still, I need to understand what I'm up against. I need facts to ground me before I tell anyone, even Donny, about the appointment. Otherwise, as soon as I hear his voice I'll begin to cry. I walk upstairs to our bedroom, where, on the floor next to our bed, there is a small library of books cataloging each phase of fetal development. I toss them onto the bed and settle myself in a circle of words.

I read that pregnancy-induced hypertension (PIH), or preeclampsia, is characterized by high blood pressure, protein in the urine, and edema, just as Dr. Bradford said. Then I read this: PIH can impair kidney and liver function, cause bleeding, seizures, pulmonary edema, stroke, and in severe forms, death.

Death.

I stare at the word until it becomes blurry, its five letters running together on the page. Then I look away, gazing at the gold walls and the pale cream curtains that I spent hours making this summer. They hang limply on either side of the open window, not even the slightest breeze moving into the room.

I close the windows and flip on the air conditioner, which roars to life, and turn back to the books. I learn that PIH is simply the latest in a series of names for the disease. Its full name is preeclamptic toxemia, but it's regularly called preeclampsia or toxemia. Its Australian name is hypertensive disease of pregnancy, or HDP, and it's also known as gestosis. "All of these names," the author writes, "reflect the uncertainty as to its cause. A nineteenth-century doctor called it a 'disease of theories,' and this remains true today."

I take a deep breath. "A disease of theories" can't be good; there are too many unknowns in a theory, and thus too many unknowns in a disease that relies on theories. I want facts, something solid, unshifting.

I read that preeclampsia comes in two forms: mild and severe. Treatment for mild preeclampsia is bed rest and fetal monitoring. Treatment for severe preeclampsia is an IV of magnesium sulfate to prevent seizures, which is followed by delivery of the fetus, no matter how far from term the pregnancy is. If severe preeclampsia is not treated, it can progress quickly to eclampsia, which is "characterized by convulsions and coma." This book goes on to say that although it's unusual for women to die of preeclampsia in the United States, worldwide it is a leading cause of death—76,000 women annually. *Holy shit!* But generally, the book goes on, preeclampsia is more dangerous for the unborn baby than the mother because it can cause growth retardation, placental failure, and premature birth.

Placental failure. Premature birth. I lean back against our pillows, feeling dazed. Dazed but not crying. Months later I'll wonder at my lack of tears. Why didn't I cry? I'll realize that even with the books spread before me spelling out our future, even as I contemplated eclampsia as a possibility, I didn't think my pregnancy would end that way—in seizures, growth retardation, premature birth.

Suddenly, I need to hear Donny's voice. I reach for the phone and dial his classroom. After four rings, he picks up. "Hello, Mr. Gramenz speaking."

I've never heard him answer the phone like this, and I'm quiet, letting his new teacher identity sink in.

"Hello," he says again, and I realize I haven't said anything.

"Hi, babe," I say slowly. "I might have preeclampsia."

"What?" he says. I'm not sure if he didn't hear me or if he's asking me to explain.

"Preeclampsia," I say, and as I explain the swelling and protein in my urine, I realize that I have adopted the outdated name for the disease. But really, pregnancy-induced hypertension doesn't seem to fit because I'm not hypertensive—I don't have high blood pressure—and I prefer preeclampsia for its prefix—it is "pre" eclampsia, "pre" seizures, "pre" coma. I like the way its name places me out ahead of these possibilities.

As I catalog my symptoms, the high-pitched chatter of Donny's students grows louder in the background. He says "Hold on" to me, then "Please be quiet" to his students. His voice sounds strained, and I picture him, hand covering the receiver, glaring the room into silence. I should have waited until the end of his school day to call, but the thought of him not knowing about the fact that I might be sick fills me with loneliness.

"Sorry," he says when he's back on the line. "I'll leave right after school." The timbre of his voice is still unfamiliar, and when he says, "Will you be okay?" I know he's scared.

"I'm sure everything will be fine," I say, suddenly reassuring, my confidence inflated by his fear. "We'll know more next week. I'm sure everything will be fine. Dr. Bradford is just being cautious."

When I hang up the phone, I still feel it, the certainty I've slipped on like a coat to counteract my husband's worry. This is the way we work.

Outwardly, Donny is unflappable, exuding calm assurance. It's one of the things that attracted me to him, though I didn't realize this until a few months after we began dating, when my friend Claire pointed out that the moment I was in his presence, I relaxed. "It's kind of amazing," she said. "It's as if the stress just seeps out of you."

Donny has been the natural antidote to my fretting, but I have also learned to be the antidote to his. I quickly realized that although he seems calm and relaxed, he simply carries his burdens more quietly, more privately, than I do. When he's worried, he seems preoccupied, his distant eyes giving no indication of the degree or severity of his stress. When he's like this, I probe and question. I become full of optimism, buoying him with my own show of confidence.

This summer, we passed the heavy mantle of worry, laden with a mortgage and bills and a baby on the way, back and forth. Our biggest fear was that Donny wouldn't get a teaching job. But, we reasoned, even that wouldn't break us. He is finishing his last season as a professional soccer player for the Minnesota Thunder, and he also coaches high school soccer. So between his playing and coaching and substitute teaching and my graduate school stipend, we'd scrape by. But now that Donny *is* teaching, he's more stressed than ever. He's trying to navigate a new profession at the same time he's juggling coaching and Thunder games and practices.

In the last weeks, I have reassured and congratulated him, trying to buttress his juggling act with a steady stream of encouragement. But now the baby, the pregnancy, has pushed the other worries aside, and it doesn't take long for my confidence to falter once I am alone with my own thoughts. I walk downstairs and stand in the middle of our bright living room, staring distractedly at the home we've created: the crowded pine bookshelves, the garage-sale entertainment center that looks new under a coat of burgundy paint, the coffee table my step-dad made for me when I moved into my first apartment at nineteen, the remnant of cream carpet that fits just perfectly, the leafy palm we adopted when one of our friends moved to Chicago.

I'm supposed to take my ninety-five-year-old grandpa, Spencer, to the eye doctor this afternoon, but the thought of spending the next few hours getting both of us in and out of the car and in and out of the heat of the afternoon exhausts me. I don't want to tell Grandpa about the possibility of preeclampsia because it would worry him, but I can't imagine feigning interest in his stories from the local par-three golf course, where he spends hours playing cribbage and devising ways to strengthen his faltering swing.

My mom can't take him because she's at work, so I pick up the phone and call my dad. I tell him that I didn't have a good doctor's appointment. I'm vague, saying that there might be a problem and that I'm not up for all the driving this afternoon. "Would you be willing to take Grandpa to his appointment?" Spencer is my mom's father, but he and my dad are good friends, even though my parents have been divorced for twenty years.

"Of course," my dad says. "But are you okay? Do you want me to stop by?"

"No, no," I say quickly. My dad and I are close—he comes over for dinner at least once a week. He's a worrier like me, but when Dad worries, he *broods:* lips pursed, forehead creased, a heavy silence weighing him down like a lead cloak. If he comes over, I'm afraid I'll need to reassure him, and I don't know if I can. "Could you just tell Grandpa I'm tired?" I ask.

But Dad *does* come over—he's at my door in fifteen minutes—and the moment I see his face, see my fear reflected in the deep lines around his eyes, I start to cry. He folds me in an awkward hug, settling next to me on the sofa. Then he grips my hand. "I'd like to say a prayer," he says gruffly, and I nod, because it's all I can manage.

My dad is a Presbyterian minister, but he's always been a theologian rather than a preacher. He never had his own congregation; instead, he taught religious studies at a small liberal arts college in St. Paul for thirty-eight years. He's retired now, and the only time he prays around my sisters and me is when we gather together around a dinner table. And even then, my sisters and I lower our heads reluctantly.

But today when he says "Let's pray," I immediately lower my head. He asks God to watch over me. His voice wavers as he asks God to watch over the baby, to keep the baby safe and healthy. His rough hand clutches my own, and when we both say "Amen," he gives my fingers a slight squeeze and my eyes fill with tears.

"Okay," he says, clearing his throat. "I can bring over dinner or groceries. Whatever you need."

I agree to call him if I need anything, and then he's gone. I listen to his car pull away from the curb, and I lie back on the couch, turning to my left side, the best position for blood circulation during pregnancy. I press my fingers into my belly and try to remember when I last felt the baby move. I look at the clock. It's only 11:30. I imagine her sleeping inside me, a snail curled in its shell. *Wake up, little one.* I give my belly a slight shake. *Wake up.* But I realize I'll drive myself crazy if I lie like this all day, waiting for her to kick, so I heave myself from the couch to water the plants.

We have a small collection of orchids on two round tables in front of our dining room windows. They were given to us by Mimi, the elderly woman for whom Donny and I were caretakers for three and a half years, beginning just after we were married. We lived in a sparsely populated St. Paul suburb in an apartment attached to Mimi's house, and in exchange for rent, we took Mimi on errands, performed seasonal chores around her house, and tended to her greenhouse full of orchids. The last was my favorite task. Every Sunday morning, I would step into the humid air of the glass room and carefully wipe down each orchid. Then I turned on the hose, filled the room with a spray of water, and inhaled the earthy smell of dirt and wood chips that, even in the coldest months, brought me relief from winter.

I carry the orchids to our kitchen sink two by two, and when the basin is full, I begin the careful work of inspection—lifting leaves, running fingertips along their edges to feel for scale—the round, seemingly innocuous parasite that will eat through the thickest leaves and wither the most dazzling petals if left on its own. I pick a dead leaf from the cymbidium and smile when I notice that the cattleya is going to bloom. Its long, elegant buds are tightly closed, like hands pressed together in prayer, but in a week it will begin to loosen its grip and become the first orchid to flower in our new house. Mimi gave it to me just before we moved, and I want to call and tell her about it, but it would be difficult to keep the news about my pregnancy to myself, so I don't. I carefully spray the plants and leave them to drip in the sink, a wet skirt of green draped over the counter.

Suddenly feeling heavy and tired, I head back to the couch. I should prepare for my class—I teach tomorrow—or work on my thesis, but writing is slow these days. I've been working on a book about a family, three generations of women in the small Costa Rican village of San Vicente, where I lived for two years after college. But I'm having trouble with it. I'm worried about the ethics of writing from a country of privilege. If it's ever published, will it seem as though I'm appropriating their stories? And then there is the question of what the book is really *about:* me or them? Is it memoir or anthropology?

The truth is that these women—Tirza and Betty and Sara—have had a hold on my mind for the six years I've been back in the States, and now they seem too large to capture in words. All I'm capable of writing are moments, flashes of memory, and at this rate, I'll never complete a draft by the time the baby comes. I need to get to work, and fast, but today I can't imagine trying to string words together to make sentences, so I just lie down and close my eyes.

I don't know how long I've been sleeping when the phone startles me awake. I reach for it, thinking it might be the doctor to tell me that there's been some mistake. But it's my older sister, Sara.

"Did I wake you?" she asks right away.

"I was just resting," I say slowly. Then, "There might be a problem with the pregnancy."

"What? What are you talking about?"

"I might have preeclampsia." My voice sounds dull, even to my own ears. This is already old news, and I recite what I know: I have signs of the disease, but I should be fine if my blood pressure remains normal.

Sara is the only member of my family who doesn't live in the Twin Cities. After the botched 2000 presidential election, she was so upset that she left the huge Minneapolis law firm where she was an associate and moved to Washington, D.C., to work on Capitol Hill. She now specializes in farm policy for an environmental organization. She feels at home in D.C., surrounded by other political junkies, but I miss her. We talk several times a week, and lately she's been calling even more, telling me about this cute outfit or that adorable toy she's found for the baby, the first grandchild in our family. I'm touched that she and my younger sister, Rachel, are so excited to be aunties.

When I'm finished telling her what I know about preeclampsia, she says, "Okay, I'm not at my desk right now, but I'll be there soon. I'm going to check this out and call you back."

"Okay," I say, although I already know what I need to know about the disease: the protein, the swelling, the things I need to watch for. I hang up the phone and drift back into dreamless sleep.

When I wake again to the phone, I'm sweating, my shoulder-length red hair stuck to my neck. It's Sara again, and she's all business this time: what was your protein level?

"The protein was one, I think." I wasn't clear what this meant, but Sara says, "Okay."

"How much weight have you gained?"

"Nine pounds since my last appointment."

"Okay," she says again, and I picture her at her desk, staring at her computer, scrolling through Web sites. Finally she says, "You should check your blood pressure every day."

"My blood pressure is fine," I say. "I don't have high blood pressure."

"Still, you should check it every day. It can spike suddenly."

"I'm going in next week," I say.

"Can you get one of those small blood pressure machines?"

Buying a blood pressure machine seems ridiculous and neurotic, even to me. "Maybe," I say. "But I think I'll be fine." I still don't believe in the power of preeclampsia. I don't understand how fast it can work.

"I have to go," Sara says, "but I'll do more reading and call you tomorrow."

"Okay," I say. "Love you."

As I wait for Donny to get home, I call my mom, who is also a teacher, and Rachel, who is in graduate school for conservation biology. I'm upbeat on the phone with both of them, saying I need to take things easy and that I'll know more in a week. But when Donny walks through the door, I crumble into his arms. Usually, I hug him tightly, the length of our bodies pressed together, but my pregnant belly sandwiched between us puts me at an angle, and I lean into him, my face in his neck. I inhale the scent of his skin, the almost sweet combination of soap and sweat that seems to belong to him alone.

After a minute, he pulls away and tucks a strand of hair behind my ear. "Show me the books."

I've carried all my pregnancy books downstairs, and we sit next to each other on the couch, moving from one book to the next, skimming the pages that detail all the things that can go wrong.

He holds a book on his lap and rereads the pages. When he looks up at me, I notice how tired he looks. Fine white lines fan from the corners of his eyes, evidence of his hours on the soccer field, squinting into the sun. But his blue eyes are clear, and he smiles reassuringly. "I think everything's going to be fine."

I can't tell if he really believes this or if he's just trying to make me feel better.

"What if something happens to the baby?" I need him to entertain the worst-case scenario, to go there and come back and tell me again that everything will be okay.

Donny runs his hand through his light brown hair, glances at the book in his lap, then back to me. "You're the sick one, right? The baby's not sick."

"Yeah, I guess," I say. "But what about this?" I point to the paragraph that says preeclampsia is more dangerous for the unborn baby than the mother.

"The baby's going to be fine," Donny says again, putting his hand on my cheek. His fingers smell like oranges, and this is strangely comforting. "You're going in next week. Dr. Bradford would've had you come in earlier if she was really worried, right?" He brushes the hair from my shoulders and kisses me gently. "Everything is going to be fine."

Just after Donny and I were married, I began to fantasize about what it would be like to have a child. I imagined us lying in bed, our bodies curled around a chubby, cooing baby. I imagined her pushing against us with thick legs, blowing spit bubbles and laughing. I imagined us spending hours tickling her, kissing her rolls of fat.

But whenever we talked about having children, my excitement was always tempered with fear, a fear that had blossomed from a mere stem of anxiety into something lush and consuming the second year we were married, when two things happened: I became seriously depressed for the first time in ten years, and Donny's mother,

Patricia, who is schizophrenic, went off her medication for the first time in thirteen years.

My depression and anxiety coupled with the schizophrenia in Donny's family seemed like too much. I fretted about our genes. Were we setting our children up for months in psych wards? A lifetime of medication?

But even with this fear rooted beneath the surface of our lives, I wanted children. So I began to research the odds. I learned that the chance of someone with a schizophrenic grandparent developing the disease is less than 2 percent. But I also learned that a child whose parent has experienced depression is three times more likely to experience depression and/or anxiety. *Three times more likely* seemed too high.

When Donny and I talked about my fears, he always assured me that our children would be okay. "We know what to watch for," he would say. "If there's a problem, we'll deal with it." His confidence in our parenting abilities reassured me, and truthfully, my fear wasn't enough to keep us from trying for children. And what was the alternative? Would we adopt because we were worried that someday our children might suffer from depression? There was nothing to guarantee that adopted children wouldn't suffer the same thing.

As I sit next to Donny now, the possibility of preeclampsia hanging between us, my worries about mental illness seem so far removed that it's difficult to believe I ever worried about it at all. Instead, this new worry stares at me from the pages of my pregnancy books, too big to digest. Donny runs his fingers along my arm. "Everything is going to be fine," he says again, and I nod.

3

I SPEND THE FOLLOWING WEEK TRYING TO TAKE IT easy—I lie on the couch in the afternoons—but each morning I still head to campus, slogging through the heat. I don't mention pre-eclampsia to my students; instead, I complain about the heat and joke about how huge I've become. I pretend that everything is fine.

But the next Wednesday, at my thirty-two-week checkup, Dr. Bradford tells me that I'm leaking more protein into my urine. Before my appointment, I paged through my pregnancy books again and read that proteinuria is the result of damaged small blood vessels in the kidneys, a sign the kidneys are stressed. I also read that if you're leaking a lot of protein in your urine, your baby will be born within two weeks. I didn't remember seeing that last week, but now I mention it to Dr. Bradford.

"That's not necessarily true," she says.

Not necessarily means possibly. It may even mean probably.

"But I'm putting you on bed rest."

"What does that mean?"

"It means no teaching. I want you to spend as much time as possible on your left side."

I nod because what else can I do? I can't tell Dr. Bradford that I don't want to give up my class or that I need to complete a draft of my thesis by the end of the semester. That would sound awful. And really, why do I care about teaching and graduate school when my kidneys are seriously stressed, when my baby might—possibly but not necessarily—be born in two weeks? I give myself a mental shake. Get your priorities straight.

"The baby?" I ask. "What if the baby were born right now, eight weeks early?" I cough hard and press my hand to my chest. I still have the same hacking cough, but neither Dr. Bradford nor I mention it this week.

"She'd survive," she says plainly. "Thirty-two weeks is a good place to be."

I suddenly feel weak all over. *She'd survive.* Why does that statement make me feel as if I could vomit? It's as if there is a split that's happened inside me: I've read the books, I understand how serious preeclampsia is—on some level I understand this because I've let it scare me—but deep down, I don't think it's going to happen to me. I don't really think that my daughter will be born two months early. I don't think I have to worry about her surviving. I'll wonder at this later, what an amazing mechanism denial is. You can let the information in enough to see it, to understand it, without really accepting it.

I must look nervous, because Dr. Bradford says, "It'll be okay. I'm going to have you do a twenty-four-hour urine test to get a more accurate reading of your protein level. I'm also going to have you do a nonstress test, just to make sure the baby is fine."

"Okay," I say, but my legs feel shaky as Dr. Bradford passes me off to a nurse in the hallway. I follow the nurse into a small, bright room and she helps me into a large leather recliner and attaches two round disks to my belly and hands me something that looks like a pen. "Push this every time you feel the baby move," she says.

I put my head back on the recliner and take a deep breath and try not to think about all the phone calls I have to make when I get home: to the head of Creative Writing, my thesis advisers, my family. Each time I feel the baby's fluttery movements, I press the button and a black slash appears on the graph paper that spills slowly from the machine next to me.

The nurse comes in a few minutes later and smiles warmly, handing me a juice box. "Have you eaten today?"

This seems like wonderful service—juice in a tiny box. "I had granola and milk with banana."

"That's a healthful breakfast," she says, and the rule follower in me is pleased. I'm healthy. I've done good work. Everything will be fine.

"Well, why don't you drink that," she says. "We'll see if it wakes this baby up." She looks at the graph paper. "You've felt her move a few times, I see?"

"Yes," I say, suddenly uneasy. Hers was clearly a question, not a statement.

She pats my arm. "I'll be back to check on you soon."

I watch the nurse leave, but now I'm nervous. No one pats your arm if everything is okay. They retain their professional distance. I take a sip of the tropical punch and stare at the closed door. I felt the baby move. Of course I did. She moved, didn't she?

When Dr. Bradford comes in a few minutes later, my mouth is coated in sugar. She tears the paper from the machine and studies it for a moment.

"How is she?" I ask, already knowing that something's not right.

"Well," she says, "We're looking for increases in the baby's heart rate. Every time she moves, her heart rate should increase, like she's exercising. But she's not showing any increases, even when you feel her move."

"What does that mean?" I ask, regretting the punch, the sickly sweetness.

Dr. Bradford folds the graph paper like an accordion. "It could mean that what you feel—the movements—are hiccups, and that she's really sleeping."

Sleeping. Okay.

"Don't worry," she says, her voice softening. "I'm going to send you to the hospital for a biophysical profile. It's a special kind of ultrasound that can tell us more than a nonstress test."

On my way out of Dr. Bradford's office, I am handed a large red jug and a white basin. "You will need to pee into the basin and then pour the urine into the jug," the nurse says.

I nod.

"And you need to keep the urine cold, so you'll need to have someone put it in the refrigerator for you while you're at the hospital." I nod again and thank her.

Suddenly, I'm in a place I don't recognize. It is midmorning, sunny and hot, and I need to go to the hospital for a test I've never heard of. I need to put my pee into a large plastic jug and keep it cold. My baby might be sleeping or there might be something wrong with her. Dr. Bradford didn't say this, of course, but I understand that it's a possibility.

As I begin driving to the hospital, slowly, carefully (as if this will make a difference), I realize I don't want to go alone. If there is something wrong with my baby, I don't want to be by myself when I hear the news. I turn in the opposite direction and drive toward my sister Rachel's house.

Ten minutes later I am standing on the front steps of her small Craftsman-style house, ringing the doorbell, hoping she's home. Her dog begins to bark, but when he looks out the window and sees me, the barking turns to slobbery panting. "Hi, Rusty," I say. "Where's your mama?" I stand there, watching the dog and hoping that Rachel will magically appear, but she doesn't. Finally, I get back into my car and drive to Abbott Northwestern Hospital by myself.

I have to pee by the time I get to the maternity ward, so before the biophysical profile, I go to the restroom and begin the Process: I pee into the basin, carefully pour the pee into the narrow-topped jug, then rinse the basin. When I emerge from the bathroom, I hold up the jug to the receptionist. "Do you have a refrigerator?" I ask, embarrassed. "I need to keep this cold."

I'm grateful when she doesn't seem at all flustered by my request. She smiles and takes the jug from me. "I'll keep it here." She points behind her desk. "In a bucket of ice."

I nod, relieved, and wonder how often she is asked to watch over people's bodily fluids.

The room where I get the biophysical profile is chilly and dark. The technician, whose name I forget as soon as she tells me, straps monitors to my abdomen and moves an ultrasound probe over the stretched skin of my belly. This is not a regular ultrasound, she tells me. It's a timed test—thirty minutes long—during which she will count the number of movements the baby makes. She explains that the baby will get points for breathing, for being surrounded by enough amniotic fluid, for bending and straightening her arms and legs. As the technician moves the probe over my belly, the baby's profile comes into focus, and I smile at her tiny nose, which turns up, just like mine. She is the color of the moon, pale against a night sky.

The technician hands me the phone, and I try to call Donny at school, but I keep getting a busy signal, and I wonder if I'm dialing the wrong number. I knew his number last week, but it's as if my brain has been addled, and every number or fact that is not directly related to my pregnancy is no longer accessible.

I hold on to the phone and stare at the screen for long minutes. The baby is asleep, not moving. But her miniature heart is beating as fast as a hummingbird's wings. She has to be okay with a heart that beats like that. She has to be.

"Let's see if we can wake her up," says the technician, pressing her fingers into the side of my belly. "Come on, baby."

I echo her words. *Come on, baby.* Ten points is the goal of this exam, and the technician says she only has four points. There are twelve minutes of the exam remaining. Move, baby. Move.

I don't know what it would mean if the baby doesn't score well on this test, but I know it wouldn't be good. When we lived with Mimi, there was a woman from a home-care agency who came out to the house a couple of times a week to help Mimi while Donny and I were at work. One day while I was chatting with her, she pulled out pictures of her sons. The younger one held a soccer ball and smiled broadly into the camera. "A happy six-year-old," she said. Then she handed me the photo of her older son, who was bent into a wheelchair, head resting on his shoulder, arms folded at unnatural angles across his chest. I stared at the picture while she told me that she'd had a "touch of toxemia" but hadn't had any real problems until one day late in her pregnancy when she stopped feeling him move. When she got to the hospital, the doctors didn't do a C-section right away, so she thought everything was fine. When they finally operated, hours later, it was clear that everything wasn't fine. Her son had been oxygen-deprived. He was born with brain damage. After a month working at Mimi's she'd had to leave to stay home full-time with her son because *his* home-care person had quit.

When this woman told me her story, I didn't know what a "touch of toxemia" was. Now, I can't help but wonder if it was the toxemia, the preeclampsia, that caused the oxygen deprivation. I can't help but wonder what I will do if my baby ends up like hers, folded into a wheelchair.

When the baby finally begins to move and ends up scoring ten points, all I can do is smile. There is plenty of amniotic fluid, and she has normal breathing patterns. I want to hug the technician whose name I don't remember. I'm back in the place where I believe everything will be fine, so when I emerge from the ultrasound room, I ask the receptionist if she will give me a quick tour of the maternity ward. We were scheduled to get a tour of the ward at our birthing class tonight, but because of the bed rest, which is certainly just a precaution, I'll miss it, and it *does* seem important to know one's way around.

The receptionist walks briskly down the hall, and it's difficult to keep up. She shows me one of the labor rooms, which is smaller than I expected, but still large by hospital standards. Then we go to a grouping of rooms called Station 54, which is where women on long-term bed rest stay. There is a communal area, where a few pregnant women recline in chairs, their huge bellies draped in hospital gowns. They look weary, and I imagine they are sick of being trapped here. One woman gives me a weak smile, and I smile back.

The Station 54 rooms are larger than the labor rooms, and each is complete with wide windows, TV, VCR, and a small refrigerator. "Wow," I say, and the receptionist nods.

"Some women are here for months," she says, "And when they finally go home, they often donate things because they are so relieved."

I nod at this, although I don't know if these women are relieved and thankful to be gone or to have been here. Probably both. My friend Margie was on bed rest for fifteen weeks with her second pregnancy because she had had an incompetent cervix. Her doctors stitched it shut and ordered her to remain horizontal for the next four months, but at least she was able to stay at home, working on her laptop in bed. The thought of having my cervix sewn shut makes me gag, but I know that would be better than having your baby fall out months too soon. I'm sure that some of the women here on Station 54 have incompetent cervixes, but some of them probably have pre-eclampsia as well. My books said that 5 to 8 percent of all pregnant women—200,000 women in the United States each year—develop it.

"You might end up here," the receptionist says casually, and I'm irritated. I want to ask how she thinks that's helpful, but instead I thank her for the tour.

At home, I settle myself on the couch on my left side with the air conditioner blowing on my feet. It's clear from the urinalysis that I'm getting sicker, but I actually feel less nervous now than I did a week ago. Partly this is because I know the baby is okay: ten out of ten on the biophysical profile. Partly it's because physically I don't feel any different. And now that I am home, being ordered on bed rest doesn't seem like such a bad idea. I can rest and work from the couch, and I can still get up to go to the bathroom and shower and make a sandwich.

When I call the director of my program, she tells me to take care of myself and not to worry. They'll figure out how to deal with my class. "Everything will work out," she says. "You just take care of yourself and that baby." My thesis advisers say the same thing, and of course I'm relieved, but I also feel a little lost without school obligations and writing deadlines dominating my schedule.

I call Donny, who sounds as though he's in a hurry. He says he'll be home as soon as he can. Then I call my parents, who both sound quietly nervous, their voices pinched. I explain about the bed rest and the twenty-four-hour urine test, but tell them that the baby is fine and that I'm okay.

When I call my sister Sara, who has been reading up on pre-eclampsia for the last week, she says, "I think you better get used to the idea that you're not going to carry this baby to term."

This is not helpful.

"Did you hear me?" she asks.

"Yeah," I say. "We'll see."

That evening, I ask Donny to go to birthing class without me because I don't want to miss anything. I know he'd rather not go—between practices and teaching we've hardly had any time together—but if he thinks my request is ridiculous, he doesn't say so. He just grabs our three-ring binder and heads out the door.

I spend a couple of hours watching reruns of *Friends,* my hand on my belly, waiting for the baby to start her evening dance, which, when she does, is more reassuring than any test. Feeling her move has been the best part of the pregnancy, the only part I really like. I'm still amazed by the fact there is *a person* inside me, a little being who will be my daughter. And for the hundredth time I wonder what she will be like, who she will look like. Will she have red hair like me? Or light brown like Donny?

When Donny comes home, he recounts what I missed: the last stages of labor and the maternity ward tour. The class even practiced changing a diaper. "I told them you were on bed rest," he says, "and everyone wished us well."

I am up and down the stairs a dozen times that night. Each time I have to pee, I waddle downstairs to collect the jug from the refrigerator. Back upstairs, I pee in the basin and pour the urine into the jug. Then I'm down the stairs again to put the jug back in the refrigerator. So much for bed rest.

Donny has been sleeping on the couch for the past two weeks because I've been snoring and coughing so much that I keep him awake. He says that sometimes my snoring even wakes him downstairs, but I find this difficult to believe. He doesn't even stir when I go up and down the stairs with my jug. He's nestled into the couch, sound asleep, and I wish, as I pass him for the eighth time, that *he* was the one who had to pee in a jug, that *he* had to lug it up and down the stairs over and over again, and that *I* was sleeping soundly on the couch.

When I drop off my jug of pee at the clinic the next day, Dr. Bradford orders some blood tests to check my platelets and liver enzymes
to make sure I'm not developing HELLP syndrome, a severe form of
preeclampsia. She also takes my blood pressure, which is still normal.

"How do you feel?" she asks.

"Okay, I guess." I still feel fine—tired and swollen, but fine.

She says she'll call me tomorrow—Friday—with the results of
the blood and urine tests.

4

ON FRIDAY MORNING, MY DAD ARRIVES AT OUR house at 4:45 to drive Donny to the airport. He's flying to Seattle for the A-League Soccer semifinals. It's a two-game total-goal series. Tonight the Minnesota Thunder will play there, and on Sunday they will play Seattle here, in Minnesota. Whichever team scores the most total goals will advance to the championship next weekend.

As I lie in bed and listen to my dad start his car, I suddenly need to see Donny one last time. He leaned down to kiss me before he left, but I was groggy. Now I'm wide-awake and I want to say good-bye again. I twist out of bed and pull the curtain back to wave, but my dad's car is already pulling away from the curb. This makes me feel like crying. It's the same feeling I experienced as a child when I frequently dreamed that I had missed the bus. In those dreams, I would run down the block after the bus, sometimes in bare feet, sometimes over broken glass, but I would never catch it. I always woke up filled with dread.

As I climb back into bed, my chest is heavy. The night before, Donny said he wished he weren't going, but we both knew this wasn't true. I know how much it would mean to him to end his soccer career as a league champion. And though I wish he were still here, in bed next to me (or rather on the couch downstairs), I couldn't have asked him not to go. And I'll be fine; I know my dad will bring over dinner, and my friend Jess said she'd come over after that and even stay the night if I wanted.

I begin to cough again, and when I finally stop, I feel light-headed. I turn on my side and tuck pillows between my knees, but it seems unlikely that I will fall back to sleep. As pale morning light fills the room, I stare at the bookshelf next to our bed. The lower shelves are lined with books. On the top shelf is a deep shadow box in which an intricately beaded purse hangs. I love this purse and its tiny beads that swirl into muted flowers of gray and gold. I love it because it's beautiful but also because it belonged to my paternal grandmother. She died two years ago, just shy of one hundred years old. In the years before her death, whenever I would visit her in Princeton, New Jersey, she would ask me which items in her house I wanted.

"Do you want this?" she would ask, holding up an item for me to inspect. She never added "after I die," but I knew that's what she meant, and it always made me uncomfortable.

One afternoon, she dug this purse from her dresser, where it was wrapped in tissue paper. "This was given to me by a member of our congregation," she said. My grandfather, who died before I was born, had been a Presbyterian minister in Cranford and Newark, New Jersey. Everything I've heard about him paints him as an austere, inflexible man who was strict with his three children but went out of his way to help his congregants. "Your grandfather helped this woman's family when their car broke down," my grandmother said, "and she gave me this purse as a way to thank us." She laid it in my open palms, and I was startled by how heavy it was, the tiny metal beads cool against my skin.

When she asked me if I wanted it, I simply said "yes" because I was embarrassed by how much I wanted it, which was in that childish, achy way I had wanted my friend's Princess Leia action figure in second grade. I didn't want to let my grandmother know this, however, because it seemed tacky, as if I would be waiting for her to die just so I could have a purse that was too precious to actually ever use. But as I sat beside my grandmother on the edge of her bed, the purse in my hands, I was awed by the way it seemed, in its careful intricacy, in the weight of its beads, to hold the lives of people I never knew, a history I hadn't lived. And now, as I stare at it in its box, I wish I could take it out and hold it in my hands, rest it on my belly, and let the coolness and weight of its beads comfort me. I wonder if someday I will carefully place it in the open hands of my own daughter or granddaughter and tell her the story of her great- or great-great-grandmother and the congregant with the broken-down car.

I wonder what my grandmother would say if I told her about the preeclampsia and the bed rest. She didn't lose any of her pregnancies the way my other grandmother had. My mom's mother, Lucille, had had two miscarriages and a stillborn child before my mother was born. Several years before she died, I interviewed her, a tape recorder propped between us on the table of my grandparents' little travel trailer, where they spent their summers parked outside my mom's cabin in northern Minnesota. I knew about the miscarriages and the stillborn baby from my mom, and during one of our interviews, I pressed my grandma into talking about them even though I could tell by the way her fingers fluttered around her china teacup that she didn't want to. I knew she would rather talk about the happy times and the greenhouse she and my grandpa had built just after the war. Still, I kept asking questions: *Did the doctors know why it happened? That must have been so hard.* At this point, my grandmother was ninety, and these losses were decades removed. To satisfy my curiosity, she told me what happened: "The baby stopped moving when I was eight months pregnant," she said. "When I went to the doctor, there was no heartbeat." She carried that dead baby for two weeks, until she finally went into labor naturally. "Those were hard times," she said. "But then your mother was born, and we couldn't believe how lucky we were."

I don't know why I pressed her into talking about this. I think I believed—though how could I have been so naïve?—that a fetus dying like that, at eight months, was something that only happened in underdeveloped countries. I believed that in the United States this was a relic of the past, even though I know that's not true.

Now I wish I could apologize to my grandma for making her tell me about her dead baby. And I wonder what my grandparents' lives looked like in the wake of that loss. How could my grandma have gotten up and gone to work in the greenhouse every day? My grandpa Spencer would later tell me that they drove all the way from Granite Falls in western Minnesota to Minneapolis to see a specialist. They didn't talk about it with their friends. It was a private loss. And I wonder how they made it through, how they kept going after their baby died. How will I keep going if *my* baby dies?

I give myself a mental shake—*stop thinking like that*—and get out of bed. I go to the bathroom, then walk downstairs, flip on the air conditioner, and lie down on the couch. I'm bored, but I don't feel like checking e-mail, and I don't want to make any phone calls because I'm afraid Dr. Bradford will call with the test results while the line is busy. I could work on my thesis, but I can't imagine sitting with the heat of my laptop on my thighs, so I just lie on my left side and wait for the phone to ring.

When I get up to make a peanut-butter sandwich, I feel dizzy and have to steady myself on the arm of a chair. My limbs are heavy and pulsing, and when I get back to the couch with my sandwich, I curse the Thunder for making it to the play-offs. Not that Donny would be home with me if he were in town, but at least he would be nearby, and he would be home by five.

I actually spend the whole day doing nothing. The baby kicks periodically, and each time she moves, I'm reassured, but I'm starting to get anxious about the tests and about the heaviness in my limbs. By midafternoon, I am short of breath just from walking to the kitchen, so finally at four I call Dr. Bradford's office and tell the receptionist I'm waiting for results that I need before the weekend.

Dr. Bradford calls back in ten minutes. I know it's her before I pick up the phone. "Well," she says, "you have more than five grams of protein in your urine."

No measurement in grams sounds very serious. Later, I'll realize that spilling five grams of protein into my urine during a twenty-four-hour period means I have severe preeclampsia. I'll realize that *more than five grams* means my kidneys are beginning to fail.

"But your blood pressure was still normal yesterday," she says. "So that's good, and your blood tests are fine."

Yes. Right. My blood pressure was still normal yesterday. The tests were fine.

"But I think you should plan on coming in tomorrow morning anyway."

"Tomorrow morning," I repeat. Tomorrow is Saturday. The office is closed.

"That way you'll be there if anything happens. And you'll get test results faster."

Oh, to the hospital. I'm going to the hospital. And then relief sets in. "Okay," I say. "That sounds good."

I can't believe I think spending the next months of my pregnancy in one of those yellow rooms or lying in one of those blue recliners on Station 54 sounds good, but suddenly it does. With Donny gone, all I want is to be watched over. "Yeah," I say, "I actually feel kind of funny today—different. More tired, out of breath."

"You're out of breath?"

"Yeah, and heavy, as if I'm going to explode or faint or something."

"Hmmm," Dr. Bradford says.

"I'm really dragging."

"Well," she says, "I think instead of waiting until tomorrow, you better go in right now. I'll let Dr. Anderson know. She's on call this weekend. I've already talked to her about your situation, but I'll tell her you'll be in tonight."

"Okay," I say, and again, I'm relieved. But I wish that Dr. Bradford was on call this weekend. I've grown used to her manner, which, when I first met her, seemed too brusque but now is the thing that comforts me most. I know and like Dr. Anderson as well, so I'm sure it will be fine, and it's not as if I'm going to deliver the baby this weekend.

"I'll check on you on Monday," Dr. Bradford says before hanging up.

Then I call my dad and tell him that instead of bringing over dinner, he will be taking me to the hospital.

"Oh?" he says. "Okay. Yes. I'll be right there." Dad's voice is thick with concern, and I know he's going to be quiet and heavy with worry by the time he gets to my house, so when I hang up, I call Rachel. She and her husband, Josh, are supposed to go out to dinner with Josh's family tonight, but when I tell her I'm going to the hospital, she says she'll go with me.

"Are you sure? I mean, you don't mind?"

"Don't be silly. I'll be there in ten minutes." This is exactly what I hoped she would say.

I walk upstairs and grab some clothes and my toothbrush and my favorite melon-scented hand lotion. I was planning on checking off all the items that my pregnancy books recommended taking to the hospital. I was planning on packing a suitcase, or at least a duffle bag—something tidy and compact—but now there's no time to search the basement for a suitcase, so instead, I throw everything into a brown paper bag. I contemplate taking my laptop so I can get some work done, but I figure I can have someone come get it for me tomorrow. Tonight, I'll just rest.

Before my dad arrives, I leave a message on Donny's cell phone: *I'm going to Abbott for bed rest. I'll call you when I get there.*

5

IN THE CAR ON THE WAY TO THE HOSPITAL, MY
dad drives and Rachel sits beside him. I'm in the back, and I don't
feel like talking to either of them. I'm not nervous, exactly, but I feel
the weight of it, of things not going the way I had planned. Hot wind
whips through the car, loosening my hair from its ponytail, and I wonder if Donny got my message. I don't have a cell phone, so he can't call
me, but as soon as I am admitted, I'll try him again. It seems wrong
that he is two thousand miles away suiting up for a soccer game while
I'm being driven to Abbott for bed rest. But really, I don't even care
that he's not here. I'm just relieved to be going to the hospital.

I tell my dad to take a left on Chicago Avenue and another left
on Twenty-eighth Street. *Okay,* he says. *Okay.* He's solemn, his lips
pursed. I'm anxious to get out of the car, so when he pulls up in
front of the hospital's entrance, I grab my purse and the paper bag
full of my clothes and tell him to meet us on the sixth floor, the
maternity ward.

The hospital is crowded, and as Rachel and I walk down the long
hallway, people blur around us. It feels as though we're moving in
slow motion, and when we get to the elevator, I take a deep breath.

"Are you doing okay?" Rachel asks, and I nod.

But a minute later, when the woman at the maternity admis-
sions window pulls my name up on her computer, and there, on her
screen, under "reason for admittance" it says, in all capital letters,
PRETERM LABOR, I feel as if I'll throw up.

"Is that right? That's you?" The woman turns to me and smiles.
Her hair is dark and cropped around her oval face. Her lips are
bright red.

"Yes," I say, "that's me." But I'm not sure that it is. I mean, that's
my name. But maybe when Dr. Bradford called to tell them I'd be

31

coming in for bed rest, the woman—or someone else—didn't understand. Yes, I'm swollen. Yes, I'm leaking protein in my urine. But I'm not having a *baby*, not yet. I'm sure that on the telephone, an hour ago, Dr. Bradford said bed rest. *Bed rest at the hospital, just to be safe.*

I turn to Rachel, who is fiddling with her hair, twisting it between her fingers and trying to clip it at the back of her head. Wisps keep escaping, and she rolls her eyes as she tries to press them between the tortoiseshell teeth of the clip. When that fails, she tucks the errant strands behind her ears. She smiles, and I look back to the computer, which Rachel can't see from where she's standing.

They're still there, white letters on a blue screen: PRETERM LABOR.

The woman passes consent forms through the window, and I sign them. Maybe the words "preeclampsia" and "pregnancy-induced hypertension" are too long for the space on the woman's computer. The column is narrow—too narrow. Why would it be so narrow?

Rachel slides my purse off my shoulder and onto her own. "Do you think Dad will be able to find us?" she asks.

"I'll let him know where you are," the woman says, emerging from behind her desk. "Follow me." She starts down the hallway I walked just two days ago on my tour of the ward, but we don't go to the labor and delivery rooms I was shown then. Instead, she leads us into a small, square room across from the nurses' station.

"Put this on," she says, handing me a blue hospital gown, "and make yourself comfortable. A nurse will be with you shortly."

"Okay," I say, trying to smile. "Thank you."

Rachel helps me out of my huge maternity blouse and pulls my overalls from my legs, and I settle myself on the hospital bed under a thin white blanket. A nurse comes in to take my blood pressure, and we greet each other cordially, politely. The cuff tightens on my arm, and my fingers prickle and throb. I've had my blood pressure taken so many times over the last week and a half that I'm getting used to this tightening and the sudden relief when the cuff deflates.

"Whew," the nurse says, looking from the blood pressure gauge to me. "Have you had high blood pressure the whole pregnancy?"

My stomach tightens. "No, no. It was fine...yesterday."

"Well," she says. "It's not fine now. It's 170 over 110."

"Oh," I say. "Oh, no." I look at Rachel, whose eyes are wide, and mouth "shit."

"Turn on your left side, and I'll take it again," the nurse says.

I obey, and as the cuff tightens on my arm again, I suddenly understand that my body has betrayed me. I read the books; I filed away the facts, just in case. I know that this kind of spike in my blood pressure means I have severe preeclampsia. There it is—I have it. I also understand that there is nothing I can do to stop what's happening; no amount of reading or worrying will help. And oddly, I almost feel light with this knowledge. I've been complaining all summer, and now, at least, there is an explanation: I'm sick, I've been sick. There is something larger than myself at work here.

The nurse takes the cuff from my arm. "It's the same: 170 over 110. I'll let the doctor know."

As she leaves, another woman comes in to insert an IV into the back of my hand. It hurts, a slow burn up my wrist. I open and close my hand, make a fist.

"Do you think she put this in right?" I ask Rachel. "Is it supposed to hurt this much?"

"Have the nurse check it," Rachel says, as she unpacks the clothes from my brown paper bag and hangs them in the small closet in the corner of the room. Rachel doesn't trust authority. She always reminds my dad to advocate for himself whenever he has to go to the doctor. She actually lived in Costa Rica at the same time I did, but while I spent my days talking to people, shooting the shit on the front porch in that small dusty village of San Vicente, Rachel tracked spider monkeys and white-faced capuchins through the tropical forest. She carried a snake-bite kit in her backpack. She owned her own machete. I'm glad she's here.

"Okay," I say, and when the nurse comes back in I hold up my hand. "Is this supposed to hurt?"

The only other time I've been in the hospital was in Iowa twelve years ago, when I was a sophomore in college and depressed for the first time. I spent months waking to a world devoid of color. Finally, one February afternoon, I had had enough. I swallowed forty-eight sleeping pills and starting walking out of town along the side of a two-lane highway, and I ended up in the emergency room in Grinnell and then in Iowa City. What I remember from those hospital stays is blurry, but the gown and the IV feel familiar, and I sense those memories hovering just out of reach as I sit in a different city in a different time.

The nurse smooths the tape around the IV and tells me it takes time to get used to it. "But let me know if it's still bothering you in an hour." She pats my arm and smiles. I imagine she cares for dozens of pregnant women every week, so she's probably used to the questioning, to the way in which, when we're scared, we point to little things and find fault.

She holds up a bag of, as she calls it, mag sulfate. I know why I'm getting magnesium. I know that with blood pressure rising as quickly as mine, seizures are likely. I remember reading that magnesium sulfate "almost always prevents seizures," but I ask her what it's for, just to be sure.

She says that it will lower my blood pressure.

"Lower my blood pressure," I repeat.

"And," she says, glancing at Rachel, who is still putting my things away, "it will keep you from having seizures."

Rachel's head snaps up. She hasn't read the books. She doesn't know about the seizures or the mag sulfate or that 77,000 women worldwide die from preeclampsia every year. I don't look her in the eye. I don't want to see her fear, don't want to see how this is becoming real for her the way it's now real for me. Instead I watch the nurse as she injects a syringe of magnesium sulfate into my bloodstream and then hooks a bag of it onto the IV stand. "I'm going to have you eat these to settle your stomach," she says, handing me two small packets of graham crackers. She motions to the bag of magnesium. "This can make you feel a little sick."

"Okay," I say, opening the packet of crackers. And I thank the nurse because I don't yet understand the power of magnesium sulfate. I don't yet understand the way it can fold you in its arms and choke you.

Rachel goes down the hall to wait for Dad, and while she's gone, the nurse comes back with a shot of betamethasone, and I blanch. "What?"

"It's called *beta-metha-sone*," she says slowly. She thinks I didn't hear her. But I *did* hear her, and I know from my books that beta-methasone is a steroid to help the baby's lungs develop. I just didn't think I would need it. I didn't think the baby would need it. Even if she is born soon, in the next few days, she is thirty-two weeks; her lungs should be developed, they should be ready for air, for breathing.

I stare at the nurse until she says, "It's just in case. We'll give you another shot in twenty-four hours."

"Okay," I say, and shift to my side so she can push the needle into my butt. It stings, a slow ache blossoming into muscle.

I call my mom, who has a bad cold and doesn't think she should come down to the hospital and risk getting me sick. I cough into the receiver. It's still there, the tightness in my chest, the dry hacking. I *am* sick, I almost say, but don't. And of course I don't want another cold on top of all of this. "Yeah," I say, "better to wait until tomorrow." It feels crowded in the room anyway, with Dad and Rachel both here, and even though it has been years since my parents' divorce and they are cordial, it's sometimes easier to be with one of them at a time.

Dad and Rachel are sitting on chairs in the corner of the room, watching me. My dad holds his khaki summer hat in his hands, and I can tell he's trying not to look worried. When Dr. Anderson comes in, both he and Rachel shake her hand.

Dr. Anderson is the most cheerful doctor I have ever met. She is small and full of energy. She flits around the room like a sparrow. "Well," she says, pulling a pair of rubber gloves from the box on the wall, "you're really sick."

At the sight of the gloves, my dad stands awkwardly and says he's going to the cafeteria.

When he's gone and the curtain is pulled around my bed, Dr. Anderson presses on my pelvis with one hand and roots around inside me with the other. She studies something on my belly as she pushes and prods, but then she looks up at me and purses her lips. "Yup," she says. "You're completely effaced. Not dilated yet, but completely effaced. The baby is getting ready." She pulls off her gloves. "She knows."

And I imagine the baby then, realizing that something has gone terribly wrong. *Unsafe environment. Must get out. Must get out.* I make her voice robotic in my mind, though I'm not sure why. This makes me feel like laughing. I must smile, because Dr. Anderson stares at me, her eyebrows raised.

She holds her hands wide apart and says that a normal pregnancy is here, her right hand, with 0 percent toxicity—did she use that word, *toxicity*? "This," she says, motioning with her left hand, "is 100 percent toxic, HELLP syndrome." Then she moves her right hand between the middle of her chest and her left hand. "You are here," she says, "at about 70 percent."

Rachel's eyes dart from Dr. Anderson to me, trying to gauge my reaction. I don't know what my reaction is, so I simply nod at Rachel and nod at Dr. Anderson, like a bobblehead.

"Do you know when the baby will be born?" I ask. "My husband plays professional soccer and he's in Seattle right now. A play-off game." It's odd, but even now, even as I just listened to the doctor tell me I'm 70 percent toxic, I experience a flash of pride: my husband plays professional soccer. He's in the play-offs. "He's supposed to be back tomorrow afternoon," I continue. "Should I have him come home sooner?"

Dr. Anderson looks startled. "Uh, you better call him. He needs to be here. You could go into labor anytime."

"Oh," I say.

"The Cervidil," says Dr. Anderson, "will help ripen your cervix, and tomorrow morning we'll start the Pitocin. I also am going to have you do another twenty-four-hour urine collection."

"Oh," I say again, subdued. I'm being induced, and I have to pee in the jug again, and Donny is two thousand miles away.

"Yikes," Rachel says after Dr. Anderson leaves.

When I reach Donny on his cell phone, he's in a van, stuck in traffic on the way to the game. I can hear his teammates in the background—they're rowdy, and I imagine them slapping each other on the back, turning around in their seats like grade-schoolers.

"I'm at the hospital," I say, oddly calm. "You need to come home. The baby might be born tomorrow. I might go into labor tonight."

Donny seems calm, as well. "Okay," he says. "Okay."

This is all we say, and this seems strange and at the same time not at all strange. What else is there to say? Months later I will ask him how he felt when I called, and he will tell me he wasn't worried. "I just started figuring out how to get home, how I would get a flight and get to the airport." He went into "dealing" mode, and he just kept going, not thinking about what was happening to me.

Rachel has agreed to spend the night at the hospital with me, so after Dad leaves, she walks over to Station 54 to borrow a movie. When I agreed to bed rest, I thought I would be going to Station 54 to be stashed away with the other women with precarious pregnancies, but things are moving too quickly now, so I will stay where I am, in the small room across from the nurses' station.

While Rachel is gone, the nurse comes in to hook me up to a monitor. She rolls me to the side and fastens two disks to my swollen belly. One of these disks measures the baby's heart rate; the other will measure the frequency of my contractions. Both are held in place with stretchy gauze straps, which I recognize from the videos in birthing class. They looked uncomfortable to me then, but I hardly feel them after they're in place. They become a part of me, just as the machine next to my bed, which spits out a graph of our heartbeats, becomes a part of me.

I ask the nurse, as she settles me on my left side, with pillows propped under me, how big a baby is at thirty-two weeks.

"It depends," she says, covering my legs with a sheet. "It depends on so many things." I will come to expect this kind of answer in the next weeks: vague, not willing to guarantee anything.

But then she pauses at the end of the bed, her hands resting lightly on my covered feet. "Maybe two pounds," she says. "Maybe two and a half." I can tell she's guessing, and I know she wants me to be prepared for how small the baby might be, but I wish I'd never asked. Two pounds is too small. I can't even imagine it, what a two-pound baby would look like, what a two-pound baby would feel like in my arms. I search my mind for something that weighs two pounds:

A cantaloupe? A basketball? I can't think of anything, so I settle for two boxes of butter. Two pounds is this: standing in the dairy section of the grocery store, cupping two boxes of butter in your palm.

I try to remember what my daily pregnancy calendar said a fetus weighed at thirty-two weeks. I'm sure it was three pounds, maybe three and a half. And I decide I'll take that. I decide I can live with three pounds.

When Donny calls, he says that the earliest flight he can get out of Seattle is at 1:00 a.m., but he promises he'll be at the hospital by 7:00.

"Are you going to play?" I ask.

"Yes," he says. "What else would I do?"

I don't know. It doesn't make sense that he would sit out the game. But there is something about my tan, muscular husband running around on a field, kicking a soccer ball, while I lie in a hospital with a suppository in my vagina to ripen my cervix that particularly annoys me.

"Whatever," I say, and hang up.

Rachel comes back with the Meg Ryan movie *French Kiss,* which I've seen before and liked, but tonight Meg Ryan is too much for me, so Rachel turns it off after only a few minutes. The nurse brings in a foldaway bed, which she and Rachel open in the corner of the room. By ten o'clock, Rachel is snoring softly.

I don't sleep at all this first night in the hospital, and it's odd that even though I spend the whole night staring at the clock on the wall, watching the second hand make its rounds, time does not move slowly. Perhaps it's the fact that I feel suspended somewhere between pregnancy and motherhood, between having my baby inside me and outside me. Or maybe it's just something about hospitals.

I remember the same thing happening with time when my grandma Lucille was dying, four years ago. She had had a stroke, and we spent ten days in the hospital waiting for her to die. I sat by her side, swabbing the inside of her mouth with a wet sponge. After five days, my grandpa decided to discontinue the nutritional supplement, which was dripping into her stomach through a clear plastic tube. My grandparents had, as a doctor told us, the most carefully written and specific living will he had ever seen. But even without the tube feedings, my grandmother didn't die. Her feet began to turn purple and swell. Her breath became sweet, smelling faintly of chocolate. My grandpa slept beside her on a pull-out couch, letting go of his wife of sixty-seven years. And we sat next to him, time suspended as my grandma's organs began to shut down.

At midnight, the nurse came in and turned down the volume on the monitor next to my bed because she thought it was keeping me awake. But now I miss the sound of our hearts beating together. Mine was slow, steady, and the baby's was doing triple time. Together they sounded like an old locomotive, clanking over rusty tracks.

By 3:00 a.m. I'm having contractions that feel like menstrual cramps. When they come, I curl into myself and try to breathe deeply. Donny should be in the air by now, and I hope, spitefully, that he's not sleeping either.

Going to the bathroom is an ordeal. I try not to disturb the needle on the back of my hand or tangle my tubes in the metal parts of the bed as I maneuver between my bed and Rachel's bed, pulling the IV stand, its wheels click-click-clicking as I inch my way along. I bump into Rachel's bed over and over again, and it's amazing that I don't wake her, but she snores through the whole thing.

In the bathroom, I begin the process of peeing into the basin and emptying this into the jug, which sits in a bucket of ice on the floor. This is complicated by my tubes and the IV stand, and I'm irritated. If the baby is going to be born soon, I don't understand why they need another protein reading.

I must eventually sleep, because at 6:30 a.m. on Saturday, I wake to the room washed in gray. When I lift my head, the room spins, and I know I'm going to be sick. I struggle from bed and push the IV into the bathroom, but by the time I get to the toilet, there is no time for the basin and the jug. I sit on the toilet and lean into the sink, simultaneously throwing up and shitting liquid. The tile floor shifts under my feet. The yellow walls tilt. I throw up again and again. This couldn't have been what the nurse meant when she said the mag sulfate would make me feel *a little sick.*

Rachel's voice through the door: *Are you okay?* She sounds far away.

"Okay," I manage. "Sick."

"I'll get the nurse," she says.

Rachel is there, then gone. A nurse comes in, then goes again. And suddenly, finally, Donny is here. He's above me, gathering my hair in his hands. He holds it back from my face, kisses my neck.

"I feel horrible," I whisper. "Thank God you're here. I feel so sick."

"I know," he says. "I know." He helps me back to bed and presses a wet washcloth to my forehead. There is a heaviness in my chest, like someone is sitting on me, pressing the air from my lungs.

Rachel is already dressed, and the bed has been folded up. "I'll leave you guys alone for a while, but I'll be back later."

"Okay," I say. I want to tell her how much I appreciate her, how much I love her for staying with me last night, but all I can manage is "thank you."

"Of course," she says, and shuts the door on her way out.

I turn to Donny and smile a little. "Hi," I say. I thought I'd be irritated with him when he got here, still angry that he wasn't here last night, but I'm so relieved I could cry.

"I didn't sleep at all on the plane," he says, rearranging the washcloth on my forehead. "I couldn't."

"Me neither," I say, and then realize it sounds as if I had been on a plane as well. "I mean, here."

"I love you," he says.

"You played," I say, trying to keep the accusation from my voice.

"It helped." He squeezes my hand. "And you never left my mind. You and the baby. You were always there, right in front of me."

"Hmmm."

"And I've never played better."

"Really," I say, and even with the mag sulfate and room spinning and the contractions, a dull ache moving across my pelvis, I understand the seriousness of this statement. Donny is really good at what he does. He's one of the best defenders in the A-League, yet he hardly ever measures up to his own impossible standard. I imagine what it must have been like for him on the field, knowing the baby would be born early. I see him running, his face set in concentration. I envy him his ability to transfer whatever worry and fear he's feeling into power, into speed, into something he can control: the ball.

"We won 1–0. The next game's here, tomorrow night."

"We'll see," I say. I want to tell him he's crazy if he thinks he's playing in that game, but all I manage is "bowl."

Donny holds the shallow bowl to my chin. I turn my head to the side, trying not to get the vomit on my hospital gown. The only thing that comes out is yellowish bile, slimy and bitter.

A nurse comes in to hook up the Pitocin, and I tell her that I didn't pee into the basin. "Diarrhea," I say, and she looks annoyed. This is a new nurse, not the nice one from last night.

"Well, there goes your urine sample," she says.

I think about flipping her off.

An hour later, my stomach is in a knot, my lower back is aching, and the pressure on my chest makes it difficult to breathe. I keep trying to sit up, but it doesn't help. Donny holds a cup to my lips, but even a sip of water makes me vomit.

Suddenly, I start to cough and can't stop. I cough and cough and then feel a rush of liquid between my legs. When I'm finally able to speak, I say, "Oh, shit."

"What?"

"I think my water just broke."

Donny's up and heading for the door. "I'll get the nurse."

When she comes in, she lifts the sheet and checks the pads under me. "Your water didn't break," she says. "You peed."

But I insist: "My water broke."

"I don't *think* so," she says. She calls another nurse, and they lift and roll me to the side and back again in order to remove the sheets and replace them with fresh ones. Then they put some kind of diaper thing on me. The nurse is terribly irritated with me, but I don't care.

When my mom shows up, she kisses me on the forehead and brushes the hair from my eyes. As she stands, I see that her face is pinched with worry. "I didn't know," she starts.

"I know," I say. Later she will tell me that she didn't understand how sick I was. She will say, "I should have been there the whole time. I should have been with you." But I'm just glad she's here now.

"I'm hot," I whisper. "I can't breathe." The mag sulfate is gaining . strength. I can feel it, burning through my veins. My mom fiddles with the thermostat on the wall, sets it to sixty degrees.

By midmorning my contractions are coming regularly, but they are still the early ones—if it weren't for the vomiting and the pressure on my chest and the incredible heat emanating from my skin, I would be in what our birthing class instructors called the "smiling stage" of labor. I try to remember the breathing exercises we practiced on the floor of our classroom, but they seem silly.

"You're doing a great job," Donny says, leaning on the edge of the bed. He breathes along with me: he he haaaa, he he haaaa.

When Dr. Anderson pushes the curtain away from the door, I scowl at her. "Why would anyone ever do this again?"

"Oh," she says, smiling, "you forget the pain. I have two kids, and I had a rough time with the first, but a couple of years later I was ready for another." She waves her hand around the room. "You'll forget all of this, and you'll want to do it again."

"I doubt it," I say. I don't tell her that I can't forget. I don't tell her that I write memoir, that I depend on my memory, that I take notes, file away the details.

She checks my cervix. "You're still not dilated at all."

"How could that be?"

"We need to get things moving here," she says. "If you're willing, I'd like to try something."

"Okay." I'd agree to just about anything right now.

She says she wants to insert a catheter into the opening of my cervix. From that, she wants to tie a rice sock, which, she says, will hang down over the edge of my hospital bed. This extra pressure, she tells me, will help pull my cervix open. "When you're dilated to three centimeters, the rice sock will drop to the floor." Dr. Anderson smiles.

"Okay," I say, though this doesn't really sound okay to me. The rice sock that she is referring to is one that normally is heated in the microwave and placed on the lower back of a laboring woman, like a heating pad. I've never heard of one being used as a weight.

"I'll need to dilate you a little in order to insert the catheter," she says.

"Fine," I say.

Donny squeezes my hand, and when I look at him I know he wants to know whether I'm really fine with this. I nod.

"It may hurt a little," Dr. Anderson says.

"Fine," I say again.

Then she sticks her hand inside me and cranks me open.

Everything turns white.

"Breathe," Donny says.

He he haaaa. He he haaaa.

"I've got it," Dr. Anderson says. "The catheter's in." She and the nurse congratulate each other. Then the nurse ties the rice sock to the rubber hose of the catheter and hangs it over the end of the bed.

When Dr. Anderson and the nurse leave, still pleased with their handiwork, Donny whispers, "What kind of medieval torture was that?" He's joking, but only partly.

I try to smile.

"Medieval torture doctor," he says. He will call Dr. Anderson this from now on. But really, after the initial pain, I don't feel the catheter unless I shift my weight to the side, which sends the sock into a slow swing, a rice pendulum pulling me open.

Donny goes to get something to eat, and my mom sits next to me, spooning ice into my mouth. A technician comes in with an ultrasound machine. Another biophysical profile. Cool gel on my belly. Baby on the screen. This time, though, I can't make her out.

When I try to focus on her, I throw up. Another ice chip dissolving on my tongue, and then the technician is gone. Baby scored eight out of ten. She's still okay, but maybe she's beginning to struggle a little?

Everything that I read in my pregnancy books is happening; it's all coming true. I know my body can't reverse the preeclampsia. I know my organs are seriously stressed. I know I can't take much more of this. Much later, I will read an article about preeclampsia in the *New Yorker* in which a doctor describes what he calls "the maternal-fetal conflict," a conflict of interest between a mother and a fetus, each attempting to survive at the cost of the other. Now, as I lie twisted in my sheets, burning up, I understand that I will recover only after the baby and the placenta are out of me. I also am acutely aware of the fact that I don't know what will happen to the baby once she *is* out of me.

But I remind myself what Dr. Bradford said: thirty-two weeks is a good place to be. And what my books said: at thirty-two weeks, a fetus's lungs are almost completely mature. In our birthing class, one of our instructors told us the story of a woman, a couple of years ago, whose water broke in class. She had been having back pain for several days, but it wasn't intense pain, so she didn't realize she had been in labor. The instructor had smiled and said, "It was okay, though. I walked her upstairs and she delivered that night. The baby was thirty-two weeks, so he had to stay here at Abbott for a couple of weeks, but he was fine."

That's what she said: he was here at Abbott for a couple of weeks and he was fine. I can handle that, a couple of weeks in the Special Care Nursery, which is just upstairs on the seventh floor.

But when I ask the nurse where the baby will go after she's born, she says she could go to Special Care or she could go across the street, to Children's Hospital. "Special Care," she says, "is a Level II Nursery, and the NICU at Children's is a Level III."

NICU. It's pronounced *Nick Q,* the Nick Q. "What?" I say.

"If your baby is breathing on her own when she's born, she'll probably go to Special Care. But if she needs to be intubated, she'll be taken to Children's."

Intubated is a word I've heard only on television. I've seen it dozens of times on *ER,* the deftness with which a doctor cradles a curve of plastic in her hand and slips a tube into a patient's trachea. But I can't imagine someone slipping a tube into *my* baby's trachea.

"Oh," I say to the nurse, because I don't know what else to say. She can't tell me where my baby will be going. She doesn't know if my baby will be breathing when she comes out.

My dad is here now, and my mom and Donny. Then my step-dad, Karl, is here, and Rachel is back and then gone again. They all, except for Donny, seem far away. Then my friend Jess is above me, and she's crying.

"It was in the paper," she manages. "In the sports section. They said you went into labor last night. That Donny didn't play." Jess and I have known each other since college. We were roommates our senior year. I know she's scared, and I want to tell her how sorry I am that she's scared. I want to tell her I'm fine. But clearly I'm not fine; I can see it in her face.

"He played," I say, as if this is the important piece of information that the paper got wrong.

Jess holds my hand, her eyes full of tears. "You'll be okay."

But I'm done with the nodding and the "okays." I look up at Jess and say, "Fuck."

It's early afternoon, and my mom has disappeared. Did she tell me she was leaving? I can't remember, but I keep asking Donny where she is.

He wipes my face with a damp cloth. "She'll be back."

Then there are three nurses in the room; they say they need to weigh me. I wonder how I will stand to be weighed. How will I keep my balance? How will I not trip on the rice sock? I'm worried that I'll accidentally yank it out. It takes me a moment to realize I won't be standing. One nurse pushes a giant hook on a stand to the edge of my bed while the other two wrap me in my sheet.

Donny says he's going to make a few phone calls.

"Okay," I say.

The nurses tie my sheet in knots. They must also secure me in some other way, but I'm not clear on this. I just know that when I am hoisted into the air, I hang there over my hospital bed suffocating in white, like a huge caterpillar unable to break free from her cocoon.

"One hundred seventy-six," a nurse says, and then they lower me back to the bed, where they resituate me on my left side. I weigh the same as I did last night, which is good. If my swelling increases suddenly, it means I am getting sicker faster.

The nurse moves around the bed to take my blood pressure, which is holding steady with the mag sulfate, and this is when my mom reappears. She's bubbly, revived from her break and whatever food she's consumed.

"I just saw the most *won*derful woman," she says.

I turn my head slowly to look at her. Any fast motion makes me throw up.

"This little old lady—a volunteer here at the hospital—was in the elevator, and she was so friendly, so *joyful*." My mom is addressing both of us, the nurse and me. Her gaze shifts between us.

I try to untangle my legs from the sheet. My skin is so hot, it's as if there is a fire somewhere deep inside me. That and still the nausea, the cough, the difficulty catching my breath.

"So joyful," my mom continues. "Spreading joy all over the place like it was her *job*."

I lift my head to look at my mother, who holds a paper cup of steaming coffee between her palms. She smiles. Her eyes even seem to sparkle. And each of these things—the coffee, the smiling, the sparkling—irritates me.

"Fuck joy," I say. "Fuck joy, Mom." And I lean back against the pillows.

"Well," my mother says.

"Well," echoes the nurse, who is fiddling with the tubes of my IV. "I didn't expect to hear that kind of thing from *you*."

I don't know what, exactly, she *did* expect to hear from me. And I don't give a fuck.

At three o'clock in the afternoon, Dr. Anderson comes in and moves close to the bed, so I don't have to turn my head to see her. But I can tell by her eyes, which hold none of the smile that they usually do, that something is wrong.

"The baby," she says slowly, "isn't doing well."

Donny reaches for my hand.

"Each time you have a contraction, the baby's heart rate drops. This is called deceleration. She's isn't getting enough oxygen."

Not enough oxygen. Oxygen deprivation causes brain damage. It causes mental retardation, learning disabilities, death. I had read somewhere that even mild oxygen deprivation at birth could cause impaired intellectual and verbal skills. I think about the woman who took care of Mimi, about the photo of her son, crumpled in a wheel-chair, head lolling to the side.

"We call it fetal intolerance of labor," she says, and I repeat her: fetal intolerance of labor.

Donny squeezes my hand.

Dr. Anderson checks my cervix, which still hasn't dilated. "Labor isn't progressing," she says. "I'm going to stop the Pitocin and remove the rice sock. I'm going to get you on oxygen and see if that helps. Then we're going to need to do a cesarean."

"Thank God," I say. "Thank you." Weeks ago, I never would have guessed this would be my response at being told I would need a C-section, this immense relief. I manage to smile at Dr. Anderson, and my gratitude hangs there, between us.

6

THE SUN HAS MOVED TO THE OTHER SIDE OF THE
hospital, and my room is cast in blue shadows. Donny and my mom
have gone down the hall to relay the news to my dad and Rachel,
who have been waiting in the family lounge. Mom will call my
friends Jess, Claire in New York, and Emily in Colorado. She will
call Sara and Grandpa, both of whom have been waiting for updates.
She will explain the decelerations, the C-section.

I'd been so smug. I'd sat in birthing class feeling superior, wanting nothing to do with the drugs, the interventions. But without the
drugs we would be dead. And even though the thought of a needle
sliding into my back, dangerously close to the nerves in my spine,
fills me with dread, I want to be awake when my daughter is born.
I can't miss that. So when the nurse, a new nurse, comes in with an
oxygen mask, I say, "I want a spinal. I need to be awake."

This nurse, whose hair is blond and curly, smiles and puts her
hand on my arm. She says they'll need to draw blood, check my levels
of something or other. "But first," she says, "let's get you on oxygen."

She unwraps a plastic mask and adjusts the elastic; then she
slides it over my head and presses it over my nose and mouth. Immediately, I feel as if I'm suffocating. I can't breathe. The nurse says, "I'll
be back," and she turns away, but the mask is too tight. "No," I say,
pulling at the straps. "No."

She comes back and lifts the mask. "Try to relax and breathe,"
she says. "The baby needs this oxygen."

"I can't do this."

"Take a deep breath."

"I can't," I say. "I feel like I'm drowning." It was the same feeling I had when I was learning to scuba dive in Costa Rica. When
I jumped into the pool for my first in-water lesson, I sank and

panicked. It didn't matter that all I had to do was breathe. I couldn't take a breath, couldn't trust the mask and the tank on my back. I kicked as hard as I could to the surface of the pool and ripped off the mask, gulping air.

The nurse smiles again and pulls the straps from my head. "How about this?" she says. "Do you think you can hold it in front of your face, like this?" She places the mask in my hand and raises it to my mouth. "If you breathe deeply, you can keep it right here as long as the baby's oxygen levels increase."

I nod, sucking at the stream of air. "Thank you."

My family has moved to the waiting lounge. I'm not sure if they sensed my need for quiet or if I asked them to go, but now Donny and I are alone in the dark of my hospital room.

The nurse comes in to tell me that the anesthesiologist has given the okay for a spinal epidural. "I'll have you watch this," she says, slipping a tape into the VCR.

It's a video of a C-section, a gory version of an after-school special, narrated by a slow, quiet voice that explains the procedure. The television screen is difficult to see around my mask, and I feel nauseous as I try to focus on the pregnant woman's belly, her skin tight and smooth. Why are we watching this? I guess they want us to know what to expect, but it doesn't really make sense. Like the woman in the video, I will be lying with my head and chest behind a curtain of blue paper. I won't see Dr. Anderson cut into me. So why do they want me to see how the doctor's knife slices through the woman's skin easily, as if he's slicing through butter? The way the doctor's hands disappear into the woman's body and pull out the baby, all covered in blood and white slime? It must be some sort of legal, covering-one's-ass protocol. I need to know what will happen so I don't complain later.

After the doctor in the video says, *It's a boy,* and the woman echoes *It's a boy!* and begins to cry, Donny turns off the television and sits with his head down on my bed. A half-hour becomes an hour which becomes two. The nurse says that the baby's oxygen levels are fine now; the baby is no longer having decelerations. I just need to keep breathing through the mask. An anesthesiologist comes in to explain the spinal. He describes how he will insert the needle into my spinal fluid. He is cocky, self-assured, and I like this. It means he won't slip up and puncture my spinal column.

Donny is restless and annoyed: *What's taking them so long? This is ridiculous. I can't believe this.* I, in turn, am annoyed with him. I want him to be quiet, to rub my feet, but he just puts his head back down on the end of my bed and closes his eyes.

The nurse comes in and apologizes for how long it's taking. "There are some more serious cases that have come in, and these have bumped you out of line."

Donny sighs, but I just nod at the nurse. Even though I still feel claustrophobic and hot all over and my arm aches from holding the mask to my face, I'm relieved to hear that there are pregnant women in more serious trouble than me. I could hold on like this forever as long as my baby is not the most serious case. I reassure myself with someone else's misfortune. I am content with their trouble. This is an awful thing to be.

The phone rings. Donny picks it up. It's Sara. She's at a Springsteen concert in Philadelphia. When Donny passes me the phone, it's so loud I have to hold the receiver a foot away. She says she feels guilty being at a concert while I'm waiting for a C-section. "But I thought you should hear this," she screams. "'Badlands.'"

And then I hear the crowd shouting the lyrics along with Bruce. It's always been my favorite Springsteen song, and it seems that right this moment, he must be singing it for me, for the baby. I imagine Sara, seven states away, standing with her arm outstretched, her phone in the air, screaming along with fifty thousand people.

Later, she'll tell me what an amazing concert it was; Bruce played the usual favorites, but he also played Johnny Cash. I didn't realize, as I lay in the hospital, waiting for a C-section, hoping that my baby will be able to breathe on her own, that Johnny Cash had died. When I learn this, I will be struck by how monumental and public his life was and, conversely, how private and seemingly inconsequential ours are.

Sara's cell phone dies, and I hand the phone back to Donny. "Bruce," is all I say.

Before I'm wheeled into the operating room, my dad comes in and stands above me. He says he wants to say a prayer, and I'm irritated. I don't want a prayer. I want a C-section. I want to be okay. I want the baby to be okay. But my dad holds my hand and asks God to watch over me, to watch over the baby. I'm not sure why this bothers me so much now when it didn't bother me at all last week. Maybe because it feels as though I'm in God's hands. And I don't want to be in God's hands; I want to be in Dr. Anderson's hands, I want to be in the anesthesiologist's hands. But I let my dad pray, and when he kisses me on the cheek, I say curtly, "Okay."

It's eight o'clock when I'm finally wheeled into the operating room. Donny isn't allowed in the room when the anesthesiologist slips the needle into my spinal fluid. When he *does* come in, I don't recognize him at first—he's in scrubs, only his eyes and glasses visible in all that blue.

On the operating table, my arms are straight out to either side, strapped down, crucifix style. In front of me hangs the curtain of blue paper. I cannot see or feel anything below my armpits. It's cold, and the lights are too bright, so I close my eyes and try to focus on the words flying between Dr. Anderson and the nurses. One names an item, the other repeats it. They count, repeat, count again. I try to follow this ritual, make sense of the special language they're speaking, but I can't.

And then it is happening—I am being cut open. I can't feel it, of course, but I know. Donny's fingers massage circles across my forehead. He is trying to keep me from thinking about the anesthesia, about the baby, about whether or not she will be breathing when she's pulled from me. He is trying to make this okay somehow, but we both know that he cannot.

I hear the doctor and nurses talking, but I can't make out what they're saying. I stare at the ceiling. And then someone is pushing hard on my rib cage, knocking the wind from me. I look up at

Donny, his fingers on my forehead. He's watching the doctor, staring over the blue curtain. I want to ask what's going on. Why are they pushing and pulling? The baby is small. Why can't you just pull her out? This didn't happen in the video. Months later I will read my chart, which says, "the fetal vertex was not easily delivered." But still I'll wonder why it was so difficult to get her out.

But then she *is* out, and she doesn't cry. I don't hear her cry. Someone says, "Time to work on her." *Work on her.* I don't know what that means.

"I'll go," Donny says.

"Go," I say, and as soon as he's gone, following the nurse or the doctor into another small room, a wave of nausea swells, rising in my throat. I tilt my head back, searching for the nurse, but this makes me dizzy. "I'm going to throw up," I whisper.

Then the nurse is there, holding a bowl to my face, and I heave and heave. I'm not sure if this is still from the mag sulfate or now the spinal or if I'm vomiting from relief. When I'm done, I feel better, and I stare up at the grid of the ceiling as Dr. Anderson pulls at me.

I realize she must be removing my placenta, because after a moment she says to a nurse, *see how small it is.* Later I will ask her about this, and she will say that preeclampsia affects how large and effective a placenta is. A smaller placenta often leads to growth retardation in the fetus. Dr. Anderson will tell me that my placenta couldn't have supported my baby much longer, that Stella wouldn't have grown any larger. "Your body," she will say, "did everything it could for that baby. She's better off out here."

Now Dr. Anderson says, "Kate, what's your daughter's name?"

"Stella," I say. "Stella Lucille."

"That's beautiful."

The nurses agree. "Is it a family name?"

"Lucille was my grandmother's name," I say slowly. "But we just liked Stella." Originally, Donny and I thought we would name a daughter Ana Lucille. It reminded me of water, of waves. But Ana didn't seem bold enough for the baby kicking in my belly. Then my friend Claire said, *what about Stella?* And it stuck: Stella Lucille.

Some people will hear Stella, always, in the eternal bellow of

Marlon Brando: *Stella!* But it is strong, too, spoken in a whisper. We hope she will be feisty and confident, someone with whom to reckon. This is what I'm counting on now, that she will be strong enough to live, to fight on her own, outside me.

Then Donny is at my shoulder. "She's going upstairs," he exclaims. "Three pounds six ounces!" I know he's smiling; I can hear it in his voice. He steps aside and someone holds Stella up for me to see. Later, I won't remember what she looked like held to my face. I do not kiss her. I do not touch her. I will remember saying, "Isn't she beautiful. *Isn't she beautiful.*" And I will remember the relief—three pounds six ounces—she's over three pounds.

Then they are gone, and I'm alone under bright light.

7

My mom and Karl are waiting outside the operating room. Their faces float above me as I'm pushed down the hall. "Did you see her?" I ask. "Isn't she beautiful?"

They're both smiling. Their floating heads nod. Yes, yes. She's beautiful. Good, we're all in agreement. I smile as well, but it's difficult for me to keep my eyes open. I close them and open them and close them. When I open them again, I'm in the recovery room. The nurse who assisted in surgery, the same one who told me I could hold the plastic mask in front of my face, is sitting near me at a desk. I'm surprised and pleased that she's here, and I want to thank her for not leaving me alone, but when I open my mouth only nonsense comes out: *I'm on my back. I feel funny. Isn't she beautiful? I'm lying on my back.*

The nurse pinches my toes, but I still can't feel them, and I hope I'm not the .02 percent who is permanently paralyzed. But then I fall back asleep. When I wake again, Donny is above me.

I reach for his hand. "Is she okay?"

"She's okay," he says, brushing away my hair. "She's okay."

"I can't feel my legs," I say.

"You will," he says, and I believe him, although I wonder how he knows.

I fall asleep and wake again as the nurse touches my feet. I can feel them now, though they are only half there.

"Do you want to go up and see her now?"

"Can I?"

"I'll take you," she says.

The ceiling spins as the nurse pushes my bed down the hall and into an elevator. We are up a floor, then down a hallway. Then we are in the Special Care Nursery and the nurse maneuvers my bed between equipment until I am next to the incubator where Stella sleeps. It's difficult to focus—she blurs before my eyes—but I turn to the nurses who stand nearby, and I say, "Isn't she beautiful?"

"She is," they say, and I nod, pleased. My daughter is alive. She's breathing. She's only one floor away.

When I am back in my hospital room, I notice the new plastic bracelet on my wrist. Pink and blue bears that look like Grateful Dead bears dance around my wrist. Under the bears are written my name and Stella's name followed by a bunch of numbers. This bracelet must be my pass into the Special Care Nursery, but I've no idea who put it on me.

When Donny comes back, I ask, "Stella?"

"I sat with her," he says. "I touched her hand. She was sleeping."

"She's okay?"

Donny nods and wipes my hands and forehead with a wet cloth. Then he helps me brush my teeth, which haven't been brushed since last night.

"I'm on my back," I say. "I'm lying on my back."

"You are."

"I'm never going to lie on my left side—ever again."

Donny smiles, and then, suddenly, he is asleep. He lies in the corner where my sister slept last night. How could that have been just last night?

Everything has soft edges, and I seem to dream without falling asleep. Stella is still inside me. I feel her kicking, doing her flips. Then suddenly she is struggling, drowning. But then I am the one who is drowning, drifting underwater. I stare up at the sun, which ripples above me, blue and green and yellow, and I know I'll never reach the surface. Then I'm back in my hospital room, and it takes me a moment to remember that I am no longer pregnant.

When a nurse comes in, I ask, "Have I slept?"

"Well, you were snoring," she says. She is a new nurse, one of those no-nonsense nurses, and I can tell I'm annoying her with my grogginess. Her black hair is pulled back from her face in long, thin braids. Her accent is thick. I ask her where she was born.

"Nigeria," she says.

"Oh." So far away.

She moves around the bed, fits a pulse oximeter onto my finger. "Why Minnesota?" I ask.

"My husband," she says. "He's in school here." In her voice I think I hear homesickness. I have never been to Nigeria—to anywhere in Africa—and I don't know if she is from a city or a small town. But I picture her home as something rural, like San Vicente: dirt roads baking under hot sun. I want to tell her I miss it, too, but that doesn't make any sense.

She lifts the bag of urine from the side of my bed. "One hundred ccs," she says.

A hundred ccs is less than four ounces—nothing. It's not enough. This means the liquid is still collecting under my skin. I am still swelling. And I remember from my books that with preeclampsia, you can still get sicker after the baby is born. You can still have seizures. You can still go into a coma. You only know you are beginning to recover when you begin to pee liters at a time.

I dip back into dreams, dreams of San Vicente, of that dusty town thousands of miles away that exists in memory, in words. I float high above the village, tilting into the wind. Strands of hair flutter behind me like the tails of a kite. The air is soft, like silt against my skin, and the whole valley is before me, burned pastures stretching out of view. Below me, San Vicente is little more than a pale road the color of bone, curving around a matapalo tree. Then I am in the center of the village, and Betty and Tirza and Sara are waving to me. At their feet are babies, lying in the dirt. They are Tirza's babies, the ones who died. They speak to me: *venga*, come.

I wake again, my throat dry. My sheets are twisted. I can't breathe. I want to call to Donny, make him tell me everything is fine with the baby, but nothing comes out when I open my mouth.

On Sunday morning, sunlight streams through the slats of the venetian blinds, and I press my hand to my eyes. "I'm melting," I say to Donny, who is folding up his bed. I'm sweating, hair stuck to my neck. I try to peel the hair away, but the movement sends the room into a slow spin. "I'm going to be sick," I say.

Donny holds the bowl to my chin. I heave and heave, vomiting the bitter slime. My hair trails in it.

"Uh," I say.

"It's okay," he says. "I'll clean it." He goes into the bathroom and fills a Styrofoam cup with water and rinses my hair.

"Cut it," I whisper.

He holds my wet hair in his palm, pats it dry with a paper towel.

"Will you cut it?"

"I don't have any scissors," he says.

"Oh."

Donny pulls the sheet up over my body and I shake my head, pulling at it.

"I'm too hot," I mutter. "It's too hot in here." If I thought I was hot yesterday, I was wrong. That was nothing.

"I'm going to go get some coffee," Donny says, "and then up to see Stella."

I nod. I don't care.

"Your mom will be here soon."

"Go," I say. He leaves, and the room spins, a tilt-a-whirl of light. I press my eyes shut. Is this still the mag sulfate? Will it continue to gain force until it kills me? Or maybe this is painkiller, whatever they inject into my bloodstream to keep my incision quiet.

I am asleep and then awake, then asleep again. I dream of Stella, still inside me. I dream of dogs, mangy dogs with clacking teeth. Then I am in San Vicente again. Betty hands me a metal pail and says, *Jocote, niña. Fetch me jocote and I'll make you jocotal.* And I run like a child, down the road to the jocote tree. I swing a stick through the air, my arms an arc of movement, hitting the tree again and again until the fruit falls into the dirt around me.

When I wake, I taste it, the sugar and milk and pulp coating the roof of my mouth. I touch my sagging belly, and pain radiates upward. I turn to press the call button, and that's when I see Stella. She's in a Polaroid, taped to the rail of my bed. I don't know who put this photo here, but I'm grateful. She's fuzzy, but her eyes are open, her head facing me. It was taken through the wall of her incubator and also the wall of the plastic box that covers her head—the plastic box pumped with oxygen and humidity, the plastic box that keeps her skin from drying out, that makes it easier for her to breathe. I don't know any of this, of course. She just looks fuzzy to me.

I try to focus on the picture. That is my daughter. I have a daughter. She is taped to the side of my bed. A nurse comes in and asks her name. Stella, I say. Stella Lucille. This is a different nurse. My Nigerian nurse is gone. The short blond who sat with me after the C-section—the one who kept checking my toes, asking can you feel them now? can you feel them now?—she is gone, as well. This nurse has light brown hair. And suddenly I think that all of these nurses with their different hair are really the same nurse. She is a shape-shifter, trying to confuse me.

"Stella," she says. "That's pretty."

"Yes," I agree. I want to ask her if she is from Nigeria.

My mom is here, sitting next to me. I'm not sure what time it is. The room is still bright. My face hurts. She tells me that Rachel has come and gone. Sara has called three times from D.C.

"Oh," I say.

I'm relieved that she's here. She is the only one I want besides Donny. And maybe I want her even more than Donny. She knows what I need before I ask. I just look at her, and she brings me the glass of ice, shakes some onto my tongue.

Pink lilies and gerbera daisies line the window. "Who brought these? When did this happen?" I ask.

Mom walks over to the ledge, pulls out each card. "These are from Sally and Richard, these are from Dick and G.G. These are from Claire's family. They smell wonderful. Nasturtiums," Mom says.

"Oh," I say. "That's nice."

There is even a balloon, but Mom doesn't know who sent it. It's pink with white cursive letters: *IT'S A GIRL! CONGRATULATIONS!*

I twist in my sheets, the room spinning. I can't breathe, can't seem to catch my breath, but I am being congratulated on my three-pound baby, my baby in an incubator. Congratulations! Congratulations! Bring in the band!

By afternoon—is it afternoon?—my ears are so sensitive that even the rasp of whispers makes me cringe. *Shhh,* I say. *Shhh.* Instead of talking, my mom now writes notes to the people coming and going from the room.

I guess Stella is doing okay, though I'm not sure. Donny is up with her, or is he? I can't keep track of him. "Where's Donny?" I ask my mom, again.

It is so bright in my room that I have to shade my eyes when I lift my head to look at her.

"He's gone with your dad," she says quietly. "To get the car."

"Oh."

Dr. Anderson comes in and asks how I'm feeling. She looks fresh, clean. She must have gotten some sleep last night, and she definitely took a shower. She reads my chart and checks the bag of urine hanging from my bed. I can tell by her face that I'm still not peeing enough.

"How long?" I ask, trying to push myself up in bed. Pain shoots into my pelvis, and I drop onto my pillows again. "How long will she be in the hospital?"

My mom and I stare at the doctor who has been here with me all weekend, who sliced me open and pulled my daughter from me last night. I feel as if I know her and she knows me, though neither of us knows each other at all, not really.

"It's hard to say," she says slowly. "A month to six weeks." She smiles. "By your due date?"

"That long?"

"It just depends on how she's doing," Dr. Anderson says, and I try to smile, try not to look disappointed.

"Of course," I whisper.

Each time I cough, mucus comes out, and I'm startled the first time I see it in a tissue, gray and slimy. "Like a chimney sweep," I say to my mom, who folds the tissue and throws it away. Why it's gray I have no idea, but I'm relieved to get it out of my lungs. Finally, the cough that has had hold of me for three weeks has loosened its grip.

This must have something to do with having the baby out of me, though I don't know how these things could be related.

The next time I wake up, my friends Jess and Laura are sitting next to my bed. Laura is a doctor and I hear her whisper to Jess, "She's not supposed to be still getting that." She points to my IV stand, then untangles the tubes until she's satisfied that the Pitocin is no longer hooked up. I want her to check me out, tell me how my incision looks, but that would be weird, especially since she's an endocrinologist, not an obstetrician.

"Aren't you cold?" Jess whispers. My mom turned the air as low as it would go, but it hasn't seemed to make a difference. I can barely breathe for the heat, for the way my legs burn against the cotton sheets. Jess and Laura have a blanket draped over their shoulders. My mom, who is grading papers in the corner, is wearing her jacket.

When Donny comes in, I lift my head from the pillows. "Where have you been?"

"I had to eat," he says, glancing at me as he hugs Jess and Laura. "How are you?" he asks them. "Thanks for coming." As if he's the host of a party. *Thanks for coming! Drive safely!* He doesn't ask how *I* am doing.

I'm suffocating, I want to say. *I'm freaking boiling.* But instead I say, "Eat?"

"My pregame," he says.

On game days, Donny eats a large pasta lunch five hours before kickoff.

"You're playing?" I ask, struggling to sit. I can't believe he is going to leave me, leave our daughter, to go play soccer.

He turns to me. "What do you want me to do?"

I think about telling him to go to hell. He and Jess and Laura tilt before my eyes. My mom looks up from her papers.

"I'm sick," I finally say.

Donny moves to the side of the bed, pushes the hair from my forehead. How many times has he done this over the last two days? "Sweetie," he says more gently, "I have to play. I'll be back here early, by eight o'clock. I promise."

If the Thunder wins against Seattle tonight, they will advance to the championship game next weekend. But if the Thunder loses by two goals, this will be Donny's last game as a professional soccer player.

"Fine," I say. "Play. But I'm really pissed." It doesn't matter to me that this could be his last game. It doesn't matter that this is his job. It doesn't matter that there is nothing he can do to quell my nausea. I want him next to me. I want him to switch places with me.

Donny turns away from me and asks Jess and Laura if they want to see Stella.

"Yes," I say to them, "go meet Stella."

Donny *does* play, and when he arrives back at the hospital after the game, he tells me they won again, 1–0.

"Great," I say, trying to muster some enthusiasm. But how can I be enthusiastic about the fact that he might be leaving town for the championship game next weekend? The Eastern Division semifinal—the Rochester Rhinos against the Charleston Battery—is also tonight; it's being played right now. If Rochester wins, the final will probably be here, in Minnesota. But if Charleston wins, it will be in Charleston because they've never hosted a championship game.

"I hope Rochester kills them," I say.

"Me too," Donny says. Then he changes into his scrubs, unfolds the bed, and climbs into it.

Tomorrow, the headline of the *Minneapolis Star Tribune*'s sports section will read: "Thunder Heads to League Final." The last paragraph of the article says that Donny Gramenz "played all 90 minutes in both matches despite getting minimal sleep while tending to his wife, who went into labor a month prematurely and delivered a daughter, Stella, Saturday night." It says, "Gramenz returned to Abbott Northwestern in Minneapolis after the match Sunday to spend the night with his wife and child, who are both fine." Then the article quotes Donny: "'I'm fighting a little fatigue,' Gramenz said. 'But everything is all right now.'"

Thank God I don't read this then, when I am too sick to swallow anything but ice, when the sound of whispering scratches against the folds of my brain, when our daughter, whom I haven't seen since just after she was born, is living in a plastic box.

Still, when I find the article two months later in a stack of papers on the sideboard in our dining room, I'm furious. A month prematurely? A month is nothing; a month would have been fine. That, clearly, was the reporter's mistake. But then I turn my rage on my husband. How could he have said that everything was *all right*? I still hadn't begun peeing. I still hadn't begun to recover from the preeclampsia. Our daughter was in an incubator, a floor away from me. What about any of that was *all right*?

8

IT'S LATE SUNDAY NIGHT WHEN I FINALLY TURN
the corner. At eleven o'clock, the nurse holds up my bag of urine
and says, "Eight hundred ccs. That's good." At that moment I know
I'm going to be okay. My kidneys are beginning to function again. I
smile at the nurse and fall back asleep.

What I don't realize is that at that very moment Stella is also
turning a corner. But I am not thinking of my daughter. I don't
know that she's having trouble breathing, that the plastic tent over
her head and the tube of oxygen blowing into her face are no longer
enough. I don't know about respiratory distress syndrome. I don't
know that Stella lacks surfactant, the slippery substance that keeps
the air sacs in her lungs from collapsing. I don't know that her skin
has become bluish, that she has begun to breathe rapidly, shallowly. I
don't know that her nostrils flare or that the skin between her ribs is
pulled inward with each ragged breath.

I don't know any of that. What I will understand later is this: I
was not with her when she faltered.

At five on Monday morning, the Special Care Nursery calls.
Barely awake, still spinning, I hold the phone to my ear.

"Stella is having trouble breathing," a woman says. She says
something about oxygen, but I'm not following her.

"We're going to move her," she says.

"Oh." This is all I say. I don't ask if she'll be okay. I don't ask what
this means.

"Send up your husband," she says. "He can go with us when we
take her."

Take her. When they take her. I hang up the phone.

Donny is sleeping. He has not heard the phone ring, has not
heard me speaking.

"Donny," I say.

He doesn't stir.

"Donny," I say more loudly.

He lifts his head.

"Stella can't breathe. You have to go up there. They're going to move her."

He fumbles with the sheets, slips out of the scrubs, and pulls on his jeans. He does this slowly, without saying anything. He struggles between the two beds and leans down to kiss me.

I stare at him. *Why are you so calm? Our baby can't breathe.*

"She'll be fine," he says, and then he leaves.

I stare at the closed door, irritated. I should be reassured by his calm, but I'm not. It's as if he doesn't care enough to be scared. I know this isn't true; it can't be true. But if he cares, why isn't he more worried?

I can't fall back to sleep. My daughter, who I thought was fine, is not. My daughter, who I thought could breathe on her own, cannot. I should be with her. I should be holding her. Suddenly I feel as if I will suffocate. I need the door open. I need to see the hallway, to breathe more air. I press the call button again and again until a woman's voice comes through the speaker, asking what I need.

"The door," I say. "I need the door open."

She sighs. "Someone will be there soon."

I realize the nurses probably have more important things to do than to go around opening doors, but I don't care. *Soon,* I want to yell, *is not good enough. I can't breathe!*

A half hour later, Donny and the nurses stop by my room on their way to Children's. They push the incubator to the door, but it's so far away that I can't really see Stella. Still, I am grateful that they thought of this. I'm grateful for a glimpse of her. "Thank you," I say. *Thank you so much.*

Last night, Donny called his school district and requested a substitute. He was worried about doing this the second week of school, but if he hadn't, he wouldn't be with Stella right now, on the way to Children's. I'm relieved that at least he is with her.

Months later, I will ask him what it was like to walk next to Stella's incubator through the long tunnel that runs between the two hospitals. He will tell me that he wasn't nervous because he knew Stella was in good hands. He trusted them. I know I wouldn't have felt this way. Yes, I trusted them, believed they knew what they were doing. But that doesn't mean anything, really. Babies die even when they have good doctors.

I will ask Donny for the details: What did Stella look like when they moved her? Were her eyes open or shut? Was she on her back or her stomach? Was her skin bluish? What did the nurses say? When you arrived at Children's, did you watch the doctor slip the tube down her throat? Did you watch them turn on the ventilator? He won't remember any of this. A fog will have descended over his memory, obliterating these details. No amount of prodding will reveal them.

It is hours before Donny calls from the NICU, and then all he says is, "She's going to be okay." I want more, but I'll have to wait. And really, for now these words are enough. More than relief, I suddenly feel hunger. But maybe this is how relief works: it loosens the knot of worry just enough to admit other sensations. And since I haven't eaten anything at all since Friday evening, it's no wonder I'm starving.

When the nurse comes in to check my blood pressure, which is now 140/90, and to hold up my bag of urine—one thousand ccs—I ask her when I can eat.

She listens to my belly with a stethoscope and tells me I can't have anything until I begin to pass gas. I can actually feel the gas moving around inside me. It's gaining force, getting ready, but none has escaped. "I'm really hungry," I say.

I don't like this nurse. She keeps shutting the door even though I have asked her to keep it open, just a crack. But when she comes back with a packet of powdered beef and a cup of hot water, I'm grateful. It's salty and hot.

Then she says she wants me to get up. "The more you move around, the faster you'll heal," she says. "And I'll take the catheter out, so you can get up to go to the bathroom."

I don't want to get up or go to the bathroom. I haven't been on my feet in forty-eight hours, and I like the way the catheter just drains the urine from me. But before I can explain this, she's on to something else: "And I assume you're going to breastfeed."

She says it as if she expects a battle, but I just nod. I always planned on breastfeeding. I'm going to nurse for a whole year. I'd signed up for a class here at the hospital, but it doesn't even meet for another three weeks. I want to tell this to the nurse, but she doesn't give me a chance.

"Good," she says, heading for the door. "I'll get a pump."

Suddenly, everything is happening too quickly. The nurse has removed my catheter and pushed a breast pump next to my bed. She tears open a bag and pulls out coils of tubing and plastic bottles and funnels. I sit up, my lower abdomen aching.

"I'll show you how this works," she says, pointing to the pump, which looks powerful, its pulleys and weights visible through its outer casing. She fits the plastic pieces together, instructs me to open my hospital gown, and hands me two bottles attached to funnels. "Breast shields," she says.

My hospital gown is around my waist, shields held to my breasts. The nurse flips the switch and I look down to see my nipples being pulled into plastic: *ba dump ba dump.* It doesn't hurt, exactly, but it makes me dizzy. On the other side of the curtain, the door is open, and I'm aware that anyone could walk in and see me like this, but it wouldn't matter. Long gone is any sense of my body as my own, as something private.

I feel as if I'll throw up, so I close my eyes and listen to the *swish swish* of the pump. *I have a baby,* I say to myself. *She is in another hospital, attached to a ventilator. She is alive, and I am pumping for her. I am doing this for her.* When I open my eyes, I notice yellowish liquid pooling in the bottles.

"Wonderful," the nurse says, coming over to the bed and peering at the funnels. "I wasn't sure you'd get any."

And this small thing—a few drops of milk—suddenly fills me with pride. I'm a good mother. I can do this.

"It's colostrum," she says. "Premilk, high in antibodies and nutrients. Your preemie will need this." She turns off the pump and empties the drops of colostrum into a small plastic jar. And this is when Donny comes in.

"Hi," I say, wiping the drips of colostrum from my breasts.

"She's okay," he says. "I'll take you to see her later."

"Okay," I say, but before I can ask him about the move, about the NICU, the nurse hands him the pieces of the pump.

"Here," she says. "I've got a job for you."

She steps into the bathroom, her back to us. Donny grimaces at me, and I roll my eyes, but I'm smiling. We are united: it's him and me against the nurse. We'll do this together.

9

ON MONDAY AFTERNOON, I'M MOVED TO A LARGE
room in the postpartum area of the maternity ward. There is a pull-
out chair where Donny can sleep and three large windows. It seems
almost luxurious after spending the last three nights in that small
square across from the nurses' station. The flowers people sent line
the window, and I'm struck by the way light pours through the glass
vases. The stems, surrounded by water, are brilliant emerald green.

When all of my things are unpacked, Donny and the nurse help
me into a wheelchair. Donny will take me to see Stella. This will be
the first time I really get to see her.

Early in my pregnancy, people told me that when I first saw my
baby, I would experience a love that called into question all the other
loves in my life. They spun tales of a world where I would spend
hours gazing into startled newborn eyes, a world where my baby
would fill an emptiness in my heart that I didn't even know existed.
And I'm ready for that, for the love to pour out of me when I see
Stella. I don't know enough to be nervous.

Donny pushes me out of the room and down the hall, and
that's when I hear tiny cries from behind closed doors. It takes me
a moment to realize there are *babies* in there. People have delivered
their babies, and now they're holding them, nursing them, in these
rooms next to mine. I'm angry for a moment, angry that I have to
listen to other people's healthy babies cry, but then the anger drains
out of me. That had been my plan, too, and I can't be angry because
they got what they wanted, because they got what *I* wanted.

Donny pushes me into the elevator. We get off in the basement, but then we are at a dead end. "No," he says. "This isn't right."
Wrong turn, wrong elevator. He just made this trip, so why he cannot
remember how to get there is beyond me. He spins the wheelchair

around. The walls slant. I lean forward, holding the hospital gown to my belly. My hand flies up: *Hey, slow down.*

We're up in the elevator and down in a different one. Then we're in the tunnel, and I'm being pushed too quickly past colorful posters on white walls. My head feels as if it will explode. I clutch the arms of my wheelchair. Regular people in street clothes—men and women in jeans and T-shirts—weave around us, and this surprises me. When did I even begin thinking in these terms: regular people, street clothes? They seem out of place, as if they have been cut out and placed here in this tunnel with me and my wheelchair and blue gown and C-section incision and spinning head. And why is this tunnel so hot and bright? This goes against everything I thought I knew about tunnels.

Then we're on the second floor of Children's and down a long hallway, where we are buzzed into the NICU. The wide door swings open, Donny pushes me into bright lights, and I'm enveloped by an antiseptic smell so floral I think I'm going to vomit. We're in a long room with shiny white floors. People in blue scrubs and colorful smocks sit at tables and stand behind counters. Donny says, "This is where the freezer is." He motions to a small room on the left with a wave of his hand, as though he's a tour guide. His voice is matter-of-fact, welcoming—the kind of voice you hear piped through speakers on a double-decker bus.

"Stella's in here," he says, still using the voice. He pushes me into the first room on the left, which is smaller, less bright. "There," he says, pointing to an open table, in the middle, on the right.

And there she is: a miniature thing, smaller than a doll, lying out in the open on the right side of the room. Station 5. Why is she lying out in the open? I glance around the room, count five incubators. Stella was in an incubator Saturday night, when I saw her in the Special Care Nursery. She was in an incubator this morning, when she was wheeled past my hospital room. Why is she out in the open now? Someone could breathe on her.

I try to look at the baby, but I can't. I close my eyes and listen to the beeping, whirring machines and to the tires of my wheelchair, which make a suctioning sound as I'm pushed across the polished floor.

When I open my eyes, I am at Stella's bedside. Donny's hand is on my arm, helping me stand. And when I look down at her, my stomach or chest—something in my center—tightens. A white ventilator is taped over her mouth, scrawny legs are splayed like a frog's, goggles cover her eyes, purple veins track across her skull like a spider web.

I take a deep breath. *This cannot be my baby. This is not how it's supposed to happen.* I look up, around the large room: nurses hovering over incubators, monitors beeping, alarms sounding. Through the windows at the end of the room the sky is blue, bright fall blue. *How can that be? How can my baby be here, in this place? How can the sun be shining outside?*

I remembered Stella being beautiful. Saturday night, and even this morning, I'm sure she was beautiful. But as I stare at her I realize I was wrong. She's not beautiful. She's yellow.

I look up at a nurse. She smiles. "I'm Kally, one of Stella's primary nurses."

"Kate," I say, though she probably already knows who I am.

"I can turn off the light so you can see her eyes," she says.

Her eyes, yes. She has eyes. Good. I nod.

"It's a phototherapy light," Kally says. "For the jaundice."

"Oh."

Donny squeezes my elbow, and I look at him. "Do you want to touch her?" he asks. He's smiling. Why is he smiling?

"Kate," he says. "Do you want to touch the baby?"

I nod then. Yes, I guess. The nurse, Kally, points to the sink in the corner of the room.

The sink is wide and metal. Foot pedals turn on the water. Donny presses the pedal with his toes, and squirts pink soap into my hands.

"Lather two minutes," he says. "Rinse fingers to wrist, hands up."

Again, I look at my husband and wonder who he is, how he knows this. But I do as he says, lather and rinse, fingers to wrist. He holds my elbow to keep me from falling, and then I stand next to him as he does the same. As we shuffle back to Station 5, I'm aware of the flimsiness of my hospital gowns, one tied in front, one in back. I feel naked, as if I'm wrapped only in a sheet.

On the counter next to Station 5, there is a can of something that looks like hair mousse. Donny sprays some into my hands and then his own. *Antibacterial foam,* he says. It's sweet, floral, and I realize that this is the source of the sweetness, the scent of the NICU. I watch how he rubs it into the grooves of his knuckles and up his wrists. I do the same, then stare at the monitor, which hangs above Stella's bed. It flashes numbers and jagged lines: red, blue, yellow, green. Red, blue, yellow, green.

"Kate," Donny says. "Look at the baby." He nods at Stella.

I don't want to look at her. I don't want to look at this tiny thing. I don't want this tiny yellow thing to be my baby.

Donny's hand is on my back. He presses it gently.

I look at Stella. The phototherapy light is off and her goggles hang, limp, from her temple. On the other temple is a circle of Velcro. Velcro on her temple. Glue and Velcro on her temple! I look at her eyes, which are closed—yellowish-red lids over bulbous eyes. Wires snake away from her chest. Her toothpick ribs shudder.

Donny cups the top of her head with his palm—dwarfs her head with his hand. "You can touch her," he says.

I nod and reach for a foot. Wrapped around one foot is a cuff with a red light on it, so I go for the other one. I close my fingers around it, and I can't get over it, how small it is, impossibly small. And hot. She's been baking under the light and the heater, which blows hot air down on her, and now her feet are on fire.

I remember the videos from birthing class, how the babies, still covered with the white slime of birth, were pressed to their mothers' chests. How the babies rested in their mothers' arms. How the babies latched on right away and nursed. That's how it's supposed to happen. But here I am, touching my two-day-old baby for the first time, and nothing is as it should be. I'm covering her foot with my fingers, rubbing her hot ankle with my thumb.

Suddenly she stretches her arms and legs, pushing against me with a force that surprises me.

"I think you're tickling her," Donny says.

I look up at him.

"You're tickling her." He nods at her foot, at my hand on her foot.

"Oh." I lift my hand away, irritated. How does he know I'm tickling her? Maybe *he's* tickling her. But as soon as I'm no longer touching her, she's still again. She settles back onto the fleece blanket. Oh. I was tickling her. He was right. He knows her better than I do. I have a baby too ticklish to touch, and I didn't even know. I feel like crying, but I don't want to cry here. "Take me back," I say. "I'm ready to go."

I say nothing on the way back to my room. Donny asks *are you okay?* over and over again, and I say *fine,* because I don't want to talk about our tiny baby. I just want to lie down. We are through the tunnel, up and down the elevators. Then I'm on my bed, gripping the metal rails, swinging up my legs. I lean back, exhausted, still nauseated. Donny hands me a Styrofoam cup of water, then puts a slash on the whiteboard on the wall under "input." We have to keep track of how much I drink and how much I pee, my input and output.

I don't know what to say now, after seeing Stella. I wasn't prepared for how small she would be. I knew she was small. Three pounds is small. But I didn't understand it, not really, what a three-pound baby hooked to a ventilator looked like. I couldn't see her mouth. I don't know what her lips look like. I'm not sure why this seems important, but it does. This is part of my problem, not feeling prepared. But the other thing that's bothering me is the fact that Donny *does* seem prepared. He's taking this—our tiny baby, the move to the NICU—in stride, as if it's no big deal. I am failing as a new parent, and he is passing with flying colors.

Donny assembles the pump pieces, hands me the bottles and funnels, and flips the switch. But I can't seem to keep the funnels in place, and colostrum drips down my belly. I lean forward to try to keep the milk in the funnels and pain slices across my abdomen. Donny turns off the pump, and we readjust the funnels. Then he turns it on again, checking for leaks. When he's satisfied that the small amount of liquid is dripping into the bottles, he heads down the hall to make me a cup of beef broth, which I've been craving.

After twenty minutes, Donny turns off the pump, collects the bottles, pours the colostrum into a jar, and washes all the pieces of the pump. I lean back and close my eyes.

The phone rings, and it's Donny's mom. She's already called twice today, and I've had enough. "Tell her not to call so much." I don't want to hear about how she's said the rosary for Stella. I don't want any of her rambling, none of her schizophrenia, not now. There's no room in my head for it.

Donny takes the phone off the hook and sits down next to me.

"I just—" I start and then begin to cry.

"I know," he says, reaching for my hand.

"She's too small," I manage. "The tube in her mouth." I had a tube down my own throat once. It was when I was nineteen, after my suicide attempt. I don't remember it being inserted, but I remember waking to the feel of plastic up my nose and down my throat. I remember gagging, struggling to get up. I remember a nurse telling me to relax. I kept shaking my head, my hand to my throat. *Relax,* she said. *Relax.* But I couldn't, and as soon as she left the room, I ripped the tube out and threw it to the floor. And now, I wonder if Stella feels the same way. "Do you think it hurts?"

"I don't know," Donny says.

"She's so far away."

I still don't understand the respiratory distress and why she needed to be intubated. It seems like something I should understand. "Tell me what happened."

"She didn't have enough surfactant," Donny says.

"What?"

"Surfactant. It's a soapy substance that coats the insides of her alveoli, the air sacs in her lungs. It keeps them from collapsing. They had to give her synthetic surfactant and then intubate her."

Donny sounds like a science textbook, and I can't believe he knows all of this. I'm sure I haven't even heard the word *alveoli* since tenth-grade biology. Usually, I am the one who pays attention to details, but now I don't know anything, and he understands why our baby needed to have the soapy stuff in her lungs. Again, I feel like a failure.

"She's getting 70 percent oxygen through the vent," he says.

I try to remember how much oxygen is in the air we breathe. "How much is normal?" I ask.

"Twenty-one percent," Donny says. "But Stella needs more than that, to keep her blood oxygen levels high enough."

"I should be with her," I say. But I can't imagine being pushed all the way back to Children's, through that steamy tunnel, to stare down at my three-pound baby with goggles over her eyes.

"We could use BabyLink," he says. Someone told me about this, how you can watch your baby on the television in your room.

I nod, and Donny calls the NICU. Then we turn on the television. For a moment there is only static, but then Stella appears. At least I think that's Stella. It's a baby, naked except for a miniature diaper and goggles over her eyes. Her skin is mottled—yellow, red, purple. She writhes on white blankets, thrashes back and forth, pulling at the tape on her mouth, like a wounded animal in a trap.

Donny climbs onto the bed next to me and pulls me to his side, but I'm still cold. He draws a blanket over our shoulders and we sit there, legs dangling over the edge of the bed, transfixed by the small creature that has been transported into the square of our television. It's as if we're hovering above her, floating through the warm air of the NICU.

No sound comes from the television. That's not part of the deal. We can't hear any of the bustle of the NICU. But we wouldn't be able to hear our daughter anyway; the ventilator has reached its slender arm down her throat and fitted itself snuggly between her vocal cords, so she cannot scream or cry.

Donny and I pull closer together. "Oh, no," he says, pressing his face into my shoulder. And for a moment, I'm reassured by his distress. This *is* hard for him. I'm not the only one.

Stella arches back, struggling. She can't see because of the goggles, but even if she could, she wouldn't know that we're here, watching her. She wouldn't know that she's not alone. And I wonder whether she will remember this. Somewhere deep in the folds of her brain, etched into her neuromuscular reflexes, will she remember this? *If* she survives, will she remember thrashing under the lights in the NICU, alone?

Dr. Anderson said Stella was better off out here rather than inside me, but that seems impossible. How can my daughter be better off on a warming bed, baking under phototherapy lights, a ventilator tube taped to her mouth? How can she be better off beamed through a television?

You can only watch your baby for twenty minutes at a time. I don't know why, but those are the rules. After a few minutes, though, I've had enough. I don't want to see our daughter, not like this. "Turn it off," I say. "Turn it off."

10

On Tuesday morning, when the nurse wakes me at seven to pump, I start crying and can't stop. Donny climbs into my narrow bed and wraps his arms around me. I press my face into his shoulder and weep into his T-shirt. I cry for Stella, lying under the unremitting glare of the phototherapy lights. I cry for myself, for the tender wound stretching between my pelvic bones. I cry because I don't know what else to do.

When Dr. Williams, one of Dr. Bradford's colleagues, rounds at nine, I'm still in tears.

"Your hormones are going wild right now," she says. "You'd be crying even under normal circumstances." She presses her fingers into the flesh of my ankles, which are still three times their normal size.

"Will they ever return to normal?" I ask.

"Eventually," she laughs. "You're getting there. Yesterday you peed three liters."

She means three liters more than I drank, three liters that I had been storing away under the layers of my skin. This seems impossible, but it's true. I've lost nineteen pounds in two days. This means my body is recovering, and I should be happy, but instead I start to cry again.

Dr. Williams hands me the box of Kleenex that's next to my bed.

"I can't stop...crying."

"That's understandable," she says, sitting down on the edge of my bed.

"But what...am I...going to do?"

"Heal and take care of yourself," she says. "With a baby in the NICU, you're at high risk for postpartum depression."

"I have a history," I say, though I'm sure it's all there in my file: the suicide attempt, the antidepressants.

She nods. "I want you to call us if you start feeling like this is more than hormones."

I nod, dabbing my eyes with a tissue.

"I'm serious," Dr. Williams says. "If you start slipping, call us right away. There are options. Zoloft is the safest for breastfeeding mothers."

"Okay," I say, though I'm not sure I'll be able to tell the difference between hormones and depression. And Zoloft would leak into my breast milk. Wouldn't that affect the baby?

Dr. Williams checks my incision, the tender scab held together by a dozen pieces of medical tape. "It looks great," she says, smiling. "You might be able to go home tomorrow."

"Oh," I say. My friend Judy had a C-section here a year ago, and she was able to stay a whole week. It's only been three days since my surgery, and I don't want to go home. If I go home, it will be as if I never had a baby, as if the baby doesn't exist.

"You'll be more comfortable at home," Dr. Williams says, as if she's trying to convince me. "People won't be in and out of your room all day."

I don't care about the people. I like the people. I just don't want to go home.

"We'll see how you're doing tomorrow," she says, and I nod.

Somewhere in the maternity ward, Donny checks e-mail, fields calls from family and friends, and talks to his principal, who has agreed to let him have the whole week off. He calls our friends, keeps people updated. While he's gone, I sleep, and finally it feels as though I'm really sleeping. I'm off the hard-core painkillers, and now I take two Percocet every four hours and three Motrin every six. The Percocet makes me a little nauseated, but nothing like the painkiller that was injected into my bloodstream on Sunday. At least now I can stand on my own. I can inch my way into the bathroom without help.

In the afternoon, Donny slowly pushes me through the tunnel to Children's, and we both stare at the colorful posters that line the wall. "I like this one," he says, pointing to a circus scene in bright reds and blues. Elephants parade in a circle, tail to trunk, in front of a big top tent.

"This one, too," I say, nodding to a fat yellow fish floating in aquamarine water.

"We should get some nice bright posters for Stella's room," he says.

"I think we should wait," I say, clutching the small plastic jars of breast milk in my lap. Her room isn't ready—the crib is still in a box—but it seems too early to fix it up.

Donny doesn't say anything. He stares at the posters that stretch the length of the tunnel. Then we are up in the elevator and heading down the long hallway on the second floor of Children's that leads to the NICU and the ICC, the Infant Care Center, which someone told me was a unit for older infants who were awaiting surgery or learning to nurse. We wear badges around our necks that say "Children's Hospital NICU/ICC."

This hallway is also lined with framed posters, but they are posters of NICU graduates—survivors. Each poster is made up of *then* and *now* photos. In one of the *then* photos, a baby is wearing one of his parent's wedding bands on her upper arm, like a bracelet. I look down at my own hand, at my wedding ring, which Donny brought from home. My hands are still a little swollen, so it's tight on my finger.

I can't imagine pulling it off and sliding it up over a miniature hand, wrist, elbow. I can't imagine a baby so small that my ring, the ring that sits snuggly on my finger, can spin loosely around her upper arm. This baby, the one in the photo, weighed 14.5 ounces at birth, less than a pound. I remember the image of standing in the dairy section of a grocery store, holding boxes of butter in my palm. But this baby didn't weigh as much as even one box of butter. And suddenly I want to cry for his parents, for everything they lived through. Their baby survived. He graduated from the NICU. But as I stare up at the *now* photo, it's clear that the hard stuff is not over. He stands with a walker, head to the side, glasses askew on his preschool face.

As we gaze up at the photos, I let it all in: the possibilities, the hope, the disappointment. I know these posters are supposed to reassure us, to prove that preemies are fighters, but they only end up frightening me. The babies don't look normal when they're born—how could they with all that tape and equipment, protruding ribs, and IVs in their heads? But they don't look normal in the later photographs either, when they're at home in the sandbox or on swings in their backyards. It's hard for me to put my finger on just what's wrong with them. Is that boy's head too big? That girl, I see, walks with crutches. She was a twenty-six-weeker. But what's going on with the girl in the poster next to her? Her eyelids are thick, heavy. And as I sit in my wheelchair, tallying imperfections, fingering the ID badge around my neck, I realize that if these babies are supposed to reassure me, nothing is guaranteed for my daughter.

Donny leans down. "I don't like these," he whispers.

"I know," I say.

"We can't look at them anymore."

But I can't look away. It's as if they hold the secret to our daughter's future.

"This one's okay," Donny says. He stops in front of the last poster on the wall. It's Amanda, born in 1982. In the early photos, Amanda's mother cradles her against her chest. Then Amanda is eight or maybe ten years old, and she looks like any other little girl standing next to a snow fort, arms and legs encased in a puffy snowsuit. Then she's an adult, and this is the photo I like best. She's in a black graduation gown, her arms outstretched, her shoulders frozen in a shrug. It's as if she's saying, *Here I am. I'm just fine. What did you expect?*

The truth is I don't know what to expect. Every expectation I had, about pregnancy and childbirth, about having a newborn baby I could cradle in my arms and smother with kisses, slipped away from me, and I don't want to be disappointed again. I don't want to count on anything.

We're buzzed into the NICU, and Donny pushes me to the freezer room, takes the jars of breast milk from my lap, and disappears for a moment before pushing me to the sink. This is only my second time in the NICU, but it already feels familiar. We lather and rinse, fingers to wrist. We spray antibacterial foam into our palms, and then we stand above Stella, who looks the same as she did yesterday: Toothpick ribs shudder up and down. Her ears, which are as thin as origami paper, are pressed flat against her head. Downy hair covers her shoulders and arms. I hadn't noticed the hair yesterday, but now that I do, I remember reading that in utero a fetus is covered with lanugo, a fine coat of hair, to keep it warm. By the time a baby is full-term, the hair has fallen out. But Stella still has hers, and it makes her look like a small woodland creature.

Kally comes over and says hello, and Donny asks Stella's weight.

"She's up fourteen grams: 1434."

I smile, even though I don't know that this translates into just over three pounds two ounces. But any weight gain, even fourteen grams, has to be a good thing.

"And her oxygen is at 25 percent," Kally says, smiling.

I nod. That's good, I guess.

I notice a picture hanging next to Stella's bed. It's a jack-in-the-box, which has been colored with bright crayons. From the jack-in-the-box's mouth is a caption bubble that reads *Happy Birthday Stella!* Above this is her birth date: 9-13-03. I don't know who colored this drawing for my daughter, and I suddenly feel a pang of jealousy. While I was sick and dizzy and vomiting, someone colored a smiling jack-in-the-box for my daughter. Someone other than me.

I glance around the room at the signs hanging by the other babies' beds, and I notice that the baby across the room has the same birthday as Stella. But under his name, Quincy, his birth weight is listed as one pound fourteen ounces. My chest tightens. He was probably one of the "more serious cases" that pushed us out of line while we were waiting for our C-section, and standing here next to my three-pound baby, I suddenly feel very lucky. For the first time in my life, I understand that luck is relative.

Kally removes Stella's goggles so we can see her eyes, which are very dark, rimmed in yellow. They open and close, open and close. I'm not surprised by the yellow or even by her lack of eyelashes and eyebrows; it's her eyes that make me draw breath. They must be blue, but they're so dark they appear black, like gleaming stones that have been mined from some deep quarry and placed here in her head.

She stretches her arms up, almost as if she's reaching for me. Can she see me? Does she know me? "Hi, Stella," I say softly.

Her hands open and close, her fingers clawing the air above her head. I catch one in my own, and it's weightless. I slide my pinky into her palm, and her fingers close around it, holding on tight.

"Oh," I say, looking at Donny, my eyes filling with tears.

Then the doctor comes up to us and asks Donny if he has any questions.

He asks her if Stella is now producing enough surfactant. He's wearing a T-shirt and jeans and is darkly tanned, as he is every year at the end of the soccer season. The doctor says something, and Donny nods. He looks so calm, as if he's talking about the weather or sports.

I am dull, silent, but I'm sure I don't look calm. With my finger in Stella's grip, I try to follow the conversation, but I can't keep my eyes free of tears, and I keep turning away to stare down at my daughter. Not that my inattentiveness to the conversation seems to matter; the doctor doesn't look at me when she talks anyway. She speaks only to Donny. She must know that everything I'm told falls immediately out of my head. But still, it seems odd that she doesn't even glance in my direction. She's a woman; I'm a woman. It seems like she should speak to *me*.

She says that Stella is having a good day and that she might be able to come off the ventilator in a couple of days. And then she nods to us, finally glancing at me. When she moves on to the next preemie, Donny stands next to me, staring down at Stella. She still holds tight to my finger, but her eyes are closed now.

Donny leans over and points to the tips of the fingers on her other hand. "Don't they look white?" That arm is the one with the IV in it, and there is a foam board taped to it to keep the arm stiff and keep her from dislodging the IV.

"This isn't right," Donny says. "Her fingers don't look right."

I shrug. My head feels so heavy. My neck aches. Her fingers may be a little white but only compared to the reddish-yellow of the rest of her body. "I'm sure they're fine," I say.

But Donny insists: her fingers are too white. He waves at the doctor, who comes back over.

I slip my finger from my daughter's grip and step back.

The doctor lifts Stella's tiny hand and gently presses her fingertips. "Good eye," she says to Donny. "Thanks for noticing that."

I stare at the doctor, who is still ignoring me. Good eye? You say "good eye" when someone finds a square of carpet that perfectly matches the hue of your dining room walls. You say "good eye" when someone spies the earring you lost on the floor of a darkened restaurant. I don't want to hear "good eye" when my husband notices that there is something wrong with our baby's hand.

The doctor is talking to Donny again, and I'm having trouble understanding what just happened. Was the tape on Stella's arm too tight? Was there something wrong with the IV? *We'll take care of this,* she says. *We'll dab a little nitroglycerin on her fingertips to bring back the circulation.*

Apparently, it's difficult for me to process anything. I stand silently at my baby's bedside, watching my husband maneuver us through this new terminology, new technology. And I don't understand any of it. All I say when we leave the NICU is, "What the fuck was that?"

All Donny says is, "I know."

When we get back to my hospital room, my friend Kate from graduate school is waiting. She gives me a hug and helps me back into bed. Donny goes out to the lounge to listen to his cell phone messages.

"Everyone has been asking how you and the baby are doing," Kate says.

She means everyone in graduate school, which seems a world away. It seems impossible that I was teaching nonfiction to undergrads just a week ago, that even a few days ago I was worried about finishing my thesis. It's all part of my life *before*—before preeclampsia, before mag sulfate, before the NICU, before a doctor dabbed nitroglycerin on my daughter's fingers. I can't imagine ever going back to that life, back to a place where school, teaching, and my thesis are important.

A man knocks on the door and pokes his head into the room. "Mrs. Hopper?" he asks.

I'm not really *Mrs.* Hopper; I'm *Ms.* Hopper. I'm married to Mr. Gramenz, not Mr. Hopper. But it doesn't seem like the time to get caught up in semantics, so I just nod.

This man introduces himself—Dr. Someone or Other—and says that the babies are doing well. "Do you have any questions?"

"No," I say, shaking my head. I just saw Stella. Just saw her white fingers, her dark, dark eyes.

"Okay," he says. "I just wanted to check in with you."

I smile. That seems awfully nice. He even looked at me when he spoke. He was talking to *me.*

He smiles as well and waits a moment, as if he expects me to say something. When I don't, he says "okay" again and awkwardly backs from the room.

But then something occurs to me. I turn to Kate. "Did he say *babies?* Plural?"

"He definitely said babies."

"Who did he say he was?"

"A doctor."

"Oh."

Later, I will realize his visit was a mistake. He was looking for Mrs. Hopper, the Mrs. Hopper married to a Mr. Hopper. I will understand this when I look up at the whiteboard in the main room of the NICU, where the babies and their doctors are listed, and see Hopper 1, Hopper 2, and Hopper 3 on the same board where Stella's last name, Hopper-Gramenz, is listed. And I will be flooded with relief. I am mother to only one premature baby.

People are in and out of my hospital room all evening. Donny's dad and step-mom, Armie, come in, and I begin to cry. I have never cried in front of them—it seems like such an intimate act—but they don't seem fazed by my tears. Donny's dad pats me on the shoulder, and Armie begins pulling Tupperware from a plastic bag. They have brought Armie's fried egg rolls and her chicken noodle soup, which I love. The egg rolls are still warm, and when I start eating them, I can't stop. They stay for a few minutes, and then Donny takes them to meet Stella.

Then my mom and my grandpa arrive. This is the first time I've seen my grandpa in over a week, and he looks older. I probably look older, as well. He sits in the chair in the corner and stares at me, his head tilted to the side, and I can tell he's trying not to cry. He asks about Stella, whether she'll be okay.

"I think so," I say, but I don't really know. No one has said anything at all about whether there will be any long-term effects. I try not to think about it, but it's always there, the not-knowing.

Later that night, Donny talks to the coach of the Minnesota Thunder. The Charleston Battery beat the Rochester Rhinos in the eastern division semifinals and Charleston won the bid to host the Saturday-night final. This means the Thunder will fly to South Carolina on Thursday night. Donny tells me that the coach has agreed to let him fly out Friday morning instead.

I shake my head. Stella will only be six days old on Friday.

"I don't want to go either," he says, but I know this isn't true. He wraps his arms around me. "I'll be back Sunday night."

"Okay," I say, because I don't feel like arguing.

11

On Wednesday morning, Donny reports that Stella is doing okay and that her oxygen is almost room-level. *That's good*, I say, though it doesn't mean I can hold her. It doesn't mean I can take her home. Dr. Williams has checked my incision and told me I'll be discharged today. I'm going home without my baby.

I change from my hospital gown into the maternity overalls I wore to the hospital on Friday. That was just five days ago, but I've lost twenty-two pounds, and I look like a deflated balloon.

I crawl back onto my bed to pick at my lunch while we wait for the nurse to bring in a rental pump that we can take home. It's taking forever, and I'm irritated. Now that I have to leave, I just want to get out of here.

I'm pushing the food around on my plate when my dad shows up. I called him to tell him not to bother visiting today, but there was no answer, and now he is here, sitting in the corner, while Donny tucks the last of my things back into a paper bag.

"You mentioned once," Dad starts, clearing his throat, "that you were thinking about having Stella baptized." He looks up at me, holding his hat in his hands, and I am filled with a rage completely out of proportion to the situation, a rage so fierce and raw that I can feel it in my teeth.

A couple of months ago, when I was still pregnant, when I still believed that things would go as planned, Dad and I were driving up to the northern suburbs for one of Donny's soccer games, and I mentioned that we had been thinking of having the baby baptized. "I thought we could have a small service," I said. "Something private, just for the family, maybe on a Saturday."

Since my dad is ordained, I thought this would be a nice gesture. Donny and I assumed he would be honored that we'd thought of it.

But in the car, Dad was quiet, his lips pursed, and I knew right away that I wasn't going to get the response I wanted.

"Private baptisms," my dad started, "are a medieval Catholic ritual." He paused, as if giving me time to absorb this. "Catholics believe that if a baby dies before it's been baptized, it won't go to heaven." He looked out over the steering wheel, at the expanse of suburb that had been farmland not long ago. "Catholics are worried about souls," he said.

Donny and I had both been baptized, and I had seen a hundred baptisms on various Sunday mornings throughout my life. I guess I had also been worried about the baby's soul, even though my faith is dubious at best. Donny, a steadfast atheist, didn't want to have the baby baptized, but he was willing to go along with it if it would make me feel better and if it would make my dad happy. But clearly, it wasn't going to make Dad happy.

"In the Protestant faith," Dad went on, his lecture voice settling in, "baptism is about asking a congregation, a group of people with whom you worship, to raise your child in faith. It's about asking them to come together and support the parents." My dad paused then, and I stared out the window, watching the suburbs slip by as we zoomed along 35W to Blaine. I wondered why he couldn't just do it anyway. Why couldn't he just baptize the baby how we wanted, for us—an exception? It didn't seem like something that would offend God.

"For Protestants, baptism isn't about a baby's soul," he went on.

"Well, in that case," I said, trying to keep the irritation from my voice, "we don't need to worry about it. We don't belong to a church, so it would be ridiculous to ask a group of strangers to raise our child in faith."

"You're still a member of Macalester Plymouth," he said.

"That's silly, Dad. We never go." I should have known there would be some rule, some doctrine, that I was breaking by even considering a private Protestant baptism. When Donny and I were planning our wedding four years earlier, we discussed the details of the ceremony with Dad, who was officiating, and we ended up going back and forth over what Dad would wear. I wanted him to walk me down the aisle in a tuxedo and then slip on his robe when he reached the altar. This gesture seemed to encompass the dual roles he was performing as father of the bride *and* officiant. But Dad is Depression-era old school; he thought it would be too showy and turn the ceremony into a circus. We discussed it for weeks, and finally he acquiesced, but I know he wasn't happy about it.

I wasn't willing to go back and forth about the baptism. There didn't seem to be a possible compromise anyway. My dad didn't want to perform a private baptism, and I wasn't about to show up at church with my baby some Sunday morning and ask a congregation of strangers to raise my non-churchgoing child in a faith about which I was doubtful and to which my husband didn't subscribe at all. It seemed hypocritical. And really, if I didn't have to worry about the baby's soul, it didn't matter. Her soul would be fine.

But the fact that my dad is bringing up the baptism again now, when I'm in the hospital and Stella is hooked to a ventilator a block away, infuriates me. Maybe he's not convinced she'll make it, and maybe he's worried about her soul after all.

I clench my jaw and drop my fork, which hits the plate with a metallic clank. "We're not getting her baptized," I say, my voice pinched. "We've already discussed this."

Dad looks down at his hat.

Donny looks up from the paper bag and glares at me.

If I could be more gracious right now, I could ask him about it, what he intended. I could ask him to explain how a baptism in the NICU would be different from the private baptism I had originally envisioned. But I can't manage *gracious*. I don't give him a chance to explain himself. I just glare at him and say, "No way. It's not going to happen."

"Okay," he says, and I know I've hurt his feelings. He stays only a few more minutes and then stands awkwardly to go. And I let him go without apologizing, without explaining my anger.

An hour later, when I am finally discharged, Donny and I walk over to the NICU. While Donny gets plastic jars to store my breast milk in at home, I wash and dry my hands, rub the foam up my wrists, and check Stella's weight, which is 1375 grams, down 59 grams, almost two ounces, from yesterday. She is hovering at three pounds.

The fact that Stella was over three pounds at birth somehow translated into her making it, into her being one of the lucky ones. It now looks as though her weight will dip below three pounds, below the arbitrary line I've drawn, and that translates into anything can happen. And though I know that babies lose weight after they're born, it somehow didn't occur to me that Stella would lose weight. She was already skin and bones.

I stare down at Stella, who is sleeping, her arms and legs flopped out to the sides. It takes me a moment to realize she looks different. Tubes now stretch away from the stub of her umbilical cord, which is waxy and purple. A nurse, one I haven't seen before, moves to my shoulder, pointing to the new tubes. "Umbilical and venous catheters," she says. "They're safer. There's a large blood vessel there, so we can draw blood without having to stick her with another needle."

I should be reassured by this. Safer is good. But I start to cry, thinking of the tiny shirts my mom bought a few months ago. They were loose and snapped on the side, designed for a newborn whose umbilical stub hasn't fallen off yet. But Stella, whose umbilical stub is covered with tubes and tape, will never wear these. By the time she gets out of here—*if* she gets out of here—she won't need them; her umbilical will have already fallen off.

It's ridiculous how careful I was during my pregnancy: I didn't use synthetic cleaners; I drank only filtered water; I ate pounds of broccoli and cheese and yogurt—calcium in any form; I bought only organic fruit; I avoided fish because of the mercury. But it didn't matter. None of it could make her stay inside me and keep growing until she was full-term. I followed the rules, I did what I was told, and it didn't matter.

The nurse, who is in her late fifties or early sixties and looks a little like my mom, her brown hair in a bob, pats me on the shoulder, which makes me cry harder. She sees me. She knows I'm struggling to make sense of this.

"I'm…leaving…today," I manage.

She gives my shoulder a slight squeeze. "You'll be okay," she says. "The most important thing to do is develop a routine. Get up in the morning and take a shower, get dressed, and then come here and see your daughter."

"But it's not fair," I say. "This isn't how it's supposed to happen." How many times has she heard this? There must be forty babies in this unit, and each parent has probably thought the same thing: This isn't fair. This isn't what we signed up for. This isn't how it was supposed to happen.

"I know," she says. Then she smiles and nods toward Stella. "But this is *your* birth story. This is your daughter's birth story, and you need to accept that."

My story, my daughter's story. Yes, that's how it works, isn't it? We each have a story. But part of me thought I could control the story. If I did the right things, if I ate the right foods, if I took the right classes, I would get to decide how the story unfolded. I would get to call the shots.

"She's having a good day," the nurse says. "She'll probably come off the ventilator later today."

"Really? Already?" That has to be good. I look down at Stella, who jerks, her arms and legs flailing at something unseen, before her body sprawls on the blankets again, arms and legs loose.

"That's normal," the nurse says. "Preemies' central nervous systems aren't fully developed, so their movements are jerky. And they don't have the muscle tone to curl into themselves, fetal position." She looks down at Stella. "She didn't have to do any of the crunching, the tucking, of a full-term baby in utero."

The nurse pats me again and moves on to the next baby. I stare down at Stella, who looks like a marionette, her body tightening and slackening, as if invisible strings are controlling her. I wonder whether her limbs will ever bend with ease, whether her movements will ever be smooth, graceful.

Donny comes back with a bag full of plastic jars and labels with Stella's name and ID number. He puts his arm around me, and we watch Stella together. A few minutes later, the doctor comes by and says Stella's oxygen needs are low, which is good, but that her right lung is damaged. "The X-ray," she says, "shows pulmonary interstitial emphysema."

Emphysema? Emphysema is for smokers. It's for the man who smokes three packs of cigarettes a day for twenty-five years and then has a hole cut in his throat. I saw a movie about it in tenth-grade health class. My baby can't have emphysema. I stare at this doctor who still will not look at me, who still will not look into my eyes and talk to me about my daughter and her damaged lung.

She and Donny speak to each other in low voices. The doctor says, "It should heal. It's just a bruise, too much pressure."

I start to cry again, even though I hate to cry in front of this doctor, as if it proves that she's right—I am too emotional to listen, to absorb her words, to ask the right questions. I turn back to my daughter with the bruised lung and let the tears run down my face.

"We'll extubate her today," I hear the doctor say to Donny.

I wipe the tears away with the back of my hand, spray more anti-bacterial foam into my palms, then slip my pinky into Stella's hand. Her fingers snap shut around mine like a miniature Venus flytrap.

12

ON OUR DRIVE HOME FROM THE HOSPITAL, I'M surprised by the leaves lining the street. The oppressive heat that made me miserable less than a week ago has vanished. It's been replaced by fallen leaves and a chill in the air. But it makes sense that the weather would turn while I was in the hospital because everything else has changed: I am someone's mother now. I have a baby, a sick baby with a bruised lung.

I stare down at my baggy overalls and remember that our last birthing class is tonight—the other expectant parents will spend the evening talking about labor and managing pain. For some reason this makes me feel spiteful. "I'd like to show up at birthing class and tell everyone a thing or two about *pain*," I say.

Donny smiles. "And medieval torture."

"It would scare the shit out of them." And part of me wishes I could do it, show up and tell all those hopeful couples to forget their birth plans. *Nothing will happen the way you expect it to, the way you plan it. There are no guarantees.* But why am I angry with *them*? They didn't do anything. Didn't I, too, spend hours and hours this summer reading pregnancy books, preparing? What a racket.

It's a dreary Wednesday afternoon, gray but not raining—my least favorite kind of day. The clouds hang low in the sky, dark and heavy, and I'm anxious to get inside, away from the way they seem to press down on me.

Donny turns onto our street, and when we pull up in front of our house, I reach for his hand. Our house looks strange—too tall, too narrow. It appears taller than the other houses on our block, which I hadn't noticed before. I stare out the car window.

Donny tucks a strand of hair behind my ear. "I love you," he says.

I turn to him. "I love you, too." I'm grateful for him, for his love, but it's not enough to make me want to walk into our house, the house I loved just a week ago. It's not enough to eliminate the heaviness that's settled in my chest.

Together we walk slowly up the sidewalk to the front door and step onto the porch. When Donny pushes open the front door, we both pause on the threshold. It feels as if we're suspended in time, teetering somewhere between *before* and *after*.

The furnishings of our old life are there: the oversized Room and Board couch we bought the week we moved in together, the hand-me-down love seat I've disguised with a slipcover, the crowded bookshelf, the garage-sale entertainment center that Donny painted burgundy two months ago. It's all there, but it looks different.

Donny drops my bag inside the door and goes back to the car for the flowers. I walk slowly upstairs and stop in front of Stella's room. The pale cream walls are naked. New, unwashed baby clothes from my one baby shower last spring are piled on the changing table and on the yellow rocking chair. The crib, which my dad bought for us a couple of weeks ago, is still in its box, leaning against the wall. It all screams *You don't have a baby! You don't have a baby!*

"I *do* have a baby," I say out loud, to quiet the room, to convince myself. *I have a baby.*

When everything is unpacked, Donny makes a list of things we need to set up a pumping station, as he calls it, in Stella's room—towels, tissues, a plastic basin in which to wash the pieces of the pump—and heads out the door to Target. I go down to the basement to check e-mail. I pull a blanket around my shoulders and watch the messages fill my inbox. Some are from the university about my maternity leave. Apparently I can start my maternity leave now, and then I can take a leave of absence for the rest of the semester, so I don't have to worry about teaching this fall, which is a huge relief. We don't know how long Stella will be in the hospital, and the thought of having to go back to teaching while she's there makes me feel sick. I scroll through the other e-mails from friends, who write that they are thinking about us. And then I get to one from a woman who is a Ph.D. student in English literature at the university. The subject line of her e-mail reads "preemies."

Kate,

Congrats on the arrival of Stella Lucille! I hope you and she are recovering quickly. My girls (twins—now four years old and healthy as horses) were seven weeks early. They spent several weeks in the NICU and in the hospital nursery before they came home. If you want to talk to another mom who has spent nights "holding" babies through the opening in the side of a clear plastic box, please feel free to e-mail or call (any hour of the day or night).

Being an English major, I immediately think of books at times like these. Of course, there are no books for this, and sometimes not even formulable questions, but I saw this and thought of you:

"Live the questions now, and perhaps even without knowing it, you will live along some distant day into the answers."
—Rainer Maria Rilke

My thoughts are with you and your family.
Leni

I cry as I read her message. Leni and I have met; we see each other in the computer lab and in the graduate assistant office, but I hardly know her. Yet she took the time to send me this message. Something in my chest expands, loosens. I write memoir, read memoir, and I know I feel less alone when I see a piece of myself reflected in someone else's story. So I shouldn't be surprised by the way I suddenly feel hopeful because Leni's daughters are four years old and healthy as horses.

I send her a response, thanking her, telling her about the preeclampsia, the magnesium sulfate, the ventilator, the bruised lung. Then I read her message again. Live the questions. *Live the questions now, and perhaps without knowing it, you will live along some distant day into the answers.* How does one live the questions? I'm not sure I can do that. I want answers. I want to know that Stella will be okay. I want to know that *I* will be okay, that we'll all make it through this.

I print out the Rilke quotation anyway, walk upstairs, and tuck it behind a magnet on the refrigerator, between photos of our family and friends. Then I walk into the dining room, where Donny has arranged the flowers from the hospital—bright gerbera daisies and pink lilies and deep purple irises. They are beautiful, of course, but they remind me of the hospital, and I'd have been just as happy to have left them behind.

I turn to my own plants, the orchids lining the windows, and that's when I notice that the cattleya, which had been closed in a tight bud when I left for the hospital, has bloomed. Its orange-yellow blossoms stretch out their long fingers to me, like a star. Like Stella, I think. I lean in to the orchid and take a deep breath, filling my lungs with its subtle sweetness. This is the first time this plant has bloomed since Mimi gave it to me, and I'm surprised by its fragrance. None of my other orchids smell like anything when they bloom. But this one is special, and I'm convinced that this is a good sign.

I jump when I hear the door open, and I turn to see Donny standing at the door, holding plastic shopping bags in each hand. When he looks up, I can tell he's been crying.

"Hey," I say, walking to him. "Are you okay?"

He puts the bags down. "I lost it," he says. "I was just sitting at a stoplight, and I started to cry and I couldn't stop."

I slide my arms around him and hug him tightly.

He presses his face into my hair. "What if she's not okay?"

"I know," I say. I hold him more tightly. This is the first time since we found out that I might be sick that Donny has cried, and oddly, I'm relieved by his tears. I don't want the man from the NICU who is calm, always in control. I want my husband, the man who, shortly after we began dating and just after I first met his mother, Patricia, sobbed in my arms.

That day, we had taken Patricia out for lunch. Donny had been quiet after we dropped her off at her apartment. Later in my studio, we lay together on my futon, and he rested his arm over his eyes. I don't think he wanted me to see him cry—we'd only been dating a couple of months—but I lifted his arm.

"I've been a horrible son," he said finally. At that point, Patricia's schizophrenia was being managed, but she was difficult to be around. She smoked packs of cigarettes a day, and just stepping into her sub-sidized apartment made me feel as if all the air had been sucked from my lungs. Patricia talked loudly about the neighbors and then about how wonderful Donny was: she told stories of how he had clung to her as a child, how he had been a mama's boy.

"I should see her more," Donny said.

I pressed myself into him, kissing his cheek.

"I remember when I was five," he started slowly. "I remember walking home from kindergarten one day. It had been raining, and I was wet." He stared at the ceiling of my apartment. I propped myself on an elbow.

"I called out to my mom when I got home, but she didn't answer, so I walked into the kitchen and she was just sitting there, facing the wall, muttering. I walked right up to her and said 'Mom,' but she didn't hear me."

Donny pressed his fingers into his temples.

"Her mouth was barely opening, but her lips were moving. The table was cluttered with cigarette butts and coffee mugs. I remember that. I wanted to get her attention, so I slid the pack of cigarettes across the table and pulled out a cigarette. I looked at her, thinking she'd tell me to stop, but she didn't notice."

"What happened?"

"I went out in the garage and smoked the cigarette, sort of. Mostly I just coughed." Donny smiled then, and I leaned over and kissed his neck.

"After that I never knew which version of her would be waiting for me when I got home. Some days she seemed fine. She'd be getting dinner started, or we'd walk down the hill behind our house to the café where we'd drink milkshakes. But some days, she was in her own world, muttering, smoking nonstop."

"Oh, sweetie," I said, my heart breaking for that five-year-old Donny. "How long did that go on?"

"I don't remember," he said. "But later, when she was gone and my brothers and Dawn and I lived with my dad, she would call sometimes and tell us that evil men were after us. We'd run to our neighbor's house and stay there until my dad got home from work."

I ran my finger over his temple, trying to imagine how scared he must have felt. "I'm so sorry," I said. "This isn't your fault."

He started to sob then, and I held him as tightly as I could.

I fell in love with Donny that day, with his willingness to be vulnerable in the face of all he had lived through. And now as we hug tightly in our small living room, I fall even more in love with him; he's human, he's tired, and he's crying because our daughter is miles away, lying in the belly of a hospital.

That night, my whole family converges on our house. Rachel and Josh arrive with a bottle of wine. My mom is in the kitchen, making a casserole. My step-dad, Karl, and my dad sit, on separate couches, in the living room. They may be uncomfortable with each other, but the only indication of this is the long moments of silence between their words.

I pump and then settle myself on the couch. The phone rings constantly. Donny and I take turns answering it, reciting the details of Stella's birth, the move to the NICU, the ventilator, the bruised lung. I sit with the NICU handbook on my lap, trying to read. On the first page is a note from the mother of a twenty-four-weeker. She says that the birth of her daughter was like "being catapulted into a dark and terrifying dream." She says they made it through the NICU by clinging to small joys and that it was "very, very slowly" that they discovered their abilities as parents. I put the handbook down. I'm not yet clinging to small joys—I don't even know what those might be—and I don't have any idea how to be a parent to my tiny daughter. I wonder if I ever will.

I feel guilty that I'm not at the hospital, although I'm so tired that I can't imagine dragging myself off the couch and into the car. But what kind of mother thinks this way? What kind of mother is too tired to get off the couch to go see her daughter?

I call the NICU to check on Stella, and the nurse tells me that she's been extubated and is doing fine. "Oh, good," I say. Then, "I'm sorry I'm not there."

"She's okay," she says. "You take care of yourself."

"Okay," I say, but I don't feel better. I can't shake the tightness in my chest or the sinking feeling that washes over me each time I think of my daughter alone under those bright lights.

My mom passes plates of casserole around, and we all eat. My whole family, except Sara, is here, surrounding me, filling my house with chatter and concern. Still, I feel alone. It's the same way I felt all those years ago when I first became depressed. I could sit in my dorm room with a group of friends, I could laugh and joke, but I felt heavy, apart.

When everyone leaves, I sit alone in Stella's room, pumping. This is a different pump, the Medela Lactina Select. It's not as sleek or glossy as the hospital pump—it is yellow and blue and has a long white arm that extends and contracts when it's turned on—but the nurse said our insurance would cover the $60 monthly rental fee for as long as Stella is in the hospital.

Donny arranged the pump on the changing table next to the rocking chair so I can position the funnels and lean down and hit the switch without getting up. I stretch my left arm across my chest, holding one funnel in place with my forearm and the other with my fingers. This way, my right hand is free to turn the pump on and off. I'm pleased that I've figured this out.

After twenty minutes, I pour the milk into a plastic jar and label it. Donny washes the pieces of the pump and then we crawl into our bed, which feels too soft after the hospital beds. We fit our bodies together, Donny curling around me as if he means to protect me. He grabs my hip and inches closer.

"You're so small," he says, wonder in his voice.

This wonder is echoed in my body, in the bones that have begun to show again at my wrists, in my hands, at the base of my neck. I'm shrinking, slowly peeing out the fluid that had puffed me up like a fish in a Japanese restaurant. I'm beginning to look like myself again. But I'm not even sure who that is, who *I* am now. I push my back into Donny's chest, and let his heat sink into me.

13

Thursday morning in the NICU, Donny and
I stare down at Stella, who is now off the ventilator. There is a plastic box over her head and a narrow tube going into her mouth; it's
taped to her cheek. Her lips are thin and yellow with jaundice, not
the lips I imagined my baby would have. But still, I'm pleased I can
see her lips.

She bats against the box with her tiny fists, furious. I don't blame
her for wanting it off—it makes me feel claustrophobic just to think
of lying under that box, not being able to breathe real air. But I'm
relieved by her feistiness. It means she's a fighter.

But is being a fighter enough? Enough to live, to survive this?
And what does survival mean? I don't want her simply to survive. I
want her to be healthy, *normal*. I hate to use that word, to even think
it, but I can't help it. I remember the posters lining the hallway outside the unit and know that some of those kids won't ever run across
a field with a kite; some won't be able to hold a book in their hands;
some won't be able to read at all. This reality fills me with dread.

I want to know whether Stella will develop normally, but I'm too
scared to ask, and I sense that I'm not supposed to ask those kinds of
questions here. It probably wouldn't matter anyway; I already know
how the nurse or doctor would respond: *Stay focused on today. Your
daughter is having a good day.* But I have never been good at living in
the moment, or as Rilke would say, living the questions. I'm always on
to the next thing, planning for the following week or month or year.

Donny opens Stella's chart and checks her weight. "She's under
three," Donny says.

My throat clenches with fear. Stella looks the same as she did
yesterday—better even, without the ventilator—but she's still losing weight. And it's as if her weight is the key, the thing that will

determine her future. I inflate the significance of the smallest weight gain or loss because it is something tangible, something that can be measured. Every ounce lost seems like a step backward.

Kally comes over and explains that the tube in her mouth sucks air from her belly. That's when I notice how Stella's belly is swollen, the roping of her intestines visible through her mottled skin. "It's a transient ileus," says Kally. "Nothing's passing through her."

Transient ileus. *Transient* is a word I associate with migrant workers, with movement, so *nothing passing through her* doesn't make any sense.

Donny quickly asks what it means.

"She was born with a lot of magnesium sulfate in her system," Kally says. She pauses, as if to let this sink in. She means my magnesium, the magnesium sulfate they pumped into me to keep me from having seizures. This is my fault.

"Oh," I say. No one told me that the mag sulfate might hurt my daughter. What if it affects her the same way it affected me? What if she feels claustrophobic, like she can't catch her breath?

"I've given her a suppository," Kally says, "and she did pass some meconium."

"Meconium," I say. "I don't get it." I associate the dark tarry stool with a baby in utero. Stella was born five days ago. Shouldn't she be having regular baby poops by now?

Kally explains to me, slowly, that since Stella is not digesting milk she will continue passing meconium.

Donny nods, but I'm dumb, not able to wrap my mind around this.

Kally points to the neon bag of liquid that hangs from the IV stand near Stella's bed. "This is hyperalimentation," she says. "It's a blend of proteins, sugars, vitamins, minerals, and fats. Each baby's hyperalimentation is different; it's made to order. This is what's going into Stella."

Hyperalimentation, a cumbersome word. How will I remember this? Hyper, Ali, Mentation. Hyper Ali Mentation. Hyper Ally works on a mint plantation. In my mind, I turn to the person who blends this just for Stella. I imagine a small woman from far away— maybe India or Turkmenistan. She received a degree in this neonatal alchemy back home. Somewhere in a cold lab in the basement of this hospital, she pulls out lists of vitamins. She grinds calcium with a mortar and pestle. She shakes in a dash of manganese, stirs in a gram of protein for good measure. She does this for my baby.

Kally points to the other bag hanging above Stella's bed. It is creamy and white, luscious. "Stella is also getting lipids," she says. "Lipids are fats."

Yes, lipids are fats. Somehow I know this. A fact recycled from high-school biology.

"Do you want to hold her?" Kally asks.

I snap to attention. Hold her? We get to hold her?

Donny and I look at each other, eyes wide. Our daughter is five days old, and we get to hold her! Kally turns off the phototherapy lights and pulls the goggles away from Stella's eyes. Donny goes to get a rocking chair from across the room.

I look at Donny. "Can I go first?"

"Of course," he says, touching my arm. I sit down in the rocking chair, smiling, nervous. I get to hold my daughter. But what if I drop her, accidentally snap her twiglike neck? I watch Kally untangle the monitor wires and the IV lines and wrap Stella in a fleece blanket. Then Donny holds the wires up, and Kally steps under them, passing Stella into my arms.

In my arms. My daughter in my arms. She's so light, it's like holding nothing, holding air. I look down at her narrow face and the miniature fist that is visible amid the fleece. Donny pulls up a stool next to me, and Kally hands him a tube of oxygen, which he holds in front of Stella's face.

"Hi, baby," I say, my eyes suddenly full of tears. I look up at Donny. He has tears in his eyes, as well. We smile at each other.

Stella's eyes open and close. Open and close. They are so dark I can't distinguish pupils from corneas. I wish I could lean down and kiss her eyelids, touch my lips to her mottled forehead. But of course I can't do that because of the germs. So I study her face: her tiny nose, her ears, thin as paper, each the shape of a continent. In the coil of one ear is Africa and in the other, South America. How can that be? How can my under-three-pound baby carry a small continent in each ear?

I look up at the monitor. I don't know when I learned about the monitor, but I did. I know that the blue numbers are her oxygen and the red numbers are her heart rate. Her heart rate is down and her oxygen is up. This is good, and maybe it means she knows me, recognizes my voice. Maybe it means she knows that I'm her mother.

I hold her for seven minutes and then it's Donny's turn. Kally takes Stella from me, and Donny and I switch places. Kally takes a Polaroid of Donny holding her and hands it to me. I wave it through the warm air of the NICU, and in the image that appears Donny is smiling widely, looking at the camera. He looks exhausted, but happy.

In another seven minutes, we have to put her back. "She can't regulate her body temperature," Kally says apologetically. "And she needs as much time under the lights as possible."

"It's okay," we say, smiling.

When we leave the hospital, I'm craving a Caesar salad, so we drive to a little café in St. Paul. It seems tasteless to go out to lunch when our daughter is in the hospital, but, we reason, we have to eat, and neither of us is ready to go home, to break the spell cast by holding Stella.

The restaurant is crowded, and we're surrounded by chatter and the clanking of silverware. But none of that touches us—it feels as if Donny and I are in a bubble. No one surrounding us knows that we have a new baby. They don't know that last night she was extubated and that this morning we held her for the first time. I'm sure they have their own troubles and joys, but today, here in this loud restaurant, they seem to embody what is normal, regular, and we have become distinct, our lives outlined in bold.

I lift my fork to my mouth and catch a whiff of the NICU. "Oh," I say. "Smell your hands."

Donny smells his and looks up, his face questioning.

"It's Stella. Can't you smell her? The sweetness?"

Donny shakes his head. "Your sense of smell is amazing."

That may be true or maybe I just want to have Stella with me, and it's this smell—the sweet scent of the NICU's antibacterial foam—that delivers her. How many times have I heard women say how they love the smell of babies, the smell of babies' scalps? I have seen them lean into newborns and breathe deeply. Perhaps I've done this very thing—bent down and inhaled—but I wouldn't be able to describe that baby smell, which is probably for the best; my baby might not ever smell that way. My baby smells like the sweet antiseptic that I must rub between my fingers and up my wrists before I can touch her.

While we're eating, it begins to rain, and by the time we get home, I'm freezing. The high I felt from holding Stella has worn off, and I'm exhausted. Donny wants to assemble the crib so Stella's room will look like a real baby room. I still think we should wait, just to be safe, but I don't say so. I nod, crawl into our bed, and pull the duvet to my chin.

I drift in and out of sleep. I listen to the rain pelting the windows, the phone ringing, and the murmur of Donny's voice. I register when he's talking to my mom, my friend Claire calling from New York, and a reporter from the Minneapolis paper, who is doing a story on Donny and our friend Amos, another Thunder player who is retiring after this season. And I feel safe, tucked in our bed, half-listening to Donny describe the texture of our current lives.

14

ON FRIDAY MORNING, THE ALARM SOUNDS AT 5:30. My dad will be here in half an hour to take Donny to the airport so he can fly to Charleston for the A-League final. Donny curls into me for a moment, and as I shift onto my side, I notice that my breasts are painful and as hard as rocks.

There is no way I'll be able to fall back asleep until I pump, so when Donny gets out of bed to shower, I slide from the bed as well, careful not to jostle my incision, which still aches. It has only been one week since my dad took Donny to the airport for the Seattle play-off game, a week since I lay in bed, listening to my dad's car pull away from the curb, believing I would be pregnant for at least a few more weeks. How could I have been so naïve?

Yesterday after Donny assembled Stella's crib, he hung two colorful Brian Andreas prints on the wall in her room. I bought them in my early twenties, but they'd been in a box in the basement and I'd forgotten about them. Each contains a figure in primary colors, outlined in black. In one, the figure is leaping through the air, her arms like two crescents reaching over her head. Next to her it says, "The first time her laughter unfurled its wings in the wind, we knew that the world would never be the same." I don't remember what this meant to me when I bought it almost a decade ago. Now, it seems it must always have been about Stella. Someday she will laugh, and the world will never be the same.

But in the next print a sad woman balances the sun on her fingertips, standing over a child in a chair. Above them it says, "The secret is not in your hand or your eye or your voice, my aunt told me once. The secret is in your heart." Below them it says, "Of course, she said, knowing that doesn't make it any easier." If the secret is in my heart, how will I access it? I have stashed my heart carefully away.

Even if I *could* access it, it wouldn't make a difference; it wouldn't make this any easier. The hopefulness of the first print is nullified by the second. I feel heavy as I sit down in the rocking chair and assemble the pieces of the pump.

Pumping has become painful, especially the first few minutes before my milk has let down. It feels as though my nipples are being shredded, rubbed raw against the plastic cylinders. The pump must be set too high, but I can't figure out how to reduce the suction power. I don't really mind the pain; it's as if it somehow brings me closer to Stella, to the pain she must experience when they take her blood, when they thread the tube up her nose and down her throat. So I grit my teeth and wait for my milk to let down, which feels like an electrical current under my skin.

When the milk begins to squirt into the cylinders, the pain subsides. I love this part of pumping. Nurses change my daughter's diaper, take her blood, watch over her. Everything that I can do for her at the hospital, at her bedside, they can do better and more efficiently. But only *I* can pump for her, only *I* can sit in this chair and feel this pain, only *I* can fill these bottles with my milk.

Donny brings me a cup of tea and leans down to kiss me.

"Call me when you get in," I say.

"I will," he says. "I love you."

"I love you, too."

I listen to his footsteps on the stairs, and when I hear the scrape of the door, I feel a rush of panic—what if his plane crashes? What if something happens to him and I'm left alone with our baby in the hospital?

The door shuts and then, a moment later, opens again. "I love you," he calls again, and I yell, "Be safe. I love you, too!"

The house is quiet then, and I feel lonely, the whoosh of the pump my only company. I wonder about the people who lived here before us. I know an elderly woman lived here for a long time, but I don't know any of her story. I don't know what happiness or heartbreak she experienced within these walls, just as the people who come after us won't know our stories. Time suddenly flashes forward, and I see a new young couple in this very room. She is pregnant. He is stenciling the walls with bears and balloons. They are expecting their first baby, and they are full of hope. They won't know—they probably won't care—that decades before, I sat here, in this very room, breathing this air, pumping for my daughter who is too small to bring home. This impermanence fills me with sadness.

I can't drive for another week and a half because of the C-section, so at 8:30 Rachel picks me up to drive me to the hospital.

When we arrive at Stella's bed, there is a doctor there, and she turns to us. "Good morning," she says. "I'm Dr. Gregor, and I'll be Stella's doctor for the next few days." She looks me in the eyes and smiles, and immediately I love her.

Rachel and I stand back as Dr. Gregor presses her fingers into Stella's belly. Her voice is quiet and gentle. She says that Stella's abdomen is still distended. "But it's looking better, and she'll probably be able to have a little breast milk in a day or two."

"Really?" I understand that I won't be able to nurse her—someone mentioned it could be three weeks before that happens because Stella doesn't yet have the ability to suck and breathe and swallow at the same time—but at least she'll get some of the milk I've been pumping. I know this will make me feel more like her mother. It will make her seem more like my baby.

"Has anyone talked to you about Stella being anemic?" Dr. Gregor asks.

I shake my head.

"We'll keep an eye on her for now, but she may end up needing a blood transfusion."

"A transfusion?"

Dr. Gregor nods, frowning slightly. "Do you know your husband's blood type?"

I shake my head. "He's out of town until Sunday night."

"Well," she says, "we'll watch it, and he can get his blood tested on Sunday. Often anemia resolves without a transfusion."

Dr. Gregor doesn't ask about my blood type, and I assume I can't donate because I just had surgery. If Stella does need a transfusion and Donny isn't a match, she'll get a stranger's blood. I can't decide if this bothers me or not. It would be a small thing considering everything she's been through, but it does give me pause, the thought of a stranger's blood coursing through my tiny daughter's veins. It's as if she would be even less mine.

"What does anemia do?" I ask.

"Well," she says, glancing at Stella, whose eyes are closed. "It makes her tired. Babies get most of the iron they need during the last twelve weeks of pregnancy. Iron is essential for making red blood cells, and red blood cells carry oxygen."

I can feel Rachel standing next to me, paying attention, absorbing this information in case I fail to take it in. But I *am* taking it in, maybe because I'm off the Percocet now, and I don't feel so fuzzy. Maybe because this doctor looks me in the eye, which helps me focus.

"If there aren't enough red blood cells," Dr. Gregor goes on, "your heart has to pump harder in order to get enough oxygen. This makes you tired." It turns out that many preemies are anemic while they're in the hospital. Each time their blood is drawn, red blood cells are removed.

"Okay," I say. And now I understand why, when I lived in San Vicente, my host-mother Betty, one of the women whose lives I was recording, was always tired. I knew she was anemic—she would send my host-brothers down the road to collect dark pods that hung, like withered bananas, from the branches of a craggy tree. Then Betty would slice the seeds from the pod with the curved blade of a knife and boil them into a tea. I knew it was supposed to help with her anemia, but I never realized that the anemia is what made her tired. I wish I could boil a tea for Stella, drip it into her mouth, and that it would keep her from having a transfusion.

Dr. Gregor smiles at Rachel and me and moves on to Emily, the baby next to Stella near the door. Kally asks if I want to hold Stella. I nod and settle into the rocker as Kally wraps Stella in a fleece blanket as she did yesterday and passes her into my arms. She hands the tube of oxygen to Rachel to hold near Stella's face.

I stare down at Stella's closed eyes and thin lips and sunken cheeks, but in each of these things I now see beauty. I adjust the miniature hat on her head, and that's when I notice that the sides of her skull don't fit together. The left side protrudes, an uneven ridge of bone.

"Feel this," I say. "Her head's uneven."

Rachel hands me the tube of oxygen and runs her hand over the back of Stella's head. "Like tectonic plates," she says.

"Great."

"Seriously," she says, pulling her hand away. "But aren't all babies' heads funny like that at first? She's not even a week old."

"Thirty-three weeks and three days," I say. I still count her gestational age, her corrected age, as well as her actual, chronological age. Her corrected age is how old she *should* be—still inside me for another six and a half weeks. All preemie parents learn to live in two time zones, which run side by side: reality and *what should have been.*

Rachel brushes her fingers along the back of Stella's head again. "I bet it will shift into place," she says.

"I hope so."

Stella's alarm sounds, and I look up at the monitor. Her oxygen has dipped to 83 percent. Rachel holds the tubes closer to Stella's face, and it rises to 90 percent, but then it dips again and won't increase. Kally comes over and punches off the alarm.

"Try holding her head up a little more," she says.

I nod, but it keeps happening, and each time the alarm blares, I feel like I'm doing something wrong. *Look at this woman. She doesn't know how to hold her baby.* Finally Kally says, "I should get her back under the lights anyway," and I hand off my daughter, both relieved and ashamed.

When Stella is resituated on the warming table, I glance around the room, making sure the other babies are still here. Joe lies to Stella's right, Emily to the left. Angel is across the room. He's been here for a month already, but he's much smaller than Stella. I catch a glimpse of him as the nurse lifts the quilt from his isolette to change his diaper. He looks like a baby squirrel. No, a fetal squirrel.

I remember a summer at the cabin when I was seven or eight and Sara, Rachel, and I found a litter of newborn squirrels. We discovered them in a flattened circle of grass near the edge of the lake, and they were curled into themselves, covered in blood. We decided that they had been abandoned so we gathered them up, pink and throbbing and wet in the palms of our hands, and carried them to the cabin, where we made a house for them out of a cardboard box and beds of shredded toilet paper. I remember we felt important for saving them. We shined a lamp down on them and dripped warm milk into their open mouths. We were diligent, but two died the first night, and one died the following day. The fourth lived for two more days before it died as well. We buried them at the base of a large pine tree.

I shudder now, over twenty years later, and stare down at my daughter, understanding all over again how lucky we are that Stella made it to thirty-two weeks, to three pounds.

You aren't supposed to ask about the other babies in the NICU. That's one of the rules in the handbook. But how do I pretend we're here alone in this room full of whirring machines and beeping alarms? I can't. I watch parents come and go. I watch nurses hover over isolettes. I listen for snippets of conversations and try to piece together each baby's story. Because each baby has a story. Even though they're small, they have stories and their parents have stories.

Joe's parents are the ones I watch most closely. Joe was born at thirty-three weeks and has been here a week longer than Stella. His parents are young and hip-looking, and I like them, though how I've decided this, I'm not sure. Maybe because it seems we could have been friends if we'd met under different circumstances. The father and I smile at each other whenever we catch each other's eye, but the mother never makes eye contact. There is a seriousness about her—I can't tell if it's rooted in irritation, anger, sadness, or simply shock. Probably all of the above. I might look like that as well. I listen to their low voices as they read to their son, and sometimes I catch snippets of their conversations. Today I hear Joe's mom ask the nurse about the Special Care Nursery. Joe must be getting ready to move, and this makes me feel envious and sad. I don't want them to go. I don't even know these people—we've never spoken—yet I feel close to them and to their baby.

When I was young and our family took annual road trips east to visit my grandma in New Jersey, I would choose friends from the pool of other travelers on the highway, deciding randomly that I liked the people in the Corolla or the rusted-out Chevy. I silently urged my dad to stay close to the cars I'd chosen. I didn't want us to be separated. If they pulled off at a rest stop and we did not, I willed them to catch us later, so we'd be reunited. I never admitted aloud what I was doing because it was a silly game. I knew that. But I also knew that I was somehow comforted by the fact that we were not alone on our journey—other cars with other people in them were traveling in the same direction. I feel the same way about the babies who lie on either side of Stella, and I feel the same about their parents.

15

AFTER RACHEL DROPS ME BACK AT HOME, I PUMP, make myself a sandwich, and go down in the basement to check e-mail and return phone calls. Then I go upstairs and crawl into bed. I remember what the nurse said to me a few days ago, on the day I was discharged from the hospital: "Develop a routine." I'm amazed how quickly I have done this.

When my mom takes me back to the hospital in the evening, I stop in the freezer room with my jars of breast milk. The freezer is lined with shelves of blue bins, each labeled with a name and ID number. Most of the bins are full, overflowing with tiny plastic jars of creamy milk. Some babies even have two bins. Stella's contains only a handful of partially full jars, and I wish it were as full as the other babies' bins. But then I realize that this doesn't make any sense. A full bin means a baby has been here a long time. A full bin means weeks—or months—of pumping. I don't want that.

My mom knows the drill: when we walk into the room, she immediately turns to the sink to wash her hands. She is one of the four people on our visitor list, one of the four people who have access to the NICU and Stella even if Donny and I aren't here. (Rachel, my dad, and Donny's dad are the other three.) She has been coming to visit Stella in the mornings on her way to teach. She stays for twenty minutes and reads *Brown Bear, Brown Bear, What Do You See?* as she holds Stella's tiny hand. Mom says the rhythm and repetition of *Brown Bear* will be good for Stella's brain development. The nurses say how sweet this is and what a wonderful family we have. I agree, of course; I'd be lost without them. But still, I feel a twinge of something when I think of my family having access to Stella when I'm not here. Most new mothers get to decide who visits when. They can say *no, not until this afternoon* or *today's not a good day*. I don't have that luxury.

Tonight, Stella is still under the plastic box. Goggles still cover her eyes. The phototherapy light still beats down on her. But for the first time, she seems relaxed; her face is turned to the side and her breathing seems steady. Mom wants to take a picture, but I don't want her to photograph Stella while she's wearing the goggles. I don't want to remember her with Velcro on her temples, just as I did not want anyone to photograph her with the ventilator tube covering her mouth.

A nurse I haven't seen before comes up and introduces herself and asks if I want to kangaroo with Stella. I've read about kangarooing in the three-ring binder, how holding your diapered baby to your bare chest, skin-to-skin, can help the baby grow. The mother's or father's heartbeat and the close contact can lower the baby's heart rate and increase her oxygen.

I nod quickly. Another first with my daughter. And it's a step forward—I know that only babies who are fairly stable can kangaroo.

"I can't let you hold her very long because she needs to be under the lights," the nurse says. "But this is good for her. There was a study in Africa—I can't remember which country—but they designed these special shirts with little pouches in them so preemies could constantly be pressed to their mothers' chests. The outcomes were pretty amazing."

I like the idea of wearing Stella like a marsupial, having her close enough that I can feel her breath on my skin.

The nurse pulls a screen around the rocking chair and the stool that my mom has pulled up next to me. It feels as if we're in a cocoon, enclosed in a permeable skin. The opaque walls of the screens don't block any of the sounds of the NICU, but they offer some privacy, so I pull off my shirt and bra.

The nurse passes Stella to me, wires and tubes trailing behind her, and helps me situate Stella, her legs tucked up into her belly, the side of her head pressed to my chest. This is the first time I have held her without the padding of the fleece blanket, and I can't believe how small she is, nestled between my breasts. The nurse drapes a blanket over her and tucks it behind my shoulders.

I hold my daughter awkwardly, and her head lolls to the side. She seems so vulnerable. I cup her back in my palm, trying to contain the heat of her small body. I'm both terrified and elated, holding her like this. I look up at my mom, whose eyes are full of tears. She takes out her camera and stands behind me. Stella seems to understand that this is a moment to document. She looks up at me and throws her arm over my breast.

"She knows you," my mom says.

"Do you think so?" I ask. In the photo, which I will stare at again and again in the coming months, it looks as if she is reaching for me, her eyes searching mine. But maybe she would have looked up at anyone; maybe it didn't matter who I was.

We sit like this for a long minute, her dark eyes opening and closing, but then her head tips back too far, and the alarm blares. The nurse comes over and adjusts Stella's head. I'm afraid to do this myself because her neck is so skinny it seems as if just moving her could break it.

The nurse has to readjust Stella's head three times, and each time I feel incompetent. I wonder if I'll ever be able to hold her unconsciously, free of the hyperawareness that she is in my arms.

My mom takes me home, then goes to the airport to get my sister Sara, who is flying in for the weekend to meet Stella and to stay with me while Donny is out of town. I pump, get ready for bed, and wait for her. When she finally arrives, we hug and go straight to bed.

On Saturday morning, Dad picks us up to go to the hospital. My dad hasn't been in the NICU yet, and both he and Sara are nervous. They wear blue masks because they're worried about germs, though neither has a cold. I understand their fear and actually appreciate their caution, but my dad stands so far back from Stella's bed that he's almost in the middle of the room. He doesn't want to touch Stella, shakes his head gruffly when I ask. But Sara is braver: she scrubs her hands, rubs foam into her palms and up her wrists, and stands next to me at Stella's warming table.

Stella is no longer under the oxygen tent, and she reaches her hands above her head. Her fingers extend and contract, swimming through the warm air above her.

"They're like starfish," Sara says quietly. "Look at her precious starfish hands."

I like that: Stella the starfish.

Sara catches one in her own hand, and Stella latches onto Sara's finger.

A few minutes later, after I have settled myself in the rocking chair and Sara has settled herself on the stool and Dad has gone to wait in the family lounge, the nurse, Angela, wraps Stella up and passes her into my arms. We are rocking, just barely, when Baby Emily's family comes in. This is the first time I've seen them, so I assume they live out of town. The father is a big, ruddy man with thick arms. The mother is small and round, and on her hip she's holding a toddler. Trailing behind her is another child, a boy of about six. The father is holding a balloon, which he awkwardly ties to his daughter's isolette. That's when the toddler begins to scream: "*I* want it! My balloon! My balloon!" The mother tries to reason with her, "This is for your sister," but it doesn't make any difference. Over and over: *My balloon! My balloon!*

I try to press Stella closer to me, wanting to shield her from the racket. "Jesus," I whisper to Sara, and she says, "Barbarian." Someone needs to get that child out of here. But Stella doesn't seem to notice anyway. Her eyes are closed, her heart rate and oxygen steady.

I glance up and notice one of the nurses glaring at Emily's family. She rolls her eyes at another nurse who walks past and whispers something that I can't hear. And I immediately change my position entirely—this poor loud family. They're the ones with a baby here, so far from home. They've probably driven half the morning to spend a few short hours with their tiny Emily, who has already been here for over a month. Poor, poor family. I turn my rage on the nurse. Does *she* know what's it like to have a baby stuck in the NICU? Does *she* know what it feels like to see your baby only once a week? How dare she judge them.

But then Stella begins squirming, and a thin, high wail escapes her mouth. Her face puckers. I look up at the monitor; her heart rate is soaring. "It's okay, sweetie," I say. "Shhh, shhhh." But it doesn't make any difference. Stella begins to cry harder, and I'm back to my original position on Emily's family: can't someone shut these people up? Who the hell do they think they are?

Their toddler with gale-force lungs continues: "I want it! I WANT IT!"

Finally the father relents, hands her the balloon, then leads her from the NICU.

"Thank fucking God," Sara says.

But it's too late. Stella's alarm blares. Angela comes over and says she better put Stella back, as if *I* have done this, as if *I* have made her cry.

"It's too loud," I say, unable to keep the defensiveness from my voice.

Angela smiles gently. "She'll be okay."

Back on the warming table, Stella is bright red and mottled, tight fists waving. Her heart rate is still too high, and I feel useless, unable to calm her. Angela pops a green pacifier into Stella's mouth, and the response is immediate: her eyes close and her cheeks become sunken with the effort of sucking. She looks like Maggie Simpson.

"She'll be okay," the nurse says again, and I feel as though this is our cue to leave. As we walk down the long hallway to the NICU lounge to collect Dad, Sara glances at the photos on the wall and then at me.

"I know," I say.

Sara wants to buy some preemie clothes for Stella, which she will be able to wear as soon as she no longer needs the bilirubin lights, so we drive to a suburb where there is a Babies R Us. But as soon as we pull into the parking lot full of SUVs, I know we've made a mistake.

The store is packed. Hugely pregnant women are everywhere, notebooks and scanners in hand. Strollers seem to be coming at me from every direction, and each is stuffed with a grotesquely fat, full-term baby. It's as if we've stepped into an alternate universe or fallen through a hole into Baby Wonderland. I'm dizzy and grab Sara's arm. We move through the store in slow motion, picking our way between stands of huge sleepers and frilly dresses. We finally find some preemie onesies, and Sara wants to look around a little more, but I can't. My incision aches, and the women with their over-sized strollers, trying to decide whether to get the bouncy chair with music or without music, to get the orange Halloween dress or the black one, make me want to scream. "We have to go," I say to Sara. "I have to get out of here."

16

Saturday night my whole family drives to Brit's Pub in downtown Minneapolis. It's dark and smoky. We make our way upstairs, where the televisions are all tuned to the A-League final. Fans with Thunder jerseys congregate around tables and in small groups, and I feel nauseated as we move through them. One of Donny's friends says, "Hey, how's it going?"

I'm not sure if he knows about the baby. If he did, he wouldn't have asked that, would he? I want to ask him how the fuck he thinks it's going, but instead I wave at my deflated belly and shrug. "Oh, you know."

I quickly move into the far room, which is less crowded. I don't want to be around these fans; I don't want to make small talk. I feel guilty that I'm at a bar when my week-old daughter is lying alone in a hospital.

Dad, Mom and Karl, Sara, Rachel, and Rachel's husband, Josh, all pull stools up, and we sit staring up at the television. I start to cry quietly when I see Donny, a tiny figure in a white jersey, running onto the bright green grass of Charleston's stadium. He's so far away. The Charleston fans are going crazy, waving flags, and through the television speakers, their cries are like the deafening hum of a thousand angry bees.

A Thunder fan, a mother whose daughters play soccer and who attends most home games, sits down next to me. "I'm so sorry," she says, and I nod, eyes full of my tears. I order a glass of wine, which makes me light-headed after three sips, and then I begin to talk. I tell this woman every detail—the magnesium sulfate and the Special Care Nursery and the respiratory distress and intubation, the jaundice and the bruised lung and the extubation, the blocked intestines, the anemia, the kangarooing. I can't stop talking. It's as if recounting every detail somehow guarantees something, though I'm not sure what.

The soccer game is a disaster. Compared to Charleston, the Thunder seems disorganized and distracted, incapable of passing the ball. It's Donny's last game as a professional soccer player, and the Thunder loses 3–0. I'm disappointed for Donny at the same time I'm irritated by the other Thunder fans' outrage. As we make our way out of the bar, I hear them complain about calls made by the referees, and I want to stop and say, really? You're really getting upset about this? You actually think this matters?

When I get home, I pump and pour my wine-tainted milk into the bathtub. I watch the milky swirl circling the drain and feel a pang of guilt for wasting it. "Whatever," I mutter, and turn on the water to rinse it away.

On Sunday morning, Dr. Gregor calls to say that Stella was given three ccs of breast milk. She doesn't drink it, of course; it's injected into the tube that's taped to her cheek and threaded up her nose and down her throat. A cc is nothing; it's like a raindrop. It takes thirty ccs to equal one ounce. But it doesn't matter; she's finally getting some of the milk I've been pumping for her. Dr. Gregor tells me that in three hours, before Stella's next feeding, the nurse will pull back on this tube with a syringe to see whether Stella is digesting the milk or whether it's still in her stomach. If she's digested it, she will get three more ccs; if not, they'll reduce the feedings.

When Sara and I get to the NICU, Stella is sleeping soundly, her arms and legs flopped to the sides. "She was just hungry," Sara says, and I nod. She looks totally different from the angry, thrashing baby of yesterday. My mom meets us there with Grandpa, and together, we all stare down at Stella. Grandpa has tears in his eyes, and he says, over and over again, his voice cracking, *Well, she has all her fingers. She has all her toes.*

I know he thinks we've been keeping something from him, not telling him the whole story. He's been worrying about her, and I imagine that his own losses—the miscarriages and the stillbirth and, of course, my grandma's death—are there, just beneath the surface. I reach for his hand, and he squeezes it tightly.

Sara leaves on Sunday afternoon, and at 5:45, my dad drops Donny off. I'm waiting by the door because we need to leave right away if we want to make it to the hospital in time for Stella's 6:00 cares. Every three hours, Stella has her diaper changed, her temperature taken, and the pulse oximeter moved from one foot to the other so the red light on the sensor won't burn her arch. If we get there in time, we can do these things for our daughter.

Donny throws his bag on the porch, and we hug tightly. I'm surprised by how rested he looks.

"How do you feel?" I ask as we walk to the car.

"Pathetic," he says, unlocking the car door for me. "I just wish it could have ended, to have had my last game..." He shrugs. "I wanted us to be the champions."

"Hmmm," I say, and it's all I can muster. I gave myself a pep talk this afternoon, convincing myself that I could be supportive, commiserate with Donny over the embarrassing loss, but I'm having trouble following through. It is, after all, just a game.

I give myself a mental shake as I buckle myself into the passenger seat. Because of course soccer is more than a game to him; it's his job, his passion. But there is a part of me that has never understood how important it is to him. The year we got married, the Thunder played the Rochester Rhinos in the championship game. The Thunder had made it to the championship before—each time against Rochester— and each time they lost. But the year of our wedding, the game was played for the first time in Minnesota. It was freezing—our breath was visible in the night air—but the stadium was packed with thousands of screaming fans. And for the first time, the Thunder won. After the game, when everyone congregated on the field, a rabid fan came up to me and said how wonderful it was that they won because now our wedding the following weekend would be a *real* celebration. I smiled thinly at the woman and wondered briefly whether she was drunk. Certainly the fact that we were getting married was reason enough to celebrate. But looking back, I think she was right; Donny was elated the week of our wedding, and it was partly because of the Thunder's victory. I didn't fully understand what it meant to him then, and I know I don't understand it now. But he has always supported me in everything—my jobs, graduate school, writing—and I know I need to do the same for him. I reach for his hand in the car, and he holds it, running his thumb over my knuckles.

When we get to the hospital, Stella is lying on her stomach, sleeping. Her legs are tucked up under her. The tube of oxygen blows into her face.

"She looks relaxed," Donny says.

"The milk," I say, pleased.

The nurse says that there wasn't any aspirate—leftover milk—in her stomach, so she was given another three ccs this afternoon. She also tells us that Stella has pulled her feeding tube out twice.

"That's good," Donny says. "She's feisty."

Donny changes Stella's diaper, which is the size of a cocktail napkin, and takes her temperature. The nurse moves the pulse oximeter from her left foot to her right and then pulls a screen around the rocking chair that Donny has moved next to Stella's warming table. There aren't enough rocking chairs in the NICU, so you have to hope that one is available when you want to hold your baby. Luckily, there aren't many people here tonight, and Donny didn't have to negotiate with another family for a chair.

He pulls off his shirt, and the nurse passes Stella into his arms. He presses her to his chest, and I cover them with the fleece blanket. This is the first time Donny has kangarooed with Stella, and she looks even smaller than usual against his wide chest, but he seems totally comfortable. He grins down at her. "Hi, sweetheart. Your daddy's back." When Stella's head slips to the side, he adjusts it all by himself, making it look easy.

After seven minutes, it's my turn. Donny goes down the hall to the lab to get his blood type tested in case Stella needs a transfusion. I lean back in the rocking chair and try to breathe her in, store away the combination of antiseptic foam and adhesive. She is curled into a tiny ball against my chest. "You are never alone," I whisper. "You are never alone." But even as I say this, I know I'm lying. I don't know all the nurses who rotate through the shifts at night. I don't know if they are kind and gentle, careful and sturdy. I don't even know their names.

A half hour later, Donny and I walk down the long hallway away from the NICU, and I glance up at the photos on the wall and then quickly away. I feel heavy, walking away from our daughter, again.

"This sucks," Donny says.

I squeeze his hand. "I know."

Later that night, after we have eaten and I have pumped, Donny and I curl into each other in bed, and I tell him how glad I am to have him home.

"Me, too," he says, but he sounds sad.

"You seem pensive," I say. He's been quiet since we left the hospital, and I know he's thinking about the game. "I'm sorry you lost," I say.

"I'm just tired," he says, and I can hear the weariness in his voice. He will go back to work tomorrow, and he'll need to leave early in order to have time to prepare his five science lessons. I know he's dreading it.

"Do you think she knows us?" he asks then, and I realize he has been quiet not because of soccer or his new job; he's been thinking about our daughter. He rubs his eyes and leaves an eyelash on his cheek.

"I don't know," I say, lifting away the eyelash and balancing it on my fingertip. "They say so." In the three-ring binder it says that a preemie recognizes the sound of its parents' voices from hearing them in utero. But how do they know for sure? She hears so many voices. How does she know that I'm her mother? That Donny is her father?

"I hate leaving her there every night."

"Me too," I say, holding my finger up to Donny.

He closes his eyes for a moment, then blows the eyelash up into the silence of our bedroom like a tiny prayer. I don't ask him what he wished for because we're both superstitious. But I don't need to ask—I know. He has saved our Stella. He has wished for her to be okay, for her to come home soon. He has wished that she will be a healthy little girl who will someday grow into a strong woman.

17

On Monday morning, Donny is out the door early. I get out of bed, make my tea, and pump with gritted teeth. The pain that I didn't mind a few days ago has intensified, and my nipples are chapped and bleeding. After fifteen minutes, I can't stand it anymore, so I turn off the pump, slather my nipples with ointment, and ease myself into my bra.

I eat breakfast and wait for Dr. Gregor's call. I appreciate the time it takes her to call me at home, and she always reassures me: Stella is having a good morning; Stella digested her milk; Stella's anemia is holding steady. But when Dr. Gregor calls at 8:30, the first thing she says is that Stella had a rough night. My body constricts, and I start to cry before I even hear the details.

"She threw up, and we had to suction her stomach," she says. "She's having a little trouble digesting your milk, so we'll suspend the feedings for now."

"Oh, no," I say.

"It's not a major setback," she says calmly. "And the good news is that her bilirubin levels are down so we can discontinue the phototherapy lights today."

A step back, a step forward. Stella will be able to wear clothes and she won't have to bake under those lights anymore. These are good things. Still, the thought that she had a rough night and I wasn't there, that I don't even know what a "rough night" looks like for her, fills me with sadness, and I can't stop crying after I've hung up the phone. I sit in the rocker in Stella's room, feeling utterly alone. I stare up at the Brian Andreas drawings sick with the knowledge that nothing is guaranteed. She could get worse and not better. She might never have the chance to unfurl her laughter in the world.

I'm still heavy and quiet when my dad comes to pick me up to take me to the hospital. We make the drive without talking, and I'm grateful that Dad doesn't press me for information—it's not his way.

When we get to the second floor, he says he'll wait in the family lounge because he's still worried that he might have a bit of a cold, and I nod, relieved. I just want to be alone with my daughter.

When I walk into the NICU, I'm surprised to see that Stella has already been transferred into an incubator, which I now know is called an isolette. I sit down on the stool next to the large plastic box covered in a quilt. I should be happy about this because it means Stella is doing better, but it feels as though she's even more inaccessible.

Dr. Gregor is across the room, but when she sees me, she comes over. She motions to the isolette. "This will help her grow," she says gently, somehow knowing that I need reassurance. She smiles. "Remember, she should be inside you still. The darkness and quiet will help her get stronger."

She lifts the quilt, and I see that Stella is wearing a tiny sack covered with yellow and blue and green diamonds.

"Your mom brought it in this morning," Kally says.

"This is a step in the right direction," Dr. Gregor says. "She might be ready to move back to Special Care in a week or so."

"Really?" I say, and suddenly I think of Joe, the baby next to Stella. He must have been moved during the night because the bed next to the window is empty. He is one week older than Stella, and he was moved today, so it makes sense that Stella will move next week. Suddenly, the Special Care Nursery becomes the goal, the light at the end of the tunnel. When Stella returns there, we will be a step closer to going home.

After I hold Stella, who sleeps the whole time she's in my arms, I lower the quilt over her isolette and walk back down the long hallway. As I turn the corner to the NICU lounge, I almost collide with another woman. We both stop short, and I take her in: a blue business suit, skirt to her knees, a doughnut with sprinkles on a napkin in her hand. We smile at each other, and that's when I realize that I know her. There is the split second of panic that I always feel when I see someone out of context, but then her story, the murmurings of her tragedy, come to me. We had seen each other at the wedding of a high school friend in May, so I knew she had been pregnant with twins, but then at some point this summer, my sister Rachel said that the babies were born early—months too soon—and one of them died.

"Amy," I say.

"How are you?" she asks, giving me a hug. She seems so calm, composed, as if we're running into each other anywhere but here. "Mark thought he saw a Hopper sister here the other night." Amy was in Rachel's class in high school, Mark was a year younger.

I should have known that her surviving son would be here at Children's, but I had been so wrapped up in *our* lives that I hadn't even thought about her. I'm suddenly filled with a sense of guilt so strong it's searing. My eyes fill with tears. "My daughter Stella is here," I say. Then, "I heard about your delivering early. I heard about... I'm so sorry."

Amy nods, her eyes filling with tears as well. "Yeah, it's been hard." She plucks some sprinkles from her doughnut and puts them in her mouth. "I have to go to work," she says, "but I want to meet Stella. And I want you to meet Noah. He's in the ICC."

"Of course," I say. Then, "You have to go to work?" I can't imagine having to sit in an office all day when my baby is in the hospital. I can't imagine ever working again after losing a baby.

We start walking back down the hall to the NICU.

"Yeah," she says. "I was off for a long time. The boys were born in July." Amy shrugs. "But it makes more sense to work now and have some time off again when Noah comes home."

I try to take this all in: a dead son, another son who has already been here for two and a half months, dressing in a suit, going to work. I look down at the long cotton maternity skirt I wear every day because I can't manage putting on anything else.

"My boss has been really amazing," Amy says. "That helps a lot."

In the NICU, we both wash our hands and then I flip up the quilt on Stella's isolette. She is sleeping on her back, her legs tucked up and flopped to the sides like a miniature yogi. "They think she might be able to go back to the Special Care Nursery in a week or so."

"Oh, she's gorgeous," Amy says, peering at Stella through the plastic wall of the isolette. I smile. No one has said that Stella is gorgeous, and I'm not sure it's a word I'd use to describe her disproportionate head and body, her vein-tracked skull, her bulbous eyes. Still, I'm pleased that Amy thinks so.

Amy looks at me. "She's going to be fine, Kate. If they're talking about moving her in a week, she's going to be just fine."

Noah and his brother weighed less than two pounds each when they were born. Stella must seem huge to her, and I must seem ridiculous.

Amy walks me over to the ICC, which is right next to the NICU. I've never been in this unit, and I'm startled to see babies in plastic bassinets and white metal cribs. "This is where less seriously ill babies stay," Amy says. "Babies who are waiting for surgery or to be transferred to regional hospitals."

She leads me into the room where Noah lies in one of the white cribs with a black and red and white mobile hanging above him. He's wrapped in a blanket, and he's huge. Amy says he weighs six pounds—he's tripled in weight since his birth at twenty-six weeks and six days.

A six-pound baby is anything but huge, but compared to Stella, Noah looks like some kind of miniature Goliath. "He looks great," I say.

"He's doing pretty well," Amy says. "Every day, they pull ten ccs of cerebral spinal fluid from his head." She motions to Noah, and I notice the bump on his skull where they must draw the fluid.

"Why?" I ask, trying to absorb the fact that ten ccs is three times more than the amount of milk Stella got per feeding yesterday.

"An intraventricular hemorrhage," Amy says. I won't remember that she called it this—a hemorrhage—until later, when I am also forced to learn this language. "There is bleeding in the ventricles of his brain."

"How did it happen?" I ask, staring at the mobile spinning slowly above Noah's head.

"I had twin-to-twin transfusion syndrome," Amy says, and she proceeds to explain that in utero, Noah and his brother, Peyton, shared a placenta and began unequally transferring blood and amniotic fluid back and forth. Peyton ended up with very little blood; Noah had too much. "When they were born," she says, "Peyton was white as a sheet and anemic, and Noah was red, filled with extra blood that stressed his heart." I imagine them, two miniature boys, one a ghost and the other a blooming poppy.

"The vessels in a preemie's brain can rupture easily. If they do, the blood can fill and scar the ventricles of the brain," Amy says. Her fingers reach for Noah's foot. "Sometime in the next two weeks, he'll have surgery and have a shunt put in, which will drain the fluid from his head into his abdomen."

"Oh, my God," I say, shaking my head, trying to keep my tears at bay, not asking what this means for Noah, for his brain development.

Suddenly Noah's alarm blares, and Amy punches a few buttons on the monitor to silence it. She rubs Noah's belly. "Okay, sweetie. Remember to breathe."

She looks up at me. "He has great doctors."

I nod, amazed by how together she seems, how upbeat. I'm also amazed by how comfortable she is with her son and the technology that surrounds him. I never punch off Stella's alarm when it blares. I never even *touch* her monitor. I don't have the faintest idea what she needs. For a moment I'm envious of Amy's level of comfort. But then I remember that comfort means you've been here for a long time. It means you know the ropes. I don't want to be comfortable here. Not ever.

Later that night, when Donny and I return to the hospital, we walk into the hospital's family resource center. I had seen a flyer about a NICU "parent connection" meeting, and I want to go. Donny would rather skip it—he's exhausted and wants to see Stella and go straight home. But I convince him. I think the more parents we meet, the better. And maybe we'll learn something about how to be good parents in the NICU. I need some instruction.

There are only two women in the small room at the back of the resource center, and as we maneuver around the table, one of them introduces herself as Jan, the facilitator.

Ready for Air   25

"I'm Anne," the other woman says.

"Hi," we both say, and then Donny turns to look at Anne again. "Oh, hey. How are you?"

It turns out Donny went to high school with this woman. She just had a thirty-two-weeker as well. She also has two children at home. She looks absolutely weary as she tells us how she became pregnant a month after her second child was born, and how, with her third being born two months early, her second and third children are only eight months apart.

"Holy shit," I say.

Donny raises his eyebrows at me, but Anne just says, "Tell me about it."

We sit in the meeting, recounting the details of our births and the first weeks in the NICU. Jan hands us folders with handouts on nursing and a preemie play group that will meet in the spring. She stresses the importance of us feeling involved in our child's care, and I try to absorb her words, but I can't get over the fact that in one day, Donny and I both have run into people here with whom we went to high school.

I know that one in eight babies is born prematurely in the United States, so it makes sense that we would know other people with preemies, but it's difficult for me to wrap my mind around the fact that we actually *do* know other preemie parents. I never could have imagined this world: the lights and alarms, the IVs and feeding tubes, the babies with bleeding brains. I never could have imagined a place that contains at once so much hope and so much fear. Yet here we are, and we aren't alone.

18

HOW MANY TIMES HAVE I BEEN TOLD BY DOCTORS and nurses about the importance of breast milk for a preemie's immune system? Pumping is my one clear-cut job, the one thing I can do for my daughter that I know is making a difference. But it has become so painful that I'm not sure what to do. I know I can't quit. Stella is back up to two ccs of my breast milk every three hours and is finally gaining a little weight. She is benefiting from my pain.

But something has to change. On Tuesday morning, I finally admit to Kally that my nipples are cracked and bleeding. My sister Rachel sits next to me, a look of disgust frozen on her face. In the car on the way to the hospital, I told Rachel that I was worried I might pump my nipples right off, and she almost threw up in her mouth.

"I can call the lactation consultant if you want," Kally says.

"Please," I say.

A few minutes later, the lactation consultant comes in, and I discreetly show her the evidence.

"Hmmm," she says, studying my torn nipples. "That shouldn't be happening. Do you have the pump set too high?"

I shrug. "Maybe. I don't know. I can't figure out how to turn it down."

"Didn't the nurse show you how it worked before you left the hospital?"

"No. She seemed confused, so I said I'd figure it out on my own."

"Looks like you were wrong about *that*," Rachel says, and we both let out a snort of laughter.

Kally and the lactation consultant give each other a look full of exasperated irritation, but I'm not sure if it's directed at the nurse who was confused by the pump or at Rachel and me. "I'll go find a pump," the lactation consultant says. Rachel and I continue to guffaw softly. I'm not sure why we think this is so funny, but laughing is better than letting the other emotions I'm feeling—stupidity and inadequacy—rise to the surface.

The lactation consultant is back in a minute with the long white cylinder of a breast pump in her hand. She holds it in front of me and points to the raised bars on the pump shaft and the little arrow that moves up and down when she twists the shaft. "Have you tried this?"

I bite my lip and feel the heat flooding my face and neck. The bars are difficult to see—white on white—and they would be even more difficult to see in a dimly lit room like Stella's, but really, I should have noticed them. I have been ripping my nipples to shreds all on my own.

"I didn't notice that," I say quietly.

The lactation consultant gives me an understanding smile, but Kally is just staring at me. I'm sure she thinks I'm a fool.

Back at home, when I look at my own pump, I see that it's set to the highest suction power. I sit down in the rocker and hold my forehead in my hands. "I'm such an idiot."

Later that night, when Donny and I go to see Stella, there are three nurses in Stella's room, and they are joking around, laughing quietly. It must be a slow night. One of them tells us that Stella pulled her feeding tube out again, but that she's calm now, sleeping on a swath of flannel. One of the other nurses comes over to peer at Stella. "Oh, yes," she says. "The princess and the pea. She knows exactly what she wants, and she wants flannel!" She laughs then, and we join in, happy that for once the nurses seem like regular people. Their nursing degrees and our situation are momentarily stripped away, and we are left with a sense of normalcy. It will dissolve, of course, the moment we leave our daughter in her isolette and go home without her. But for those few minutes, we are simply people, laughing together over the sleeping form of our baby.

When I kangaroo with Stella, her tiny body pressed against my chest, one of the laughing nurses comes over and says that I can try to get Stella to latch on.

"Really? I thought I had to wait." I can't remember what the binder said, something about babies not being able to coordinate their sucking and swallowing until thirty-four or thirty-five weeks? Stella isn't even thirty-four weeks yet.

"Well," she says quietly, "I think it's a good idea." She glances around the room. "Not everyone agrees on that, but I think the sooner the better."

I have been waiting to nurse, as if this act will solidify something between me and Stella, give me some ownership over her. But I'm also sure that the binder said *at least thirty-four weeks*. What if Stella *does* get some of my milk and chokes on it? The rule follower in me wants the official okay to nurse my daughter. I don't want to be seen as some rogue parent sneaking around trying to breastfeed under the radar.

The nurse helps position Stella at my breast. I cradle her head in my left hand. Her body lies across my left forearm. I look up at Donny, who is smiling down at us, and then back to Stella. Her eyes are closed, her spindly arm thrown up onto the mountain of my breast. I wonder whether she knows this is where she's supposed to be. She doesn't seem to really notice. She sleeps with her cheek pressed into my breast.

"Don't worry about her getting a good latch yet," the nurse says, leaning over me. "But this will get her used to the idea."

I can feel the electricity under my skin as my milk lets down. My body is clearly ready to nurse my daughter, but Stella is sound asleep. Both of my breasts begin dripping, and the nurse hands me tissues to staunch the flow. I thank her, and look back down at Stella, whose cheek is covered in milk, her lips parted slightly. She looks so precious, sleeping in my arms. I want nothing more than to lean down and kiss her temple, feel her skin on my lips.

When the nurse comes back, she seems pleased about my milky breasts, but I'm sticky and uncomfortable. I let Donny have his turn holding Stella while I walk down the hall to the pumping room.

On Wednesday morning, Rachel drives me to the hospital again—I have no idea what I would do without her—and a nurse I've never seen tells me that Stella is up to five ccs of breast milk every three hours. I beam as I check her weight, which is up thirty grams from yesterday. She's now three pounds five ounces, almost back to her birth weight!

The nurse, who is very tall—big-boned—passes Stella into my arms, then moves on to Emily. Most NICU nurses are petite, as if delicate hands and arms are a prerequisite for caring for preemies. This nurse doesn't fit the bill, and she looks out of place among these tiny lives.

Rachel sits next to me, taking pictures of Stella, who is wrapped in fleece. "I need some new ones now that she's not so yellow," she says. She has been showing photos of Stella to her fellow graduate students, but their reactions vary from uncomfortable to speechless when Rachel says, "My niece—isn't she adorable?" If they think Stella looks like an alien, I wonder what they would think of the tiniest babies here, the twenty-three- and twenty-four-week micropreemies.

"Have you wondered what would have happened if you'd been in Costa Rica?" Rachel asks suddenly.

"Yes," I say, my stomach sinking at the thought. Before I knew I was pregnant, I had applied for a grant to return to San Vicente, the Costa Rican village where I lived in my early twenties, to do more research, to immerse myself in the details of daily life there. I didn't get the grant, which was a relief because I would have been worried about being so far from home and my doctors while I was pregnant. But what if I had gotten the grant and had spent the summer in the unrelenting heat and humidity of the rainy season? Would I have even made it to thirty-two weeks? Would the doctors have realized I was sick? What if I had gone into labor down there? Or began to have seizures? What if Stella didn't make it? Just thinking about the possibility of our deaths somehow makes our lives feel more tenuous, as if we're here on borrowed time.

"Have you called Betty yet?" Rachel asks.

"No," I say. Betty, who is like a second mother to me, was ecstatic when I told her I was pregnant, and I know I need to call and tell her what's happened, but I'm dreading it because I know she'll be worried. Besides, I don't have the right vocabulary to describe what happened: my swollen body, the protein in my urine, Stella's intubation, her bilirubin levels. My vocabulary in San Vicente was the language of the earth: *barro, polvo, lluvia*—clay, dust, rain. I can't translate our new reality.

I'm sure if Betty saw me now, she would hardly recognize me. When I lived in San Vicente, I was relaxed, easygoing. Sent on an errand, I would ride my host-brother's much-too-small bike through the center of town yelling *¡Adiós!* to everyone I passed. I spent hours behind the house, listening to Betty tell stories from her childhood as flames licked the rim of the concave plate where a tortilla sizzled. And every Saturday night I rode with friends in the back of a truck to the nearest dance, where I flipped and swayed, spun and floated to a rhythm that worked its way inside me.

It's difficult for me to reconcile that Kate with the one I am here. There was a strength and independence that took root in me in San Vicente, and I wish I could tap into that confidence now, in *this* foreign land. Instead, I'm barely holding my head above water.

The too-tall nurse comes over and says she should put Stella back in the isolette. "Okay," I say, though I'm not ready. Stella seems relaxed, her oxygen and heart rate steady, and I want to hold her a little longer. But I pass her to the nurse, who resituates her in the isolette. When I begin to lower the quilt, Stella turns to me, her dark eyes wide—as if she knows me and doesn't want me to leave. Then she reaches out her spindly arm, toward the wall of her isolette. She's reaching for me!

"She knows you!" Rachel says.

Something—love? guilt?—expands in my chest like air. I open the armhole, the smaller door on the side of the isolette, and slip the pacifier into her mouth. "It's okay, sweetie," I say. "I'll be back later." Then I close the armhole and begin to lower the quilt.

Stella begins to cry—a high, thin wail—so I lift the quilt again. Her head is still turned toward me, and the pacifier is lying next to her. The nurse comes up behind me. "She's fine," she says brusquely.

I glance at her and slowly lower the quilt.

"It'll be good practice for you to hear her cry," she says.

Stella's muffled cry comes from the isolette.

"We can stay if you want," Rachel says, glaring at the nurse.

"If you get used to it now, it will be easier to let her cry when she's older," the nurse says, bustling past us to check on Emily, whose alarm is blaring.

Rachel and I both stand staring at the isolette, listening to Stella's thin cries. I feel stuck somewhere between being an adult and a child, unsure of my role. The part of me that is a rule follower thinks we should go. The part of me that is a mother feels a spark of anger. But I am cowed by this large woman who has dominion over my daughter. Finally I say, "I'm okay. We can go."

As we walk away from the NICU, down that long hallway, I feel pathetic. I should have said something, done something. But maybe that woman knows what's best for my daughter. Maybe she was right.

Rachel walks quietly beside me, but when we get to the parking lot, she opens my car door and says matter-of-factly, "Well, that woman sure was a bitch."

"She *was* a bitch, wasn't she?" And my guilt intensifies: I should have insisted on holding Stella again, cradling her against my chest. I should have told the nurse to go to hell. I should have asked to speak with a supervisor. I vow if I see her again, I'll tell her off.

Rachel drops me off at home with a hug, and I make a sandwich, then go down into the basement to check e-mail. There is a message from a grade-school friend who has two children. She says she's thinking about us and she's sure Stella will be fine. She writes, "Isn't being a mom amazing? Isn't it amazing how much you love her? It's indescribable. I didn't know how much my mom loved me until I had a child."

I stare at the computer screen, trying to reconcile her words and what I had thought motherhood would be like—the instant bond, the baby latching on immediately, falling head over heels in love—with our reality. How do I explain it without sounding heartless? I raise my fingers to the keyboard:

When Stella was born, I was so relieved that she was okay and I was okay that I couldn't think of anything else. Then I was so sick for a couple of days that I couldn't focus on her at all. Now, each time I visit her it's more difficult for me to leave. But I think there is a part of me that's still holding back. It's so hard to have other people caring for my baby. I know she's in good hands, but still, I can't wait to bring her home and be the one taking care of her.

I hit "send" and lean back in my chair. Then I turn off the computer and walk upstairs to wait for my dad, who will be picking me up soon to take me to a trendy salon in the Uptown neighborhood of Minneapolis. I've decided to get my hair chopped off.

A half hour later, Dad and I sit on a bench in the hair salon surrounded by hair and fashion magazines. Dad unfolds the newspaper he brought along and begins to read, but I just stare at the people checking in and paying at the front desk. I'm still angry about the nurse this morning, and my mind has transformed her into a giant who clumsily knocks over isolettes as she lopes through the NICU. I rehearse what I'll say if she happens to be Stella's nurse again: *Do you know what it feels like to have a baby in the NICU? You're too fucking tall to work here!*

Eliza, my stylist, appears around the corner, and I stand. She's been cutting my hair for the past four years, so I know her fairly well. By the time I'm seated in front of the mirror, it's all out: the preeclampsia, the C-section, the nurse this morning. "So," I add, "I want you to chop it all off."

Eliza, who has a different hair color every time I see her, lets strands of my red hair slip between her fingers. Then she takes a bottle of oil and drips it along the part in my hair and begins working her fingers in small circles across my scalp. She does this before each haircut, but today, the gentle pressure makes me want to cry.

"Usually I don't like to drastically alter a hairstyle when a client has undergone a major life change..." Eliza starts.

It hadn't even occurred to me that she might *not* cut my hair, and I'm ready to fight her.

"But you've had your hair short before, so you know you like it..."

I nod. "It will be easier to manage as I go back and forth to the hospital," I say, relieved. But that's not the only reason I want to cut it. I haven't forgotten the feeling of hair on my neck while the magnesium sulfate pulsed in my veins, and I still hold a grudge. Getting rid of it will feel as if I'm following through on a promise I made to myself.

I remember reading an article once about how chemicals we're exposed to are stored in the strands of our hair. Testing can reveal what drugs people have ingested and, if you compare the chemicals in their hair with various chemical levels in drinking water across the country, you can even tell where in the United States they've lived. For me, hair also seems to store memory and experience. So, contrary to what Eliza says, a big life change seems to be the perfect time to change one's hair. The first time I cut it short was when I was nineteen, after my suicide attempt, after I had left Grinnell College on a medical leave of absence. I decided not to return to Grinnell, and instead I transferred to Macalester College in St. Paul, which was where my dad taught, just down the block from where I grew up. Cutting all my hair off helped me start over. It helped me see myself differently. I was still struggling with depression, but I felt stronger with short hair. I cut it again after a particularly difficult breakup in my early twenties, just before I went to Costa Rica. And now it's time to cut it again.

I imagine that most women undergo some kind of shift in their identities when they become mothers—some morphing from woman into mother. But I don't feel like a mother yet. How can I when I don't even have the power to decide if I want to let her cry or not? Cutting my hair will help me make a clean break with the parts of me that existed before Stella. And maybe it will somehow help me feel like her mother.

I close my eyes as Eliza snips away. I feel chunks of hair slide down the cape I'm wearing, and when I glance down, I see it carpeting the floor below me. When Eliza is finished, I stare at myself in the wide mirror. My hair is short all over, a pixie with wispy curls at my neckline and cheekbones. It's a good haircut, but I'm not sure I look more like a mother; I just look really young. But over the next few days, every time I catch a glimpse of myself in the mirror, I'm startled, and this jolt *does* help remind me that I am changed.

Thursday afternoon, my mom picks me up and drives me the twenty minutes to the suburb where Mimi, for whom Donny and I were caretakers, lives. Mimi has left two messages, and Kim and Dave, who replaced us as Mimi's caretakers, have called to let us know that Mimi is beside herself with worry. I imagine her sitting in her brown leather chair, fretting, and I know that the only thing that will ease her worries is to see me.

Mom and I let ourselves in through the garage, just as Donny and I did when we lived there. As we walk into the familiarity of Mimi's kitchen, I'm struck by how much my life has changed in the last few months. Yet as I move through her kitchen and into her living room, I feel myself sliding back in time, into my role as Mimi's caretaker.

"Kate!" she cries when she sees me.

I lean down and give her a hug, kissing her papery cheek.

"Your hair!" she says. "I've been worried sick!" As if these two things are connected.

"I cut it." Then, "I know. I'm sorry."

"What can I get you? Tea? Coffee?" She looks from my mom to me, placing her hands on the arms of her chair as if she's planning to stand.

"No, no," I say, waving my hand. "I'll get it. How about tea?" I slip on a cheerfulness that I haven't felt in weeks and move into her kitchen, where I put water on the stove and pull mugs and boxes of tea from the cupboards. I line everything up on a tray. And it's odd, but I really do feel almost cheerful. I can see why people "stay busy" when their lives are falling apart. It is so much easier than thinking about what's happening and about how little control you have over it.

I stand in front of the stove as the pot of water begins to sizzle and crack. From the other room I hear my mom talking about Stella, about the book she reads to her in the mornings on her way to work.

I could go back into the living room and describe the texture of my new life, but instead I lean against the counter and stare out the window at Mimi's wooded lot, where three cardinals perch at the bird feeder. I can't count the number of times I hauled birdseed to that feeder. It made Mimi crazy when the squirrels and raccoons would eat the seed, and she was always devising new methods to repel them. One time, she insisted I rub olive oil and cayenne pepper on the feeder post. But it didn't work. Nothing worked.

Oddly, I miss hauling birdseed. I miss taking Mimi's dog, Maggie, for a walk every day. I miss all the clear-cut jobs I had while Donny and I lived here. I knew what to do. I knew what Mimi needed. I made a difference.

When the water boils, I pour it over the teabags, and carry the tray with the cups and a plate of cookies into the living room. My mom shows Mimi the photos she's taken of Stella, the ones in which Stella is still very yellow, Velcro goggles dangling from her temple. "Oh, Kate," Mimi says over and over.

"I know," I say, taking a bite of my cookie. "But she's doing okay. The doctor said she might move back to the Special Care Nursery in a week."

Mimi nods. "I have something for her." She points to a huge gift bag on the floor next to her chair and slides it toward me. I sit with it at my feet and pull out onesies and blankets and frilly bibs and burp cloths covered in butterflies—all pink and purple and flowered.

"This is excessive," I say. And I know that she made Kim drive her to Babies R Us. I can imagine Mimi leaning on the shopping cart, pointing to item after item. I know she did this even though she hasn't been feeling well. "Thank you," I say as I hug Mimi. "They're perfect."

Mimi shrugs. "Go take a look at the greenhouse," she says. "Kim and Dave are doing a wonderful job. But I think the orchids miss you."

I push open the glass door and step down into the greenhouse and take a deep breath. The warm, humid air and the scent of dirt fill my lungs. How many hours did I spend here during the three and a half years that Donny and I lived with Mimi? Certainly over three hundred. Now, a couple dozen orchids are in bloom and their yellow and violet and scarlet flowers are like shouts amid a quiet sea of green. I walk slowly around the center table, lifting leaves to check for parasitic scale. I flick one onto the floor with my thumbnail. Then I walk along the outside wall, where the vandas, my favorite orchids—and Mimi's as well—perch along the window like gangly prehistoric birds. One of them is about to open, and through the pale green of the buds I can tell the petals will be magenta.

Mimi always gave me credit when her orchids bloomed. "Kate, you're a genius," she'd say. I would smile and shrug off her compliment, but secretly I was pleased that she thought I was responsible for the silky petals, the blasts of color. Week after week I groomed and watered these plants, but I didn't do anything special. Mostly, I just watched and waited.

And suddenly, as I stand in Mimi's greenhouse, surrounded by all that throbbing color, I understand that this is what I must do with Stella as well. I must wait. I must be patient. And eventually, she will come home. Eventually, I will feel like her mother.

19

When I raise the quilt on the isolette on Friday morning, Stella is tucked into herself, sleeping. Rachel, who has driven me to the hospital again, says, "Aww, she's so cute."

She actually does look cute. She's filling out, which almost makes her look like a regular baby. I have an urge to pick her up and press her to my chest. But I need to check in with Kally, who is on the other side of the room talking to another nurse, Kris. Though Kris has never been Stella's nurse, I like her. She has blond hair and wears dark eyeliner and lots of mascara and has a warm, gentle voice. To parents she says, "Oh, you *guys*," in a way that makes them seem like her friends. I saw her hugging the mother of Sam, a new baby on the warming bed by the window. Kally never touches me, which is fine, I guess, but some days I could use a hand on my shoulder.

Kally smiles when she catches my eye and walks over to us. She lifts the side of the isolette. "Why don't you try to flip her?"

The nurses change Stella's position every few hours so she doesn't get a flat head, and I'm supposed to be able to do this—flip her from stomach to back or back to stomach—but it terrifies me. Three different nurses have demonstrated how to do it. I purposely ask a different nurse each time, pretending that I've never seen it done before. But Kally is one of those nurses, so I can't play dumb.

Donny isn't at all nervous about flipping Stella. He steps up to the isolette like he owns it, reaches in, and flips our daughter in one fluid motion. Like everything we've experienced in the last weeks, he seems confident, calm, steady. Last night, after he flipped Stella and changed her diaper, I whispered, "How did you do that?"

He shrugged. "You just need to try."

But as I stand before my daughter now, flipping her seems like an impossible task. The wires snake across her body. What if I twist her chicken neck? What if I drop her? Panic rises in my chest, and my hands begin to shake. Kally hovers behind me. Rachel waits at my side.

Finally, I step back. "Could you do it for me?"

Kally moves in and places one hand over Stella's diapered butt, one hand at the side of her head, and *flip*. I'm sure she thinks I'm a coward, maybe even a loser. She'll probably make a note in Stella's chart: *mother afraid to flip baby*. "You can go ahead and change her diaper," Kally says, and I nod. At least I can do that.

I unbutton one of the miniature sleep sacks my mom bought for her, place a new diaper underneath, and unfasten the old diaper. I'm pleased to see there is a little bit of poop in the diaper. Not quite the yellowish baby poop of a normal baby—she's not getting enough of my milk yet—but at least it's not meconium. I wipe Stella clean, fasten the new diaper, and hand the old one to Kally. Then I slide the thermometer under Stella's arm. She begins to squirm and arch her back, and I place my hand on her belly. "It's okay, little one. Almost done."

"She hates that," Rachel observes.

It's odd that with everything she's been through—the bright lights, the goggles Velcroed to her temples, the brace taped to her arm to keep her IV in place—she can't stand the imposition of a thermometer under her arm. Stella bucks, and I smile at my spunky girl, sliding my pinky into her palm. Her fingers close tightly around mine.

Kally wraps Stella in fleece and passes her into my arms, and I begin to rock slowly in the chair. Rachel pulls up a stool and sits next to us. Stella gazes up at me with those dark, dark eyes, and I lean close to her, running my finger over her forehead and down her tiny nose. "Hi, sweetheart."

I can't wait until there is no tube taped to her cheek and snaking into a nostril. I can't wait until her right arm is free of the IV and the brace that holds it in place, when her sleeve can be pulled down to her wrist. I can't wait until I no longer have to worry about germs, when I can lean down and kiss the blue crescents of her closed eyes.

Dr. Gregor comes up to us and smiles. I pass Stella to her, and she places her back in the isolette, unwraps the fleece, and presses her fingers into Stella's abdomen. "Her anemia seems to be resolving slowly on its own," Dr. Gregor says, talking to me over her shoulder as she examines Stella. "So for now, we don't need to worry about a transfusion."

"Oh, good," I say.

"She's still a little distended, but that's improving as well."

I nod. Everything is going well. Stella is gaining weight gram by gram. They are increasing her feedings, and soon I'll be able to nurse her. Each of these things means we are a step closer to the Special Care Nursery, a step closer to home.

Dr. Gregor closes the side of the isolette and turns to Rachel and me. "I wanted to let you know that this will be my last day as Stella's doctor. I'll be leaving for vacation tomorrow."

What do you mean you're going on vacation? "Oh," I say.

"Stella is doing great, though."

"Where are you going?" I ask, trying to sound casual and pleased for her.

"California. We're going to get a little golf in before winter."

I want to tell her that she could golf here, that it's the perfect time of year to golf in Minnesota, but I bite my lip.

"Dr. Brown is wonderful," she says, and puts her hand on my arm. "She'll be Stella's doctor for the next week."

I nod, but I don't want Dr. Brown. I want Dr. Gregor. What if Dr. Brown doesn't look me in the eye? What if she doesn't call me at home every morning with an update?

I smile and thank Dr. Gregor before she moves on to the baby next to Stella, the one who took Baby Joe's place. This baby—I don't know his name yet—has a high, thin cry, the kind that puts your nerves on edge. He has a ton of white-blond hair, which is visible through the plastic oxygen tent as he thrashes his head back and forth. Last night, when he first arrived, he wailed and wailed. The nurse propped him up and turned him on his side. She kept returning to his bed, but nothing worked. I thought Donny, who was holding Stella to his chest, would roll his eyes or swear under his breath, but instead he looked as though he would cry as well. "Poor thing," he said. "Can't they do something for him?"

Today, the baby is more settled, and while I stand by Stella's iso-lette, my finger still in her grip, I see the mother being wheeled in, pushed by an older woman, maybe *her* mother. She washes her hands at the sink in the corner and then is pushed to her baby's bedside. Her face is drawn and grayish. She looks like she had a C-section, and I wonder how much pain she's in. My own incision is less than two weeks old, and though it still sends pain shooting down my legs if I move too quickly, I'm amazed by how little attention I pay to it.

I turn around to see this mother standing over the little wailer, who is sleeping now. She stares at him as tears stream down her cheeks. The other woman puts her arm around her. I turn back to Stella.

Stella isn't even two weeks old, yet it feels as if we've been here for months. But time has taken on a new quality since her birth. This is probably because I'm back and forth to the hospital twice a day, and each visit seems like a new day. And sometimes, it's as if three days have been compacted into one.

I suddenly remember that scene in *The Jerk* when Steve Martin's character is in bed with his sleeping girlfriend and he's chattering away, reviewing each day that they've known each other.

I smile and turn to Rachel. "Do you remember that scene from *The Jerk* when Steve Martin is talking about how long he's known his girlfriend?"

"I don't think I've ever seen that whole movie," Rachel says.

"Me neither, but you must have seen the part when he says, 'The third day was like a week, and the fourth day was like eight days...' and he goes on and on."

"Oh, yeah," Rachel says, nodding.

"That's what it's like here," I say. "Except not funny."

We both start to laugh then, and we're still laughing when a doctor I've never seen walks up to us. He's smiling broadly, and he reaches out to shake my hand. He has to be Dr. Levine, my friend Laura's pediatrician. We had exchanged phone messages a month ago, before I knew I was sick. I was trying to set up a time to meet him before Stella was born, but we didn't connect, and then I forgot about him until a couple of days ago when one of the nurses asked who Stella's pediatrician would be. So I called the clinic again yesterday, and when we spoke I explained that Stella had been born early and was in the NICU.

"At Children's?"

"Yes," I said.

"I'll be in tomorrow," he said, "and I'll come down to meet her."

"Really?"

"Absolutely. I can just pop down and see her. It's only a floor away."

I didn't know what I expected him to say, but I hadn't expected that kind of generosity.

Now, after he shakes my hand and then Rachel's hand, he bends down to gaze into the isolette. "Oh, you guys," he exclaims, "she's absolutely beautiful! She's gorgeous!" He's bursting with gentle good humor, and immediately I fall for him: he's the one, the pediatrician of our dreams.

And then Dr. Gregor is there, too. "Dr. Levine!"

"Dr. Gregor!" They shake hands, both smiling broadly.

Dr. Levine turns to me. "You have wonderful taste in neonatologists."

I smile and nod, though I'm sure I can't take any credit for choosing her; she was just here one day, and she'll be on vacation tomorrow.

"And you have wonderful taste in pediatricians," says Dr. Gregor, smiling at Dr. Levine.

I nod again. I'm pleased that everyone agrees Stella is in good hands. I glance at Rachel and she raises her eyebrows.

Dr. Levine looks at Stella again, and says, "I'll see you again when you have this little darling home." Then he and Dr. Gregor walk into the hall.

"He's perfect," I say to Rachel.

"That was a veritable pediatric love fest."

We both start laughing again.

20

I'VE RUN INTO AMY A FEW TIMES IN THE HALLWAY, and I know they're getting ready for Noah's surgery, during which a shunt will be placed in his head to drain the cerebral spinal fluid from his brain into his abdomen. Amy must be nervous about it, but she doesn't *seem* nervous. Last time I saw her, she said, "Well, Noah has one of the best surgeons in the country." She held up a folder. "I did my research."

I wonder if it's the fact that she's already been through so much that gives her that air of calm assurance, or if it's just her personality. Probably a little of both. Even in high school, she seemed more mature than her age warranted.

On Friday night, when Donny and I see her, I ask her how she handles all the people who want to see Noah.

"Most of our friends are waiting until he comes home," she says, "but our families are here a lot. They can come whenever they want."

"What about when you're kangarooing or trying to nurse?"

She laughs. "Oh, I have no modesty anymore. I don't care if people are around." She shrugs. "And really, it takes so long to get Noah to nurse that no one would ever be able to see him otherwise."

My mom visits Stella every weekday morning on her way to work, and she wants to visit on the weekends, too, but this morning on the phone, I told her she couldn't.

"Oh," Mom said quietly.

"It's just that there are other people who want to visit—Donny's dad and Armie—and I don't want Stella to have too many visitors."

"Okay," my mom said. "I understand." I could hear the hurt in her voice.

I'm not even sure why I did that. It's true that I don't want Stella overstimulated. I don't want too many people hovering over her isolette. But part of it is that I just want to be there with Donny, just the two of us. I know I'm being possessive, but visiting Stella, holding her, is all we have. Still, I feel as if I'm brandishing around a tiny baby brand, trying to lay claim to my daughter. *She's mine. She's mine.*

Amy shrugs. "I figure that this is the only time my family will have unrestricted visitation rights. As soon as Noah's home, they will have to call before they come over, so I might as well give them this time with him." She clearly doesn't feel resentful and overprotective. I feel myself grow smaller as we walk down the hall together.

But even Donny agrees that we should minimize visitors. His mom has been calling two or three times a day, and she wants to see Stella, but Donny told her she'd have to wait until Stella was home. "The smoke on her clothes wouldn't be good," he said, and I nodded, relieved that he was making this call. The smoke, yes. But also, Patricia has been on and off her medication in the last two years, and the last thing we need is for her to involve Stella in one of her schizophrenic delusions. I can imagine her trying to break Stella out of the NICU because she thinks someone is trying to kill her granddaughter. She wouldn't stand a chance, of course; the hospital has amazing security. But still, the thought sends a chill through me.

On Saturday night, Donny's dad and step-mom, Armie, come to see Stella. We have just finished Stella's cares, and Donny is holding her.

Dave and Armie are jovial people, and we always laugh a lot together, but tonight their voices seem to clatter around the room. We should have been clear about the rules: quiet voices, go directly to the baby's bedside. Luckily, there aren't many other visitors; it's just Sam's mother with two other women. I've never talked with Sam's mother, but I've watched her, and I gather that the other women are her mother- and sister-in-law. The mother-in-law is sitting in a chair, holding Sam, rocking just slightly.

Armie and Dave peer down at Stella in Donny's arms. "She's bigger," Armie says, and I smile. Even though Stella weighs only a few ounces more than she did when she was born, she does seem bigger. Maybe this is only next to the two-pound babies that are in the other isolettes. Or maybe this is just our normal now.

Donny looks up at his dad, motioning with Stella in his arms. "Do you want to hold her?"

At first I don't think I could have heard correctly. I stand up very straight and move a step closer to Donny. Did he just offer her up? Did he just ask his dad if he wanted to hold our less-than-four-pounds baby?

Donny's dad backs away, hands up, fingers spread wide. "No, no, that's okay." He's shaking his head. "When she's bigger."

I let out my breath, which I realize I've been holding. Yes, Dave knows that Stella is still too small, that only Donny and I are supposed to hold her. Donny and I never discussed this, but I thought we agreed—only we can hold Stella.

I'm still thinking, trying to figure out why Donny offered up our daughter, when Armie steps forward. "I'll hold her," she says. And I blanch again.

This time Donny will get it right. He'll say no. He'll explain that this privilege is reserved for us, for her parents. But he doesn't. I'm paralyzed, unable to stop him as he stands up with Stella in his arms. I don't say anything as Armie rubs foam into her hands and sits down in the rocker. I don't say anything as Donny passes our daughter, bundled in fleece, into Armie's outstretched arms. I just stare at Donny, his face gray with fluorescence and exhaustion, his eyes glittering dully. He doesn't look at me.

Why don't I say something?

I move to Armie's shoulder, hover behind her. Stella is sleeping. I look up at the monitor—her oxygen and heart rate are fine—then back to her face. It's going to be okay. It's going to be okay. But then Armie begins rocking. The wooden runners of the chair make a clicking sound—back and forth, back and forth—across the polished floor.

I want to reach out my hand, press the chair into submission. Stella is too small for all this commotion.

And suddenly my heart is beating so fast that I feel faint. I take a step back, lean against the counter next to Stella's bed. Breathe, Kate. Breathe. Everything will be fine. But the chair clicks clicks clicks, wood against linoleum. And I can't slow my heart, which is like a sparrow trapped in my chest, fluttering, frantic.

Ready for Air   145

Donny glances up at me, and I glare at him, my lips pursed. Then I nod to Armie, who has picked up even more speed in the rocker. I glare at Donny again, and he gets it, finally.

"Okay," Donny says. "We can only hold her for a little while, so Kate will hold her now." His voice is steady, leached of emotion.

Armie nods. "She likes me," she says.

Armie passes Stella to Donny; I spray foam into my hands and quickly take Armie's place in the rocker. When Stella is in my arms again, I hold her as still as I can. My hands tremble. "It's okay," I whisper. She's still sleeping and has no idea she was not being held by me the whole time, no idea that she was being rocked too quickly.

Later, I am quiet on the drive home. I don't want to open my mouth because I'm not sure how to put my anger into words without exploding. I'm not even sure why I'm so angry. Because I thought Donny understood? Because he didn't check with me first? I'm not sure, but I know if I can't pinpoint the reason for my rage, I should keep quiet. If I open my mouth, it will rush out of me, all sparks and flashes. I won't be able to tamp out the fires I start.

We've driven halfway home and are stopped at the light across from the Poodle Club, a dinner club announcing in white signs with green lettering: Dinner! Dancing! Breakfast! It's early for Saturday night, but people are congregated outside, smoking cigarettes, laughing.

I open my mouth and close it again. I can feel the storm in my throat, fierce and electrical.

"I don't understand," he says then.

I take a deep breath, and then it's out. "I can't believe you let Armie hold Stella! I can't believe you did that! She's *our* baby. We didn't even talk about it." I hit the window with my fist, and all of a sudden I want to smash my hand through it. It's as if I separate from myself—I can feel the anger spark and tingle under my skin at the same time I wonder what's wrong with me. Why am I so angry? What's going on here?

Donny turns to me. "Are you *serious?*"

This is clearly not the right thing to say, and in that moment

I lose sight of the part of me that still has a grip. "Are *you* fucking serious?"

Donny shakes his head and turns away from me. I stare at his profile. His lips are a tight line.

"We didn't talk about this!" I almost shout.

Donny runs his hand through his short hair. "I wasn't thinking," he says then, quietly. "I saw that other woman holding her grandson." He means Sam's grandmother. "I saw her holding the baby and I thought, *wouldn't that be nice.*"

"No," I say. "No, it wouldn't be nice. It. Was. Not. Nice. It was too much rocking. Stella is our baby, our baby. This is all we have, holding her." I start to cry, sob—long racking sobs that seem to have bubbled up from somewhere deep in my belly. "She's...our...baby," I wail.

Donny glances at me, and I know I'm freaking him out.

"What could I say?"

"You could have said no! You shouldn't have offered her up at all!" This is one of those moments when I wish I could reel myself in, suck the words back into my mouth, dissolve them on my tongue.

We pull up in front of our house, which is glowing warmly. My mom is inside, making us dinner, and I hate that she's here and she'll see me crying. She'll ask what's wrong, and I know if I tell her what happened, she'll be upset that she wasn't the first grandparent to hold Stella. She was upset that Donny's sister, Dawn, was the first to take pictures of Stella through the plastic wall of her isolette the day after she was born, when she was still in the Special Care Nursery. She wanted to be the first to photograph her granddaughter, and I know she wanted to be the first person besides us to hold her. And I know if she's upset, I'll be angry with her, and I don't want to be. I forbade her to visit Stella on the weekends, and instead of being mad at me, she's here, making us dinner so we have something warm waiting for us when we get home.

Donny leans back in his seat. "I'm sorry," he says. He turns to me. "I wasn't thinking."

I look past him, at our house. "I don't want to deal with my mom right now."

"Don't tell her," he says, and there is something conspiratorial in his voice. It seems to say: this is private. This is our marriage, our fight. Don't tell. He puts his hand on my arm. I don't move away. I don't want to fight with him, I really don't, but I'm still angry, and I can feel this breathing between us, taking on a life of its own.

"I'm sorry," he says again. He looks as if he is going to cry, too, and I wonder if he thinks I'm crazy, out of line, or if he really believes he made a mistake.

"It's just—" I start, then shake my head. "I just want it to be us holding her. While she's in the hospital, it should just be us."

He pulls his hand away. "I got it."

My mom calls out *hello!* as soon as she hears the door open. The house smells warm, meaty, as it always seemed to when I was young, when my parents were still married. I put down my purse next to the stairs and walk into the kitchen. Mom is standing in front of the stove, stirring beef stroganoff, sipping a glass of wine.

She looks up, her smile becoming a worried frown. "What's the matter?"

I have to give her some explanation for my red eyes or she'll think something happened to Stella. I could say that Donny and I had a fight and leave it at that. I could tell her that everything is fine.

But I don't feel fine. I start to cry and before I know it, the whole story is out: Donny's offer, Stella in Armie's arms, the wild rocking of the chair. I betray Donny just like that.

"Oh," she says, reaching for me.

"I'm fine," I say, hugging her back.

"Oh," she says again.

I pull away. Her eyes are full of tears. "But don't *you* feel bad." And immediately I transfer my anger to her. "I know you wanted to hold her first." I don't give her a chance to deny it, to surprise me. "But this isn't about you."

She steps back suddenly, as if I slapped her. Her arms rise and fall at her sides like small gasps. "No, sweetie," she says. "I just feel bad because you feel so bad."

But I don't believe her. "I need to pump," I say, and turn my back on her.

In the living room, Donny slouches on the couch. His face is set, and he's staring into the middle of the room, at nothing. He knows I've tattled on him.

I slide down next to him, and he opens his arms to me anyway. Now it's my turn to apologize. I press my face into his neck. "I'm sorry," I say.

"I wasn't thinking," he says again.

"I should have said something," I say. And this is it, why I'm so upset. I didn't do or say anything. I should have spoken up, said no. Stella is my baby too. But instead, I said nothing.

The basement door opens and shuts, and I hear my mom's feet on the stairs. And I know she's going down there to cry. "Fuck," I say.

"Your mom's upset now, too," Donny says, his voice full of weariness.

"She could tell I'd been crying," I say, as if this excuses my betrayal. "But she doesn't have a right to be upset." I stand up.

"Leave it," he says. But of course I don't.

Back in the kitchen, Mom is emerging from the basement. Now *I* can tell that *she's* been crying. She has a crumpled tissue in her hand.

"Mom, this isn't about you!"

"No. Honey." My mom is imploring, reaching for me again. "I just feel bad for you."

Why can't I believe her? Why can't I listen to her words? I'm like a two-year-old—it's impossible to reason with me. "Whatever," I say coldly, and I walk out of the kitchen, walk past Donny, who is still slumped on the couch. I walk upstairs into Stella's room, flip on the little light, and assemble the pieces of the pump. When I sit down in the chair, I'm crying again.

I know that in a few days, in a month, even years from now, this will be one of those evenings I will wish I could redo. I stare at Stella's empty crib, its naked mattress, the pile of blankets neatly folded in its corner, and I wish I could channel some of Amy's graciousness. I wish I could be a different person.

I take deep breaths, listening to the whoosh of the pump. Then I twist the pump handle until the suction power is as high as it will go, and I grit my teeth in pain and watch my milk spray into the cylinders.

21

On Sunday morning, I call my mom to apologize again. I had said I was sorry last night after I pumped, but I knew it was too late. The hurt in her face was still there when she left our house. So this morning I call and tell her she can visit Stella today if she wants. I use my daughter to barter for forgiveness.

"No, no," she says. "I'll see her tomorrow."

"Okay," I say. "I'm sorry."

Donny and I are also subdued. We step carefully around each other, as if we know that any collision will result in more sparks, more tears. We get dressed, slip our NICU/ICC badges over our necks, and stop at the coffee shop near our house for lattes on our way to the hospital.

The coffee shop is full of sunshine and people congregated around tables. I recognize some of their faces. There is the group of women who row on the Mississippi every Sunday morning. They always sit at the large table in the middle of the room. Their arms are thick, muscled, as I imagine they must be to propel their boat through the strong currents of the river. A few other regulars sit in front of their laptops, absorbed in their work.

I came here every morning this past summer to drink decaf and work on my thesis about San Vicente. I can almost see myself, hugely pregnant, puffy, sitting on the wooden bench along the wall. I wish I could walk up to that other version of myself, the version that doesn't know anything about preeclampsia and NICUs and what it feels like to have your three-pound baby grip your pinky finger in her tiny fist. What would I say? I'd acknowledge that it's hard. *But relax*, I'd tell myself. *Keep things in perspective. Don't overreact.*

After Donny and I get our drinks, we drive down Lake Street, which is mostly deserted. We drive under the bridge at Hiawatha, where the tracks for the new light-rail train are being laid. We're quiet as we turn on Chicago Avenue and park in front of the hospital at a meter that doesn't need to be plugged on Sunday.

Then we walk through the wide front doors of the hospital, take the elevator to the second floor, and walk down the long hallway to the NICU, as we do every day. We toss our empty coffee cups into the trash and greet the attendant behind the desk, showing her our badges.

"You have a blessed day," she says.

"You, too," I say. But as the NICU doors swing toward us, and we are enveloped by the sweet antiseptic of the unit, I wonder what a "blessed" day would look like for us. And who would be blessing it? I don't broach the topic with Donny, who would probably just roll his eyes.

We stop at the milk room, and I go in and open the refrigerator, dropping the small containers of my milk into Stella's bin, which is now half full. Funny to think I had wanted a full bin, as if it were a competition. As if it were a good thing.

When I close the milk room door behind me, Donny is waiting for me, looking so tired, so worn down. He reaches for my hand, and together we walk to the sink, wash our hands, fingers to wrist, and walk to Stella's isolette.

When we flip up the quilt on her isolette, I smile. Stella is on her tummy, legs tucked up, head turned toward us, eyes closed. "Oh," Donny says, and I can hear the wistfulness in his voice. I feel it in my own throat.

A nurse we don't know well comes over and says good morning. Then she says, "You can try to nurse her today if you want."

"What? Really?" I'm sure I look like a child whose mother has told her they're going to spend the day at the fair. All of the little joys in the NICU—holding Stella for the first time, getting to kangaroo with her, and now being able to officially nurse her, finally—come as surprises. They are sprung on us when we get to the hospital. But I'll take them however I get them. And we definitely need something today, something to bring us together again.

I look at Donny, who flashes me an excited smile. "I'll get a chair," he says, and goes to snag the unused rocking chair from baby Sam's bedside.

After I am situated in the chair, the nurse pulls the white screens around the chair and the stool where Donny is perched. Then she passes Stella into my arms.

"Hold her like this," the nurse says, demonstrating how I should lay Stella across the forearm of my left arm and support her tiny head with my left hand, just as the nurse had shown me a few days ago. "That leaves your right hand to support your breast."

I nod, balancing the back of Stella's head in my fingers.

"Now, tickle her lower lip with your nipple."

I do as I'm told, and Stella opens her eyes. She looks annoyed, as if she's wondering who is shoving this mountain of flesh into her mouth. *I'm sleeping for God's sake.*

"Once her mouth opens wide, press her onto your breast."

I've studied the handouts I've been given about breastfeeding and made note of the way a baby's mouth needs to be wide open before she latches on. I've read that if a baby is sleepy, you are supposed to rub her cheek, tickle her chin.

The nurse presses Stella's chin down and her mouth opens; then she presses Stella to me, and my nipple slips into her mouth. But as soon as the nurse leaves our small pod of privacy, my nipple pops out, and Stella is asleep again.

I try to tickle her chin with my nipple, but nothing happens. "Shit," I say.

Donny lets out a quiet breath of laughter.

The nurse pops back in. "How's it going?"

"She's sleepy. Nothing's happening." And then I picture this scene—the bare-breasted mama, the attentive husband leaning over her shoulder, the four-square feet of privacy, the nurse, and the sleeping baby—as some *Saturday Night Live* skit gone awry. Except in the skit the baby would be a grown man—John Belushi or Will Ferrell. Eeew.

I probably look disgusted because the nurse says, "It's okay. Let's try again. Rub her cheek."

I rub Stella's cheek with my fingertip. She opens her dark eyes and looks up at me.

"Okay, great," says the nurse. "Now hold your breast like this. Good. Now place your nipple here. Good. Good. Great!"

And just like that I'm breastfeeding my baby. Stella sucks and stops. Sucks and stops. When she closes her eyes, I rub her cheek with my finger and she starts sucking again. I stare down at her sunken cheeks, her tiny nose, the veins tracking across her eyelids. She's nursing. I'm nursing my baby. My eyes fill with tears. I look up at Donny, and he beams down at us.

"How does it feel?" he asks.

"Good. Weird. Good. It doesn't hurt the way pumping does. It's because it's supposed to happen this way, right?" There is a part of me that doesn't believe it *is* happening. And there's also a part of me that feels like a fraud. I'm doing this thing that is supposed to be the most natural thing in the world, and it doesn't actually feel natural. It's as if I'm watching us from above, looking at it as a clinician would, with distance. I wonder if it (and I) would have felt different if Stella had been pulled from me and placed directly on my chest, if she had been able to follow her instincts, root around until she found my breast. Both of our instincts have been dulled by the lights, the alarms, and the miles that separate us from each other most of the time. But maybe instincts can somehow be resuscitated.

I stare down at Stella, who starts and stops, as if each gulp of milk makes her tired and she needs to rest between drags. When she stops sucking and closes her eyes, I rub her cheek again. I smile, because really, if it weren't for the tube that's taped to her cheek and threaded into her nostril, if it weren't for the IV line taped to her arm and the alarms and bright lights and low voices on the other side of the privacy screen, this would be like it's supposed to be—just a mother nursing her baby. I stare down at my daughter, eyes opening and shutting, and decide it's close enough.

The nurse pops backs in and says that if Stella actively nurses for a total of five minutes, she'll only need to get half a tube feeding. If she nurses for ten minutes, she won't need a tube feeding at all. Ten minutes of active nursing would take over an hour at this rate, though, and the thought of her not getting a tube feeding, carefully measured out and slowly injected into her feeding tube, makes me nervous. Who knows how much she's actually getting from me?

"You should be able to hear her swallow," the nurse says. But I can't hear her swallowing, and Donny can't either. I can't even hear myself swallow in the NICU.

After a few more minutes of Stella's on-and-off nursing, my other breast begins to flow, a steady river of milk. Donny hands me some tissues and I make a small dam. The tissues are soaked in less than a minute, so Donny hands me more. That's good; my body knows she's there, latched on, and it wants to feed her.

Over the next two days, I'm allowed to try to nurse Stella twice a day. Sometimes, she seems to get it, sucking on and off. Other days, I can't keep her awake; it's as if the whole process is just too much for her. The nurses peek their heads around the screens, and I either smile and nod or shake my head. Regardless, the pressure is on to get Stella to actively nurse for five minutes per session. It's hardly the vision I had of what nursing would be: long, lazy hours at home, cuddling my newborn in our padded rocking chair or sunk into our deep couch downstairs, pressing my lips to her temple. Tea and soft lights and maybe even music. Instead, I'm on the clock: I have fifteen more minutes to get her to latch on and nurse or she'll get a full tube feeding.

But she does seem to be getting better at it. On Monday, when Kally comes over to check on me, I report that Stella has nursed for a total of five minutes.

"Great," Kally says.

Then I tell her what Stella's new doctor, Dr. Brown, told me on the phone that morning—that if Stella continues to do well, we might be able to move back to the Special Care Nursery in a few days.

Kally furrows her brow. "I don't know why you're so excited to move."

Now it's my turn to furrow my brow. "Well, it means she's getting stronger, that we're closer to going home."

"But she'll get less attention there," Kally says.

I shrug. Um, duh. Less attention is good, right? It means Stella is doing better.

22

TUESDAY MORNING IS CLEAR AND SUNNY. IT'S SEP-
tember 30. Stella is seventeen days old. I get up with Donny, as I
always do. He gets ready for work, and I pump. Then Donny kisses
me good-bye, and I shower quickly. I'm scheduled to see Dr. Anderson this morning before I go to the hospital. If my incision is healing
properly, I'll be able to drive again, which means I'll be able to go to
see Stella whenever I want, without having to arrange a ride. I also
have a list of questions for Dr. Anderson about preeclampsia, about
what actually happened in my body, what inside me failed.

Bright sunlight saturates our bedroom as I step into the black
maternity skirt I'm still wearing, and I realize I feel good, rested. I'm
determined to get Stella to nurse at least five minutes this morning,
maybe even ten. The sooner she gets the hang of it, the sooner we
can bring her home.

I'm slipping my arms into the sleeves of my loose sweater when
the phone rings. I look at the clock. It's 7:30. The doctor doesn't usually call until 9:00.

I lift the phone from its cradle. "Hello?"

But it's not the doctor; it's Donny, and as soon as I hear his
voice—*Hi, Hon*—I know something's wrong.

"Don't panic," he says. "But something happened."

Something happened. Donny always calls the NICU on his way
to work to see how Stella's night went. *Something happened* means
something happened to our daughter. No, I won't go there. It's
something else. My mind ticks through other possibilities: a dead
aunt; an injured dog on the side of the road; a car accident on the
highway, cars tangled in a mess of metal. But even as I settle on
another tragedy, I know none of these is the *something* he means.

"Kate?"

"What?" I say. The phone, which is old, crackles at the sound of my voice.

"The IV line in her arm. It slipped out of her vein. There's fluid in her shoulder."

Fluid in her shoulder. That doesn't sound so bad. Our bodies are made up of fluid. Aren't we 98 percent water? What's a little more?

The space between our voices fills with the flat buzz of static.

"She has a blood infection," Donny says.

A blood infection. I stare at the phone cord, a coil of plastic in my palm.

"Kate."

"Yes?" I say.

"Did you hear me?"

The pale curtains flutter into our bedroom like sails. The walls glow with bright morning light. I squeeze the tangled nest of plastic in my fist.

"I heard you," I say. And suddenly I understand why the nurses never say things like "your baby is going to be fine." I understand why they say, always cautiously, that Stella "had a good day." *She is having a good day.* They know—they always knew—that tomorrow she might not be so lucky.

"She's on antibiotics already," Donny says. He sounds far away. "Call Kally."

"Okay," I say. And then I hang up.

I stare at the golden walls of our bedroom. I stare at our bed, which is still a mess of sheets. Then I pick up the phone again and dial the NICU. I ask for Station 5. I wait on the line, phone pressed to my ear.

"Hello," Kally says.

"It's Kate," I say. "What happened?" My voice is steady, dull.

"Don't panic," Kally says. "She's okay."

People keep telling me not to panic. That can't be a good sign.

"She started having trouble last night," Kally says. "She was really fussy."

Yes, she was fussy last night when Donny and I were there. She struggled in my arms, wouldn't nurse at all.

"Later, she became mottled. The nurse wasn't one of her primaries, but she asked another nurse if that was typical for Stella. Of course it wasn't."

"Of course," I repeat. But I wouldn't have known if it was typical. Maybe Stella fusses late at night. Maybe she becomes mottled. I don't even know. I sit down on the edge of our bed. I feel the pull of my incision, the pieces of tape that still cling to it catching on each other, tugging.

"Finally, they called a doctor," Kally says. "But by that point, Stella's shoulder had begun to swell with fluid from her IV line, which had slipped out of her vein." Again, the fluid in the shoulder. Then Kally says something about infiltration, an infection in her blood, sepsis.

I feel my heart pounding in my chest. I feel my lungs. My rib cage. A tingling in my breasts—my milk letting down. I grip the bookcase, clench the solidness of wood in my fingers.

"They started her on antibiotics right away, which should take care of the infection."

Should. It should.

"I have to get my incision checked," I say. "And then I'll be in. I'll be there as soon as I can." I can hardly breathe, but I do not cry. But maybe I should skip my appointment? Go to the hospital right away? No. I need to be able to drive. And it's just fluid in her shoulder. She's already on antibiotics.

"Okay," Kally says.

When I hang up, I look up at the swirls of stucco on our ceiling. Like seashells, like fossils. If I leaned back on the bed, I could stare up at the ceiling and lose myself in those ancient-looking whorls. But I don't. I look at the clock. Twenty minutes until my appointment with Dr. Anderson. Five minutes until Dad is here to pick me up. I stand up, smooth my damp hair flat against my head, and walk downstairs to wait.

When the phone rings again, I jump.

But it's not the hospital; it's my mom. "What happened?"

She was there. She saw Stella. The nurses wouldn't tell her what happened. "I couldn't stay by her," she said. "They asked me to leave."

"An infection," I say slowly. "The IV line slipped out of her vein."

I repeat what Kally told me: sepsis, antibiotics. Then I say, "I have to go, Mom. I'll call you later."

Five minutes later in the car, I tell Dad what I know: sepsis, infection, blood, antibiotics. Dad just says, "Oh?" in that worried way I've heard a thousand times. Then we are quiet. I stare out my window. The sun glints off cars, and the flashes of light make me squint and close my eyes. I don't know what sepsis can do. Can it kill my daughter? Is she going to die? Is this it? Suddenly, my eyes fill with tears, and I know I need to get to the hospital.

"Faster, Dad," I say, my throat tight. "I need you to get me there faster. Drop me at the door, but don't park. Drive around. Come back in fifteen minutes." I am desperate to get out of the car, and a few minutes later when Dad pulls up in front of the building where my doctor's office is, I open the door before we are fully stopped.

Then I am through the doors, up the elevator, and standing in front of the receptionist. And as she looks up at me, her smile freezes. I have started crying now and I can't stop. "My daughter is sick. An infection. In the NICU. I need to get to the hospital. I need to see Dr. Anderson right now."

The response is amazing. In less than a minute, I am ushered into the same room where I sat four weeks ago on the day I found out I might have preeclampsia. The same room—blue walls, medical school diplomas on the wall, the pink map of a uterus on the clipboard on the table—but everything has changed.

The nurse takes my blood pressure, which is normal, then leaves. I lie back on the exam table and stare up at the ceiling, where the fluorescent lights flicker. What if Stella dies now, now that I have gotten to hold her and kangaroo her and nurse her? Now that I have felt her skin against mine? What if she never comes home? Tears run down my face and drip onto the paper on the table.

Suddenly the door opens and Dr. Anderson is above me, her brow furrowed. "What kind of infection?" she asks before she even says hello.

I pull myself to a sitting position. "I don't know. Something with the IV line. Sepsis."

Dr. Anderson nods.

I register that she looks good—much fresher and more rested than she did while I was in the hospital. She smiles slightly and presses my arm. "An infection from her perc line is better than other kinds of infections."

I'm still crying, but I nod. It's not as bad as it could be. Okay.

"Let's take a look at that incision so you can get to the hospital."

I lean back again, and Dr. Anderson folds down the waist of my skirt. She presses her fingers into my abdomen, above and below the incision. The narrow strips of tape still cling to my milky skin, and she begins to pull them off one by one. I hadn't wanted to pull them off myself, as if they were the only things holding me together.

I had meant to ask Dr. Anderson questions, but now I can't remember what they were. Questions about my health, my body, no longer seem important anyway.

"This looks great," she says, folding my skirt back up. "It's healing beautifully."

She jots something in my chart, and I stare at her narrow face, her cropped hair. I love this small doctor. She has seen me at my worst, and there is something powerful in that, in witnessing a person in crisis. I have forgiven her the medieval torture, and I want her to understand the depth of my appreciation. "Thank you," I say slowly. "For everything, for saving her. For getting her out of me alive." I can feel tears coming again.

Dr. Anderson pulls me into a hug. "She's going to be okay," she says.

I start to cry harder, clinging to her.

When I pull away, she puts her hands on my shoulders and looks into my eyes. "You can drive again, but not today. Not while you're this upset."

"Okay," I say, though I'm planning to drive anyway.

Twenty minutes later, Dad and I part with a hug and he tells me to call him later. I go straight to my car and drive to the hospital. My incision aches when I press the clutch. But at least I'm in control of something.

When I get to the NICU, I walk to the sink. I go through the motions as I always do. After I dry my hands, I walk toward Stella.

Kally is talking to another parent, the blond-haired crier's mom, but she glances up and smiles at me.

There is no quilt on Stella's isolette, so I pull up a stool and peer in at her. An IV juts from her head, taped to a dark swirl of hair. She's naked except for her tiny diaper, and her skin is mottled: red, purple. Her arms are flung out to the side, her eyes closed, her body slack.

My body is pulsing as I open the armhole of the isolette and tickle Stella's palm with my fingernail. But she doesn't move. I will her to grip my finger, to close her tiny hand around my pinky, but nothing happens. It's as if I'm not there.

Just yesterday, Kris, the nurse I like from across the room, came over and remarked how well Stella was doing. We talked about how she might even move back to the Special Care Nursery in a few days. Now, a day later, Stella looks dead. I start to cry silently, wiping tears away with the back of my hand, and look up at the monitor.

Her heart rate is high, her oxygen a little low, but she's still here, blipping away. Her chest, narrow as a pop can, rises and falls, rises and falls. There is an ache in my own chest, and I realize that this is how it feels to have my heart break.

I thought I had protected myself. I thought I had hidden my heart carefully away. But I guess I didn't. Without realizing it, I began to imagine the day I would be able to lean down and kiss the vein-tracked crescents of Stella's closed eyes. I began to imagine the day we would take her home. I started to fall in love with my daughter.

When had it happened? Was it the first day I saw her, when she held tight to my pinky, her hand impossibly small, her grip so surprisingly strong? Was it when she was five days old and I first held her against my skin and felt the rhythm of her breath? Was it when she was a week old and she opened her eyes and seemed to recognize me? I don't know, but now I feel sick to my stomach.

Suddenly, there is an alarm, a flashing light above Stella's bed. I look at the monitor to see her oxygen and heart rate plummeting. Then I look at Stella, her chest unmoving. She's not breathing. I spin on my stool, my heart pounding behind my eyes, in my neck, my wrists. The alarm blares above us. Where is Kally?

I shake Stella's limp hand. *Move, baby. Move.* I stand up, ready to shake the breath into her, but suddenly Kally is there, rubbing Stella's tummy, rubbing the bottoms of her feet—everything in slow motion. *Breathe, baby. You have to breathe.* Finally, my daughter's ribs stutter to life again: up and down, up and down.

Kally steps away. "Apnea and bradycardia are common with sepsis," she says, so calm, so steady. "She's okay."

I shake my head and look back down at my daughter. *This is not okay. It's not okay.* Kally goes back to the crier's bedside, and I hear her tell his mother that they will be ready to move him later today. I look up at the mother, who is smiling down at her tiny boy. The baby that wailed and wailed is moving and we—we who have been here longer, who were doing just fine yesterday—will be staying. His mother looks up at me and smiles a sad smile. I imagine she is wondering what has happened. I would be wondering the same if she were in tears. All sorrow is public here.

I sit back down on the stool and look at Stella, who is flopped in her isolette, unmoving except for her chest, which is doing its work, up and down. I reach my hand in again through the armhole and rest my fingers on her palm, which is hot and dry, her skin sloughing off as if she's had a bad sunburn. *Oh Stella,* I think. *If we were home, I would take you in my arms, and I would slather you with lotion. I would be so careful.* My eyes fill with tears again. Will I ever be able to do that? Will I ever get to decide on my own what she needs?

I notice her unmoving chest just as I hear the alarm blare again. My fingers clutch her hand and I shake it. My gaze swings to the monitor: heart rate and oxygen plummeting. Apnea. Bradycardia. I know those words from the handbook. Periods of stopped breathing. Drop in heart rate. I turn to Stella again. *Breathe, goddammit. I will not breathe until you breathe. You cannot leave me. I love you, okay? I love you.*

I scan the room. "Kally?" I say loudly.

Then Kally is there again, and I am three steps back. She opens the side of the isolette. She is rubbing Stella's tummy, the bottoms of her feet. Time stops. Tears run down my face.

And then, finally, Stella's chest is up and down again. Up and down.

"Let's leave this open," Kally says, nodding to the wall of the isolette. I must be staring at her in some wild, uncomprehending way, because she raises her eyebrows. "We'll leave this open," she says again, and I nod. She means because this is going to happen again. Because I have to watch my daughter stop breathing again. How many times?

"Apnea is really common in preemies, especially when they have infections," she says.

She already told me this. Didn't she?

Kally moves away, and I just stand there, staring at Stella, not touching her. And when I look up again, Dr. Brown is there, spraying foam into her hands. She's a petite woman, professional in her blue scrubs but kind, gentle. She nods to Stella. "It's a setback," she says. "Just yesterday we talked about her being ready to have the IV removed, and if we had taken it out yesterday—" She shrugs. "You just never know."

A setback. I resist the urge to get angry. If the IV could have been taken out yesterday, why wasn't it? But Dr. Brown is sympathetic, her head tilted to the side.

"We started her on two different kinds of antibiotics right away. We're not sure which one is the right one, but we'll know when we get her labs back. Then we'll discontinue the one she doesn't need."

I stare at Stella, at the IV jutting from her skull, and imagine all that medicine being injected into her bloodstream. Some of it will wage war against her infection, some of it will do nothing—a useless bystander on the sidelines of a bloody battle.

I'll learn later that anything that breaks a preemie's skin barrier— IV lines, ventilators, feeding tubes, blood tests—becomes a path for infection to enter the body. I'll learn that a preemie's veins are brittle, fragile, like strands of hair encased in glistening ice. When they crack, an IV can break free, filling an arm or head with fluid. A preemie is too weak to contain a localized infection, so it sweeps the tiny body, plunders, invades the blood.

Dr. Brown puts her hand on my shoulder. "The antibiotics should take care of this."

I nod, my eyes full of tears. *They should. Should.*

Dr. Brown moves on to Emily, and Kris comes over from the other side of the room and gives me a hug. "Oh, sweetie," she says. "I'm so sorry. She was doing so well."

I start to cry harder, enveloped in Kris's floral perfume. Why can't Kris be Stella's nurse? Why can't Kally tell me she's sorry? I pull away and brush the hair from my eyes.

"Thank you," I manage.

"The antibiotics will help," she says, and she presses her lips into a smile. "You're such a wonderful mother."

"Thank you," I say again, although I wonder how she's decided this. If I were a wonderful mother, wouldn't I have known that something was wrong with Stella last night? I should have known. She was fussier than usual. She refused to latch on. Donny and I had never met the nurse on duty, but we should have mentioned that Stella seemed off. She *was* off. It's something a mother—a good mother—would know. If we had said something, maybe they would have caught the infection sooner, started the antibiotics sooner. Maybe Stella wouldn't look dead now.

Again, the alarm flashes red, screams. This is all my fault, I think suddenly. I don't even know my daughter, and now she has forgotten how to breathe. I start to cry helplessly, waiting for Kally. I press my eyes shut. *Please,* I think. *Please let my daughter be okay.* I don't direct my prayers to anyone in particular. I just send them up because I don't know what else to do.

While Kally does her magic again, I sit on the stool crying. I can tell I'm irritating her with my tears, but there is no stopping them now.

"This is odd," Kally says. "She wasn't having any spells earlier."

She means before I arrived. Am I causing my daughter to stop breathing? Is this my fault too?

Years from now, some friends will describe how powerful meditation can be for patients in critical condition. Donny and I will be sitting in Juanita and George's dining room sipping wine, and George will tell us about the research. "The sick person doesn't even need to be the one meditating," he'll say. "His or her breathing and heart rate will calm if there is someone else meditating in the room. That's how powerful it is."

When he says this, I'll wonder whether panic has the same effect with opposite results. Is desperation also that powerful? Could I inadvertently shoot it, an electric current of panic, into my daughter's palm?

Kally picks up the phone. "I'm going to have to call the respiration specialists. We'll try an oxygen tent first. If that doesn't work, a cannula. If that doesn't work, CPAP." Each of these things is a step backward. I've seen babies on CPAP; the device is bigger than a cannula, and it forces oxygenated air into the baby's lungs. Kally doesn't say this, but I know that if CPAP doesn't work, they will put Stella back on a ventilator.

Ten minutes later, the respiratory specialist arrives. "She's having a little trouble breathing?" she asks gently, and I nod. She first tries to fit a tent over Stella's head, but the tent is too small. I watch as she struggles over my daughter. Kally comes over, and the specialist says, "A cannula would be easier."

Kally nods, and I feel a sudden panic. They just skipped a step—now we are two steps back, just like that. But when Stella is situated with the thin tube of oxygen under her nose, I'm grateful. At least I don't have to look at her through another layer of plastic. And the oxygen should help.

But it doesn't help. A few minutes later, Stella stops breathing again. My skin begins to tingle, as if my whole body has fallen asleep. *Breathe, sweetie,* I whisper. *You have to breathe.* I stand up and Kally comes over and rubs her feet. Nothing happens. I hold my breath and listen to my heart pounding. Yesterday, yesterday morning, Stella nursed. Her eyes were wide, her arms outstretched. She seemed to know me. Now, nothing. What if this is it?

When Stella finally takes a breath, I know I can't take this any longer. I cannot sit here all day and watch my daughter breathe and then not breathe. "I'm going to call Donny," I say slowly, "and then I'm going home."

"Yes, that's a good idea," Kally says quickly. She looks relieved.

And just like that I abandon my daughter. I walk out of the NICU, past the photographs of miracle babies on the wall, and into the lounge, which is empty except for a couple of teenagers who are eating bagels and doughnuts from the box on the counter. I wonder if they even know anyone here—do they have a sick sibling?—or if they just discovered the free food and stop by on their way to school. But then, who really gives a fuck?

I dial Donny's classroom number on the phone in the corner of the room, and when he answers I say, "She keeps forgetting to breathe. She has a cannula now." I start to cry. "It's awful. She looks dead."

I hear the chatter of his students in the background. He shushes them.

What does he say? Not to worry? That everything will be okay? I won't remember. All I know is that he's useless to me right now. He's not here. He hasn't seen our daughter stop breathing. Nothing he says can make this better.

"I'm going home," I say, as if I expect him to say *no, stay.*

"Okay," he says. "I'll be home early."

And then I leave the hospital. I get in my car and turn the key. I don't think of my daughter. I don't think of how horrible it is that I'm leaving her. I just drive. I drive past the run-down houses on Twenty-eighth Street. I drive past the corner fourplex that's probably a crack house. I turn onto Hiawatha and then onto Lake Street. Finally, I turn onto our street.

When I step into our porch, there are Japanese ladybugs all over the windows and ceiling. I had heard there was some kind of infestation this fall, but I hadn't seen any. And now—in the few hours I've been gone—there are dozens of them, their orange and black bodies bright against the pale yellow walls of our porch. I look around, dazed. How did they get in here? How did it happen so fast?

Suddenly, I'm so exhausted that it feels as if I'll collapse. I shut the door to keep the bugs out, slowly climb our stairs, peel off my clothes, and fall into bed. I sleep for three hours.

23

Y EARS LATER, I WON'T REMEMBER EXACTLY WHAT
I did when I woke from my nap. I know I called the hospital and
was told that Stella was stable—that she'd only had a few apnea
spells since I left. Maybe I also went down to the basement and
searched "sepsis, infant, NICU" and scared myself all over again
with the possibility of her death. Maybe I checked e-mail. I probably made myself a sandwich. I must have pumped. The only thing
I will remember clearly is a feeling: guilt. Thick and slow in my
veins. Sitting like a rock in my stomach. How could I have left my
daughter? What if she had gotten worse? What if that was the last
time I saw her alive?

And somehow, over the course of the afternoon, my guilt turns
into something else: self-righteousness. As I wait for Donny, my failure as a mother transforms into anger. *I* am the one who had to
watch her stop breathing. *I* am the one who sat next to her and cried.
How many times has Donny said, *I think she's going to be okay. I can
feel it?* How many times have I believed him? But now I understand
that he can't be trusted. We can't know whether or not Stella will
make it out of the NICU. We can't take anything for granted. We
need to be vigilant. We need to pay attention.

When Donny pulls up in front of the house, I'm ready to give
him the full force of my anger, to blame him for lulling me into
complacency. To blame him for not being at the hospital with me,
for not seeing Stella like that. But when I get into the car, Donny
opens his arms, his eyes tired and full of worry, and my anger dissolves into exhaustion. I pass him the sandwich I've made, and we
drive the route that is now automatic, Donny eating and driving,
me staring out the window.

Ten minutes later, as we walk through the doors to the NICU,

Donny reaches for my hand and squeezes it. We're both nervous. I am because I know what to expect; Donny is because he doesn't.

We wash our hands, rub foam into our knuckles and up our wrists. Why bother with this, anyway? Washing our hands didn't keep Stella from getting sepsis. We did what we were told, and she still got an infection.

Stella's isolette is covered with a quilt, which is a good sign. If she were still having regular apnea spells, it would have been removed to give the nurses easier access. I hang back while Donny flips it up and opens the armhole.

"Oh," he says.

Stella is still mottled, eyes closed, arms flung to the sides. She doesn't look good, but she looks better than she did this morning. The cannula is now gone, replaced with a tube of oxygen blowing into her face. I glance up at the monitor. Her heart rate is steady and her oxygen is at 95 percent.

"She looks a lot better," I say. And then, to make sure Donny understands how bad it was, I add, "This is nothing compared to this morning."

Donny nods, but doesn't say anything. He's staring at Stella, his finger resting in her palm.

A nurse comes by and opens the side of her isolette so we can see her better, and Donny pulls up two stools. We sit side by side, watching our daughter.

And then it happens. The alarm blares. Stella's chest stops moving. I turn to Donny. His face—full of panic—swings up to the monitor and back to Stella. He's moving in slow motion. I must have looked the same way this morning.

But now, instead of turning my back on my daughter, instead of searching the room for the nurse as I had earlier in the day, I reach my hand out and rub Stella's belly with my fingertips. "It's okay, sweetie. Breathe." Her chest is still unmoving, so I reach for a foot, rubbing her sole with my thumb. *I can do this.* Then I put my palm on her stomach, and nudge her slightly. "Breathe now," I say.

Her chest bucks into action again. Up and down. "Good girl," I whisper. "Good girl."

I watch her breathe for a moment, making sure that whatever I did sticks, and then I smile, realizing that this is the first time I have been able to meet one of my daughter's needs without the help of a nurse. It's the first time that I knew what she needed—a hand on her belly to remind her to breathe—and I gave it to her without asking someone for permission. I *am* her mother, I think suddenly.

I turn to Donny to share this realization, but my smile freezes when I see his face, which is drained of color. "Oh, babe," I say, reaching for his hand. "It's awful, isn't it?" I had wanted him to witness this, to feel the racing dread, to understand how time stops when she stops breathing, but now, seeing his face makes me feel sick.

"Oh, my God," he says slowly. He doesn't take his eyes from Stella's chest.

The nurse comes over and checks Stella's monitor, and I nod to her. But Donny looks as if he'll vomit. That's how I felt this morning. That place is actually more familiar than the place I'm in now, the place where apnea is old hat, where suddenly I know what to do and I do it.

"Do you think this is my fault?" Donny asks, turning to me.

"What?" I say, startled, searching his face. "Of course not. How could this be your fault?"

Donny's eyes are brimming with tears. "Maybe when I was holding her last night. Maybe I did something, and that's when the IV pulled out of her vein?"

This thought hadn't occurred to me, but now a tiny shard of me wonders if this is possible. Could this be his fault? Could Donny have done this? Did he jostle her? I try to remember if anything happened last night while he was holding her, but it didn't. No, nothing happened. And the IV line was deep in her arm. Holding her couldn't dislodge it. And anyway, it should have been removed yesterday.

Donny wipes tears away with the back of his hand, and I feel another pang of guilt for wanting him to witness our daughter like this. "This wasn't your fault," I say softly, reaching for him. "It just happened."

Donny nods slightly.

"Hey," I say, standing up and putting my hands on his shoulders.

He slides his arms around me slowly, and I press my lips into his neck, breathing in the muted smell of soap on his skin. "This wasn't your fault," I repeat.

"Yeah," he says quietly, but I can tell he doesn't believe me.

When I sit back down, we hold hands and stare at Stella, who is stable for the rest of our visit. Donny is quiet next to me, his fingernail dwarfing Stella's palm. I know he is probably urging her to close her fingers around his own. I know he needs a sign from her that she's okay. But he's not going to get one, not tonight.

It's probably better that he wasn't here earlier today. If we had seen her at her worst together, we might have collapsed. Who would have been the strong one? One of us needs to be—that's how we work. Donny has definitely been the solid one since Stella was born. In those first days he was the one gathering information, talking to the doctors. He has been the one to insist she will be fine. Now, he's no longer certain of this, so I need to step up. I need to be strong. I give Donny's hand a squeeze.

He turns to me, his eyes distant the way they always are when he's worried.

"The antibiotics are working," I say. "She's better than she was."

He nods.

"This wasn't your fault."

He nods again, and we sit silently for another half hour. Then we leave the NICU again, walking slowly down the long hallway, away from our daughter.

24

On Wednesday morning, I arrive at the NICU prepared to be feisty, to speak my mind, not let the nurses cow me. I'll stay by Stella's bedside as long as I want and not let Kally make me feel as though I'm in the way. I am Stella's mother, after all.

I open the armhole of the isolette, and Stella stretches an arm above her head and opens her eyes. I take a deep breath, inhaling relief. *Yes, good girl. You're doing better now.* If it weren't for the IV jutting from her head, she would almost look like herself again. "Hi, sweetie," I say. "You're awake." I want to drink her in—her dark eyes, her spindly arms, her narrow chest.

I notice that there is a peach-colored Beanie Baby perched on top of her isolette. At first I think my mom brought it in on her way to work, but then I glance around the room and see an identical Beanie Baby sitting on every isolette in the room.

"Good morning," Kally says. "She's doing much better today. No spells since last night."

"Thank God," I say quietly. Then, nodding at the little bear, "Where did this come from?"

"Someone brought them in—one for each baby in the NICU."

"Wow. That's nice. That's a lot of bears." At least forty, maybe more.

Kally nods. "Former NICU families often bring in gifts for the current babies and families—usually on the anniversary of a birth."

"That's sweet," I say, feeling another surge of relief. People make it out of here and return bearing gifts.

"Or sometimes," Kally adds, "on the anniversary of a death."

And just like that the cold rock of fear is back, wedging itself under my rib cage. I glance up at Kally, but she's turned away and is jotting something in Stella's chart. I feel a spark of anger. Why would she say that? Does she think I don't know, after yesterday, that some babies don't make it out of here? Does she think I've forgotten what it feels like to watch my daughter stop breathing over and over again?

I should say something to her. Hadn't I planned to speak my mind? But I can't; there is something about this place—my lack of control, having to listen to a twenty-five-year-old nurse tell me about my daughter and about the babies that don't make it out alive—that immobilizes me. There is a kind of desperation here, thrumming like a machine, and it makes me question my authority as a mother.

I lean toward Stella and press my finger into her palm. My eyes fill with tears, and I make a vow: if Stella dies here, I will never step foot in this place again. Not to bring frilly peach-colored bears, not to bring a rocking chair to ease the competition among nursing mothers. Why would any parent want to revisit the place their child died? I run my fingernail over Stella's tiny knuckles. "You need to make it, little one," I whisper. "Deal?" Then I lean closer and blow lightly on her arm. She closes her fingers around my own, and I smile. "Okay, then," I say. "It's a deal."

I sit by Stella's bedside longer than usual, unwilling to leave her side. I watch her sleep. I watch her stretch her skinny arms over her head. At noon, I change her diaper and take her temperature. As I sit there, I take inventory, making sure the other babies haven't been moved (which could be a good sign or a very bad sign).

I'm relieved to note that Emily is still next to Stella, Sam is still by the window, and the two tiny, tiny babies next to Sam, Quincy and Elijah, are still there as well. The blond-haired crier is gone, but I don't need to worry about him because I know he's been transferred to the Special Care Nursery. In his place is another baby, a boy, and he's gargantuan—so big that he's almost obscene, his chubby arms and legs flopped to the sides, taking up most of the space on his warming table. Tubes are taped across his chest, and there is a machine next to his bed, which looks like a water pump, whirring, whirring. I don't know what's wrong with him. I won't realize until much later that he was probably born with a diaphragmatic hernia, a hole in his diaphragm through which his intestines migrated into his chest cavity, putting pressure on his underdeveloped lungs—a serious, sometimes fatal condition. Today, all I think is how chubby and healthy he looks, even with all the equipment.

I see a social worker walk up to Kris, who is Sam's nurse, and I feel a surge of panic. She and Kris are talking quietly so I can't make out their words. But then Kris says more loudly, "I'll let her know that you stopped by." The social worker gives Kris one of her cards. I wonder what's wrong with Sam; there must be some diagnosis, some illness that was revealed in an ultrasound or blood test. Whenever something bad happens, a social worker appears. I've seen them talking softly to families, hands on shoulders, heads lowered.

As this one turns to leave, she catches my eye and smiles. I nod, giving her a pursed smile in return, but I urge her not to stop, not to say anything to me. *We're fine. Stella's fine. You don't need to talk to me.* It doesn't occur to me that I could seek her out, that she might be able to help me process everything that's happening.

I do feel the need to talk to someone, but when I'm home, I'm too exhausted to call my friends. And I couldn't begin to explain it all anyway—what it feels like to watch my daughter stop breathing, what it feels like to make her breathe all on my own.

A few days ago, three of my graduate school friends stopped by with a huge lasagna. I showed them Polaroid photos of Stella, and they kept saying, "Oh, Kate." But I was quick to assure them that she was okay, that we were okay. Why I needed to do this, I'm not sure.

"How is everything going? Tell me about your classes," I said, suddenly desperate for news that didn't have anything to do with babies or hospitals.

They gave a collective growl about their thesis projects, about how much writing they still needed to do, and then they started gossiping about the other students in the program. "I don't know who that is," I kept saying when they began telling stories about the first-year students. I had met a few of them briefly at the annual kickoff party the week before I was admitted to the hospital, but I was so hot and swollen that I'd left early.

I felt a little left out as they cataloged the transgressions of our classmates. It was as if I'd accidentally locked myself out of the house, and through the window I could see people laughing and flirting and drinking huge glasses of wine in the warm glow of the living room. I couldn't get in, so I stood on the front step shivering. Their lives were moving ahead while mine had ground to an uncomfortable halt. Or rather, my life as an MFA student had halted, and I'd taken off in a totally different direction, stumbling along.

I felt like an outsider during their visit, yet I didn't have any desire to rejoin them in school. I can't imagine having to read and write and critique another person's work. It seems impossible that words still string together to make sentences, that sentences make paragraphs, that paragraphs make chapters.

My world has become so small: home and the hospital and the roads in between. And apparently this is the only world in which I'm capable of living right now. So I was almost relieved when my friends left and I could get back to my current life: pumping and eating and heading back to Stella's bedside.

The only people I want to talk to are those who have also gone through this—I don't need to explain anything to them. I think of Leni, the mother of preemie twins and the English Ph.D. student who sent me the Rilke quote. She continues to check in with me via e-mail each week, but I know she's busy with teaching and her dissertation, so I try not to ask her too many questions. I think of Amy and little Noah, of the other parents I've seen huddled together in the lounge. But their situations are often so much worse than ours that I often end up feeling guilty for my tears.

Just after I was discharged from the hospital, an acquaintance, Jen, called to see how I was doing. We don't know each other very well, but we're friendly, and when she lost her son, Avner, a couple of years ago, I went to the memorial service. Avner was full-term. It was a normal labor, and she and her husband thought everything was fine. But it turned out that Avner had inhaled meconium during labor. This isn't always fatal, but because Jen didn't have much amniotic fluid, the meconium Avner breathed was superconcentrated, poisoning his body. He spent five days in the NICU at Children's, and then he died.

I started crying when I heard her voice on the phone, partly because I cried all the time in those early days, and partly because I felt awful for her all over again. At that point I couldn't imagine losing Stella—I wouldn't even let myself entertain that possibility—and I didn't know what kind of strength it must have taken for her to call me.

"Stella has the best care," she said. "And remember that you're lucky. You're going to take your baby home."

I felt an awful wave of guilt. "I know," I said quietly.

"But it's still hard," she said. "No one should have to start motherhood in the NICU. Go talk to one of the chaplains. They're wonderful."

I thought about doing this. I even walked slowly by their office a few days ago. But it seemed like such a big step—admitting to a stranger that I needed help, asking a minister for his or her time when my beliefs are dubious and when other parents here must need them more than I do. Who am I, with my three-pound baby and lack of faith, to seek the help of a chaplain? Also, I was worried that a chaplain might tell me to pray or that this was God's will. But I doubt they'd say that. When my grandmother Lucille died, the chaplain was respectful and warm. She held my hand lightly and told me it was okay for me to say good-bye. There was no mention of heaven or hell. There was no chastising me into prayer. I don't know why I'm so worried that someone will tell me I need to pray. On some level do I believe that if I had been praying, if I had believed more strongly, this wouldn't have happened?

Just last week, my dad and I got in an argument about this very thing. He had driven me to the hospital but had waited in the lounge. As we were leaving he said, "There was a woman in the lounge who asked me whether I'd accepted Jesus Christ as my Savior." He laughed a little as he said it, so I almost thought he was joking, but Dad doesn't joke about that sort of thing.

We'd reached the entrance of the hospital, and I stopped in the middle of the foyer, the automatic glass sliding doors frozen open in front of and behind me. "She asked you *what*?"

Dad stopped and turned around. "I told her that I was a Presbyterian minister." He shrugged. "She didn't have too much to say after that."

He started walking again and I hurried to catch up. The sky above us was bright blue.

"Let me get this straight," I said, my voice rising, my anger already fiery, like gasoline in my veins. "There was a woman in the NICU family lounge who asked you if you believed in Jesus? If you'd accepted Jesus as your *savior*?"

Looking back on this moment years later, I'll remember what it felt like to move from fine to furious in a split second. It's as if all that time sitting by my daughter's bedside, trying to be calm, had primed me to explode as soon as I walked through the hospital doors and back into real life. As if each of my nerve endings was exposed, making my reactions—to the slightest provocation—extreme. And I'll wonder how other parents—those with children who have terminal illnesses and severe disabilities—manage the stress of the hospital. How do they release the pressure?

I followed my dad to the sidewalk. As he pulled his car keys from his pocket, he said, "She was just concerned."

"Concerned?" I said, incredulous. *Did he really believe that?* "How is asking a stranger about his religious views in the NICU waiting lounge an act of concern? What the fuck?"

I stood on the sidewalk, my fists clenched, as Dad unlocked my car door. When he turned to look at me, his eyes were soft. "I don't think she meant—" he started.

"I don't give a fuck what she meant."

A bus rumbled by, spewing exhaust, and my dad shook his head slightly, walking around to open his own door.

I knew he didn't understand why I was so angry. I took a deep breath. "Anyone," I started, trying to keep my voice calm, "who is in that lounge is either in crisis or knows someone in crisis. It's not the time or place to shove Jesus down someone's throat."

When we both got into the car, Dad placed his hands on the steering wheel. Mine were clenched in my lap. I wasn't sure why I needed to make him understand how wrong this was.

"She was probably just trying to offer comfort. For her, that's the answer," he said slowly.

"For her. Exactly. Not for me. Not even for you. When my baby is a captive in the NICU, when she has an IV taped to her arm, when she's too small to take home, I don't need some Bible banger telling me to pray. Telling me that this is God's fucking will. Or that if I believed Jesus was my savior, this wouldn't have happened."

I was in tears then, gasping for air. But even in that moment, I realized it felt good to direct my anger, one of my unbearable outbursts, at someone other than the people I love (and even someone other than the nurses and doctors who were caring for my daughter). This woman—this woman with her religious pushiness, her dense insensitivity—she was the perfect person to hate.

Dad pulled away from the curb. His lips were pursed. I knew he didn't understand why I was so angry. But he should have. He believes in Jesus—he's an ordained minister for God's sake—but he would never tell another person that *they* needed to believe. He would never spew his convictions all over a stranger.

"She was just trying to offer support," Dad said again, quietly.

"That's bullshit, Dad. Complete bullshit, and you know it. She was trying to convert you. She was proselytizing. In the NICU lounge!"

I wiped the angry tears from my eyes and turned to the window, watching as we passed one run-down house after another along Chicago Avenue. I knew it disappointed him that none of his daughters were believers, that the church wasn't important in any of our lives.

It wasn't always this way, of course. When I was nine or ten, I loved to think of everyone in the world as distantly related, all of us descendants of Adam and Eve. Something about this connectedness reassured me. And though I was often bored by sermons, I lapped up the ancient lives we learned about in Sunday school; I loved to imagine houses made of sun-baked stones, dinners prepared over open flames, women pulverizing grain on wide, flat rocks.

At some point in high school I stopped believing that the Bible was the Word of God. But even then, I believed there was a God. It was only when I went to college and became depressed and woke with thoughts of suicide spinning in my head for months on end, that I thought, no, there was no God. If there were, I wouldn't wake with that heaviness in my chest. I wouldn't want to die.

I remember trying to explain this to my dad once. We were sitting at his kitchen table, and he wanted to know what had happened to my faith. Dad, who had also had bouts of depression, shook his head at me. When he was struggling with depression, he said, his faith offered him comfort. "Faith is about believing, even in those moments of uncertainty, of not-knowing."

"I still believe in something," I had said then, in the face of his disappointment. "It's more spiritual, less institutional, less Presbyterian."

As I sit next to Stella now, a day after she developed sepsis, I realize that my dad probably thinks "spiritual" is a crock of shit. But spiritual is all I can do, and I don't need anyone threatening me with God, not while my daughter is attached to tubes and wires, flashing lights, and oxygen sensors, when yesterday she developed an infection that could have killed her.

But I know I need something, and Jen said the chaplains were great, so that afternoon, after I leave Stella sleeping soundly, her legs tucked up under her belly, I walk slowly by their office again. But again, no one is there, and I feel relieved that I don't need to explain myself.

On my way home, I stop by a restaurant owned by a couple of friends to get a gift certificate for my mom. I want to thank her for all her help with dinners and for visiting Stella every morning. It's also an offering: an apology for my bad behavior last weekend after the Holding Incident.

It's early afternoon, so the restaurant is empty except for my friend Scott and two other men, who are sitting at a table crowded with glasses and bottles of wine. When I walk in, Scott and Lou, a wine rep I know from the years I worked in restaurants, stand. I give them hugs, and before they have a chance to ask why I'm there in the middle of the day, I blurt out the whole story: the preeclampsia, Stella's birth, the NICU, sepsis, the gift certificate.

As I'm winding down, the other man at the table stands and moves around the table. He holds out his hand, and as I shake it, he says, "Congratulations on your daughter."

I'm not sure anyone has congratulated me yet. Not like this, with a warm smile and no apology attached. Perhaps someone has, but this is the first time I've been ready to hear it, to accept those words.

Scott introduces the man, Stephan, a winemaker from the West Coast. He smiles again, reaching into his pocket for his wallet, pulling out a photo.

"My daughters," he says, holding out the photo to me.

I wonder briefly why he is showing me, a complete stranger, a picture of his children.

"This is Emily," he says, pointing at the younger daughter, who is seven or eight, sitting in a wicker chair with her legs crossed at the ankle. "And this," he says, pointing at the older girl, who is holding onto the back of the chair, "is Grace." They both have wide, toothy smiles. "Grace was a preemie, too. Three months early."

I look up at this man, who is watching me with a gentle smile in his eyes, then back to his daughter: her long dark hair, her narrow face, beautiful blue eyes. "She's okay?" I ask. My voice sounds small.

"Perfect," he says. "A normal twelve-year-old."

A rush of hope. I know my eyes are full of tears as I stare down at the photo again, which blurs in front of me. I can't imagine Stella like this—a girl, almost a young woman. I can't imagine a sister, another daughter. How could I ever do this again? How did he? I want to sit down with this man and get the whole story. I want to know how they made it through, how he got where he is.

"She's going to be okay," he says then. He's watching me, intent. He recognizes something in my eyes, my face. For the first time in a long time, I feel as though someone is really seeing me.

I slowly hand the photo back, and he shakes my hand again, his palm warm against mine. "It gets easier," he says.

"Thank you," I say, and then, because I know I have interrupted their tasting, I say good-bye to him and Lou and follow Scott into the bar for the gift certificate. The men return to their wine, and I walk out to my car. But on the way home, Grace is there with me. I wish I had told the man that I wouldn't forget him, that I wouldn't forget his daughter. I wish I had told him how much his words and the photo meant to me. I hope he knows.

25

THE NEXT COUPLE OF DAYS ARE A BLUR. THE BLOOD
tests reveal that Stella's infection was a coagulase-negative staph infection, and one of the antibiotics is discontinued. The one she needs is
still injected into the IV in her head every day, but since she's stable,
I get the okay to nurse her again. Dr. Brown rotates off Stella's care,
and Dr. Lanning takes over. I'm not sure I like Dr. Lanning—she's
brusque and doesn't call me at home in the mornings the way Dr.
Brown and Dr. Gregor had—but when she starts talking about moving Stella back to the Special Care Nursery, I forgive her this lapse.

On Saturday morning, when Donny and I arrive at the NICU,
Donny checks Stella's chart for her weight. "Four pounds!" he says,
beaming.

"Four pounds?" I ask, almost not believing it. Stella is three
weeks old and now half the size of most babies at birth. But she
doesn't seem small anymore—four pounds feels solid—and I wish I
could let myself give in to the feeling that we're in the clear.

Donny rubs foam on his hands and then opens Stella's isolette
to take her temperature. She's sleeping, and I watch as he maneuvers comfortably around the wires, unsnapping Stella's onesie. He
seems to have recovered from his fear, from blaming himself for Stella's sepsis; he has returned to being the steady, confident one of our
pair. I'm both impressed by his recovery and relieved to have Strong
Donny back; it means I'm free to fall apart if necessary.

When Dr. Lanning makes her rounds, she says that today is the
day Stella will move back to the Special Care Nursery. We are all
smiles and agreement. And I let myself float through the day on this
new optimism. She'll be with the other preemies growing and learning to eat and the full-term babies who are just a little jaundiced,
who need a few days under the lights. There will be no ventilators,

no babies waiting for complicated surgeries, no micropreemies, the smallest of the small. We'll be a step closer to going home, surrounded by others in the same situation.

My memories of the Special Care Nursery are so fuzzy that on Sunday morning when we arrive there for the first time since Stella's move (which happened after we left the NICU for the night), it's as if it's the first time I've ever been there.

It was disorienting to park in the Abbott Northwestern parking lot rather than across the street at Children's. And it felt odd that instead of walking down the long hallway toward the NICU, we weave our way through Abbott's hallways, finally taking the elevator up to the seventh floor. I was certainly ready to be done with the NICU, to have Stella a step closer to home, but still, everything is now foreign to me again, and I realize that this—however long she'll be here—won't be easy either.

Donny and I stand in front of the brown hospital-room door of the Special Care Nursery and ring the bell on the wall. A nurse who is sitting at a long desk peers at us through the window and holds up her arm.

"What does she want?" I whisper to Donny, but he understands right away, holding up his own arm, flashing his wristband at the nurse. Oh, right. We're both still wearing the wristbands we received the night Stella was born three weeks ago; they're tattered, held together by a few threads of plastic, but they are still there, and they are our tickets into the nursery.

The Special Care Nursery is smaller and more intimate than the NICU. The door opens into a main area where the nursing station is located. The rooms where the babies stay shoot off from the main room like the petals of a flower.

Donny tells the nurse behind the desk who we are, and she stands and smiles.

"This is where Stella was last time," Donny says, pointing to a room on the left, and I nod, though truthfully, I have no memory of it. The only time I visited her here was just after my C-section, and

I was lying down on a gurney, the ceiling lights spinning above my head. That none of this looks at all familiar makes me feel guilty, as if not remembering Stella's first home is an acknowledgment of how much more concerned I was with my own discomfort, with the thick pressure of magnesium sulfate in my chest, than I was with my own daughter, whose breathing during those hours was becoming more and more labored.

Stella is now in Room C, which is much smaller than her room in the NICU. It's divided in half by a low wall lined with a sink and small refrigerator. We wash our hands, and the nurse points to an isolette next to the window. As we walk toward our daughter, I notice that there are two babies on Stella's side of the room, three on the other side. When we get to Stella's station, I glance over the wall and see a jack-in-the-box sign that reads "Joe." He has to be the same Joe who was next to Stella for a week in the NICU. *They're reunited,* I think, pleased to know another baby here.

We lift the quilt from Stella's isolette, and she turns to us, squinting into the sunlight that slants through the venetian blinds. Her face is filling out, and she almost looks like a regular baby now—even with the IV still taped to her head and the feeding tube threaded up her nose and taped across her cheek.

We sign admission papers, and then Donny and I take turns holding Stella. She nurses for a total of five minutes, which means she only needs half of a tube feeding. "It's so quiet here," Donny says, and I nod. We're tucked in the corner, and no one walks by. A few alarms go off, but there is none of the thrumming desperation, the sense that lives are on the line, that exists in the NICU. It's just me and Donny and the other babies sleeping in their isolettes.

The nurse tells us that the sooner Stella gets the hang of nursing, the sooner we'll be able to take her home; it's like a gigantic breast-shaped carrot dangling in front of us. We decide that I'll be there for at least three feedings a day: 9:00 a.m., noon, and 6:00 p.m.

Sometimes Stella seems to get it; she latches on and nurses on and off, on and off. I try to keep track of the minutes she's actually

actively nursing, but it's not as if I have a stopwatch at my fingertips. Ideally, I could just hook something up to my breasts that
would gauge how many ccs were leaving my body. But some days it
wouldn't make any difference. Stella is sleepy and disinterested when
I try to get her to latch on, and she ends up with a full tube feeding.
And as I watch my milk snake its way up the plastic tube into her
nose, I feel an intense sense of failure. Why can't I get her to nurse?

I reread all the handouts we were given on breastfeeding, and I
read that section in the handbook. I mention to Donny that I think
we should still attend the breastfeeding class that I signed us up for
months ago when I thought everything would go according to plan.

Donny shrugs. "Sure."

So on Monday evening, after we have each held Stella for fifteen
minutes, we take the elevator downstairs and follow the hallways
leading to the auditorium. It's a brightly lit lecture room filled with
very pregnant women and their partners, whose faces register emotions ranging from excitement to boredom to discomfort.

Two couples move their knees to the side so Donny and I can
squeeze past them. As we inch along to the center seats, it seems
that everyone is staring at us. They probably either think I am a
few months pregnant and super-anal, trying to get a jump on the
information, or they know my baby has already been born, and they
think I didn't plan ahead: *You're supposed to take this class* before *the
birth*. I don't know why what these people think matters to me, but
it does. I want them to know that we *do* have a baby, a baby who was
born too soon. I did plan ahead, and it didn't matter.

I push my right sleeve up to reveal my Special Care wristband
and wave my arm around.

Donny gives me a look.

"What?" I say.

"Maybe you should just have a T-shirt made," he says.

"Smart-ass," I say. But a T-shirt doesn't sound like a bad idea. If
people knew our story, they would be especially nice; they would
stand up to let us pass rather than making us squeeze by their legs
and huge bellies. They would stop staring at us.

"I *do* feel out of place, though," Donny admits, scanning the room. The pregnant women mostly look tired, weary. But there is also a glow about them, a glow I don't think I ever emitted, even before I got sick.

"They have no idea how much can go wrong," I say, as if I hadn't been in their position just a month before.

One of the same women who taught our birthing class is teaching this class as well, and her optimism reminds me of the hours this summer that I spent reading and planning. I should have been working on my thesis, writing as fast as I could in the face of the impending deadline of Stella's birth, but instead I spent most afternoons poring over birthing books. What a waste of time.

Donny and I hold hands through the overheads illustrating different nursing positions and a proper latch. I let my gaze wander around the auditorium, and without realizing it, I begin searching out women who are as pregnant as I should be: eight months. I stare at one after another, settling on a petite, dark-haired woman whose belly is a mountain in her lap. She's probably eight months. And in my imagination, I switch places with her. I am the hugely pregnant woman and she is the preemie mom. I am the one who is writing up my birth plan and fretting about my labor and spending my evenings folding onesies and miniature washcloths smelling of Dreft. It's as if I've been given a tiny window into my parallel life, one in which I am still pregnant, still waiting for Stella to be born.

I glance at Donny, whose eyes are opening and closing and opening again in a painfully slow and tired way.

"Let's leave at the break," I whisper.

He opens his eyes and gives me a relieved smile.

On our way out, we stop to say hello to the instructor. It takes a moment for her to recognize us, but then she says, "Oh, we were worried when you didn't come back to class."

I almost make a joke about being birthing class dropouts, but I don't. I tell her about the preeclampsia, the respiratory distress, and the sepsis, condensing the last three weeks into two lines of narrative. "But she's back in the Special Care Nursery now," I say, suddenly remembering this woman's story in birthing class about the thirty-two-weeker who was just fine, the one who was in the nursery for a "couple of weeks." I hope she'll remember our story, too, and use it as a warning: watch out for swelling, for protein in your urine. And I hope she won't make it seem as though having a thirty-two-weeker is a breeze.

"You're probably getting more breastfeeding support than we can offer here," she says.

I nod. "Yeah, we're going back up to see Stella now."

She shakes our hands. "Good luck."

As we walk out of the lecture hall, pregnant gazes follow us, and Donny says, "That was fun."

I wrinkle my nose. "We should have gone out to dinner instead."

When we get back to the nursery, I feel so discouraged and tired that I can't stand the thought of trying to nurse Stella again. Is it because seeing all those pregnant women in the same place made me remember what it felt like to still be pregnant? Because it reminded me that my due date is still a month away? I'm not sure; it's not something I can articulate, so I don't say anything at all. Donny and I simply hold Stella's tiny hands.

When Dr. Lanning rounds the next morning, I explain that breast-feeding is still a challenge. I'm sitting in the rocker holding Stella, who is sleeping soundly after a forty-five-minute nursing session that ended in half a tube feeding.

"She'll get the hang of it," she says. She checks Stella's chart, and then looks up at me. "I want to move Stella into a bassinette today to see how she regulates her body temperature."

"Great!" I say, imagining Stella wrapped like the other burrito babies in the nursery.

Dr. Lanning nods. "I also think we should start giving her two bottles at night."

I bite my lip. Everything I've read about breastfeeding says that giving bottles too soon can interfere with a baby's latch. "I don't know," I say slowly. "Won't that make breastfeeding even more difficult?"

Dr. Lanning shrugs, her face impassive. "Two bottles at night won't make a difference." She adjusts her tortoiseshell glasses on the bridge of her nose. "You have to decide whether you want to strictly breastfeed and stay in the hospital a week longer or give her bottles now and work on breastfeeding later. You'll have plenty of time to practice at home." She gives me a long look, as if she's willing me to be reasonable. "She'll catch on."

I look down at my daughter, her cheek pressed to my chest. Of course I don't want her here any longer than necessary—how could she even suggest that?—but I *do* want her to be able to nurse, to experience that bonding. What if giving her bottles now makes it even more difficult than it already is?

But it doesn't sound as though I have a choice. Will the nurses give her bottles even if I ask them not to? How would I know if they gave her a bottle in the middle of the night?

"Okay," I say finally. "I guess."

Dr. Lanning nods with a curt "good" and moves on to the next baby.

I rock back and forth slightly and worry that I just agreed to something I shouldn't have. I run my fingertip over Stella's impossibly soft temple and into her hair, which is matted with adhesive.

Across the room, Joe's mother is standing above her son's bassinette. Her face is still grim, just as it was while they were in the NICU. I try to catch her eye, but what would I say anyway? Hi, remember me? Our babies were next to each other for a whole week? It seems odd to be trying to make friends in this place, but I can't tamp out the urge to connect with people.

The day before Stella was discharged from the NICU, I ran into Amy in the hallway. She had spent the night with Noah in one of the parent overnight rooms—a requirement before the hospital will discharge your baby. They want to make sure you can feed and handle your baby on your own, unplugged from all the machines—or in Noah's case, still plugged in; he'll go home with an apnea monitor.

Amy looked exhausted but elated. I can't even imagine how relieved I'd feel to take Stella home if we'd been here as long as Noah has been, three months now. But Amy also had a little of the deer-in-the-headlights look about her, and I know it must be scary to anticipate leaving. I imagine that being home with Noah will make the absence of Noah's twin, Peyton, even more palpable.

Now I glance up when I hear Joe's mother say, "Oh, hello."

A doctor whom I've never seen before walks up to her, nodding. "The brain scan was clear," he says. "Perfectly normal. No problems."

Her face breaks into a smile, and she looks like a different person. I see a glimpse of the woman she was before her days and nights were filled with pumping and driving back and forth to the hospital to hold her tiny boy.

"So," the doctor says, nodding in Joe's direction. "I'll discharge him tomorrow."

I smile and smooth the tape that secures Stella's IV to the crown of her head. Joe seems to be a week ahead of Stella in everything, so the news that his brain scan is clear and he'll go home tomorrow somehow translates in my mind into a clear brain scan and an upcoming discharge for Stella, as well.

I hear the low voices of Joe's mother and the doctor as they continue to talk, but I can't make out what they're saying. Stella stretches her arm, pushes it against my chest. Her eyelids flutter, and her thin lips part. I think of Dr. Lanning's words. "Of course I want to take you home," I whisper.

26

On Wednesday morning, Stella is in a bassinette when I arrive at the hospital. It's not actually a bassinette, not one of those white wicker cradles with frilly pink sheets; it's just a Plexiglas box. The nurse, Martha, tells me that Stella had a good night and that she sucked down each of her two bottles in less than five minutes. "She did great," she adds, and I nod.

But at nine o'clock when I try to get Stella to nurse, she swings her head from side to side and refuses to latch on. I wait a few minutes, rocking her, smoothing the wisps of hair at the base of her neck. When I try again, I'm able to get her to latch on, but after a minute she pulls away, arching her back and thrashing her head back and forth again. I grit my teeth. It has to be the fucking bottles. She tried them and loved them—*sucked them down in less than five minutes!*—and now she wants nothing to do with me.

When Martha comes over to see how I'm doing, my body is taut with frustration. "She's not nursing. She won't stay latched on. She keeps pulling away." Each sentence is an accusation.

Martha shrugs. "Some days are better than others. You can hold her while she gets her tube feeding."

I watch Martha as she moves over to the refrigerator and fills one of the plastic syringes with my pumped milk. When she clips the syringe into the machine that will depress it slowly into Stella's feeding tube, I'm fuming. "It's because of the bottles. She didn't do this before she got bottles."

Martha turns the machine on. "I doubt that," she says calmly. "Two bottles in a twenty-four-hour period doesn't make a difference." She looks as if she's daring me to challenge her, and I have a sudden urge to reach up and slap her.

My anger must be visible in my eyes because then she adds, smiling, "She'll do better this afternoon."

But the noon feeding is worse. And Martha starts to pass Stella into my arms before the folding privacy screen is in place, so I quickly whip my shirt and bra off. What else am I supposed to do? I don't feel comfortable holding Stella while I take off all my clothes. She's just a slip of a baby; she could slide off my lap as I try to wiggle from them.

But Martha purses her lips and yanks the screen around us in a clatter of metal. "You really should wait until this is up before you take off your shirt."

I stare at her.

"You might make some of the husbands uncomfortable," she says, motioning to my bare breasts.

I look around slowly, taking in the fact I'm the only parent in the room. And even if there *were* someone else around, it would be unlikely for them to catch sight of me considering I'm tucked in the corner, sitting in a low chair behind Stella's basinette.

"Some of the dads might feel uncomfortable," she says again, as if she expects an apology.

I'm clearly being reprimanded, but I refuse to apologize to her. What does she want me to do? Wear a nursing bra and discreetly lift my shirt to nurse my four-pound baby? (I don't even own a nursing bra yet.) Or does she expect me to be able to hold Stella, pull off my shirt and bra, and arrange the screen around us all by myself?

If any of the dads had caught sight of my stretch-marked breasts, I'm sure they wouldn't have cared or even noticed. We have been stripped bare by circumstance, and the fact that Martha wants me to be discreet and hide myself is infuriating.

Stella ends up getting another full tube feeding, and I feel totally defeated. So instead of staying for Stella's three o'clock feeding, which will probably be more of the same, I decide to go and buy a damn nursing bra. Stella is scheduled for her brain scan this afternoon anyway, and she might be pulled out just as I'm ready to feed her. So I tell Pam, the nurse I like who always has a wide smile for me, that I'll be back in the evening, and she says, "Yes, go get some air."

As I walk to my car, I do as Pam suggests and try to take deep breaths, filling my lungs with crisp fall air. *Everything is going to be fine,* I think, holding the air in my lungs until I can feel each of my ribs. When I exhale I think, *we just have to get Stella home.* I take another deep breath and hold it until it burns. *We need to get her home.*

When I get in my car, I pull a Pixies CD from its case and slide it into the stereo. Then I roll down the windows and crank the music until I can feel the bass guitar and drums beat in my chest. I sing along to "Where Is My Mind?," grateful for Frank Black's and Kim Deal's careening voices. And by the time I get to Rosedale Mall, I feel lighter. I'm going to a mall. To buy a bra. What a normalizing act.

But when I walk through the wide doors into the brightly lit mall filled with women pushing strollers, running toddlers, and thirty-somethings in business casuals talking on their cell phones, I feel totally disoriented. It's Wednesday afternoon. What are all these people doing here? Doesn't anyone work anymore?

I search out Motherhood Maternity on the map and make my way there as quickly as I can.

I was here the weekend before Stella was born, and I remember feeling that the clothes should be bigger—why was everything so tight on me? But as I enter the store, the billowing dresses and blouses and stretchy pants all look ridiculously huge, like obscene and faceless caricatures of real pregnant women.

I hurry to the back of the store, where two women are clipping gigantic white bras onto hangers. They look up when they see me rushing toward them, and I blurt, "I need nursing bras. I don't know what size. I was 36C while I was pregnant."

One of the women looks me up and down, her bifocals perched on the tip of her nose. "Well," she says, smiling slowly, "one thing I know for sure is that you ain't no C." Both women laugh loudly then, and I look down at my huge chest, disproportionate to the rest of my body.

"I guess not," I agree, relieved by their laughter.

"You have a baby in the hospital?" The other woman asks then, and my head snaps up. How did she know?

"Your wristband," she says, pointing at my Special Care bracelet. Oh, of course. My badge.

"A preemie," I say, by way of explanation. "A thirty-two-weeker. But she's three weeks old now."

The women nod their heads and move around to different racks, pulling down one huge white granny bra after another—nothing I ever thought I'd wear. When I have a pile in my arms, they lead me into a curtained dressing room with a full-length mirror. I pull off my shirt and bra, and stare at myself in the mirror. My breasts *are* huge, and for a second I feel like a porn star. Then I let out a snort. My belly is slack, and my milk-swollen breasts are tracked with red stretch marks. They're hard as rocks because I didn't pump before leaving the hospital, and they'll probably start leaking soon; definitely not the breasts of a porn star. How did I think bra shopping would make me feel normal? I sigh and stuff myself into a 38D that makes me look like a busty 1950s housewife.

That evening when Donny and I are at the hospital and I try to nurse Stella, she does the head-wagging thing again and refuses to latch on. It's as if she's decided to strike; she's made up her mind that breast-feeding is overrated. Stubborn girl.

Donny peers over my shoulder, shaking his head. "She was doing so well."

"I know," I say. In the car on the way to the hospital, I'd told him about the morning and noon feedings, and about Martha and the screen. "Would you care if you saw some woman's breasts as she was trying to nurse?"

"I wouldn't even notice," Donny had said, and I leaned over and kissed his cheek.

Pam, the bubbly nurse, comes over to see how we're doing. Stella has actively nursed for maybe two minutes out of the half hour we've been attempting it. "It has to be the bottles," I say again to Pam, desperate for someone to believe me.

Pam nods, her brow furrowed. "That's possible," she says. "Most babies do fine with a couple of bottles during the night, but some don't."

Thank fucking God. Someone believes me.

"Tomorrow let's try a nipple shield."

"A what?" The image of old-school female superheroes pops into my head: Wonder Woman and Dyna Girl with their huge pointed breasts sheathed in vinyl.

"It's a plastic shield that slips over your nipple. It's easier for the baby to latch on to. I'll find one for you tomorrow."

"Thank you so much," I say. At this point I'll try anything. And I'm relieved that someone here is taking me seriously.

27

STELLA IS GAINING WEIGHT—SHE'S ALMOST FOUR
and a half pounds—and she'll get the last dose of antibiotics to treat
her sepsis today. If she continues to grow, the only thing keeping her
from going home is her refusal to nurse.

When I'm buzzed into the Special Care Nursery in the morning,
I'm grateful to see that Pam is there. As soon as I'm situated in the
rocking chair, she brings me a nipple shield. It's not exactly the Dyna
Girl version I'd conjured the night before. It's a flimsy plastic thing
that I dip in water and adhere to my breast.

Stella latches on for a minute, but my milk hasn't let down, so
she's sucking air through the shield. She pulls back, red-faced and
furious. *I know,* I whisper. I put her to my breast again, but the nipple shield falls off. I'm awkward, trying to re-adhere it while Stella
flaps in my arms. We try again and again, but each time Stella pulls
away, swinging her head. I take off the shield and reattach it, take it
off and reattach it, like some kind of bovine Sisyphus. After fifteen
minutes, milk is dripping down my belly, and Stella ends up with a
full tube feeding.

The noon feeding goes a little better. I make sure the shield is
smoothed down and secure before I try to get Stella to latch on,
and this helps. Stella nurses and stops, nurses and stops, but nurses
enough so that she only needs half a tube feeding. Nurse Martha
walks by and nods, her eyebrows raised. *See,* she seems to be saying,
I told you she'd be fine.

I glare at her as she walks away, hoping that she can guess what
I am thinking. It goes something like this: fuck off.

As my pumped milk is slowly pushed into the tube snaking up
Stella's nose and down her throat, I take the elevator down to the cafeteria for something to eat.

Everything looks bland and congealed, and I realize I'm not even hungry. But I end up ordering a cup of tomato soup, which makes my mouth feel thick and metallic, as if I drank it straight from the can. On my way back to the nursery, I run into the mother of the blond crier from the NICU.

"Hi!" she says, stepping in front of me. "Your baby was in the NICU, wasn't she?"

She has that desperate be-my-friend-please-talk-to-me look about her that I'm sure is on my face most of the time.

"Yes," I say. "How is your baby?"

"He's doing really well," she says, nodding. "We're just trying to get him to nurse."

"God, me too," I say. "It's awful, isn't it?"

"So different than my first," she says. "My older son was full-term and this is a whole new world."

I can't imagine having a preemie after having a full-term baby, after knowing what it's supposed to be like—the birth, nursing, holding your baby right away. "I'm so sorry," I say, but she just shrugs.

She's heading to the cafeteria for her lunch and I'm heading back to the nursery, but neither of us is ready to say good-bye. We stand awkwardly in the crowded hallway until she finally says, "Well, good luck."

"Yeah, you too."

When I get back to the nursery, Stella is sleeping, wrapped in fleece. Her IV has been removed from her scalp and her head is covered with the tiniest wool hat I've ever seen. She seems relaxed, sucking occasionally on the huge green pacifier in her little mouth. I glance at the monitor, and note that her heart rate and oxygen are normal. She's doing fine, so I sit down and pull a novel, Charles Baxter's *First Light,* from my purse. This is the first time I've tried to read something that isn't about preemies or how to avoid mastitis and increase my milk supply since before Stella was born, and it feels almost sacrilegious—a novel, of all things, in the Special Care Nursery!

But if anything is grounding for me, it's reading—being able to lose myself in a narrative so removed from my own. So this morning as I was eating breakfast, I decided I should always carry a book with me. I know I'll be able to stay at the hospital longer—all day even—if I can dip into a novel throughout the day.

I open *First Light* and pause at the epigraph: *Life can only be understood backwards; but it must be lived forwards.* Kierkegaard. It seems like the perfect quote for a memoirist, and I'm surprised I've never seen it before. But I've always steered clear of Kierkegaard because he's one of my dad's heroes. Dad taught an undergraduate Kierkegaard seminar for over a decade, and I knew if I started reading Kierkegaard, I'd end up getting long lectures at my dad's kitchen table. This probably would have been good for me.

I turn the page and start to read: "On the Fourth of July, Hugh agrees to drive—"

An alarm blares, and I look up to search the room for the flashing light. It's the baby by the door. A nurse walks to the isolette, punches the buttons on the monitor, and raises the quilt to check on her.

Back to the book: "Hugh agrees to drive out to Mrs. LaMonte's house to get 'the explosives,' as he likes to—"

Another alarm. I search the room again, but I can't tell which baby's oxygen levels have dipped. A woman walks over to the baby boy who is in Joe's old spot on the other side of the room.

"How much longer?" she asks a nurse.

"Probably a couple of days," the nurse replies.

"They're so bright," the woman says, and I gather she's talking about the phototherapy lights beaming down on her baby in all their ultraviolet glory. Little purple boy, I think. Another mother with a glowing purple baby.

I turn back to my book, but I've forgotten where I was, so I start at the beginning again. It's slow work, reading in the Special Care Nursery. But in the moments between alarms and the nurses' conversations, when the words really enter my brain, it feels as if I've returned home. "June," I whisper, reading aloud, "a hot and rainless month, had paled the natural greens in the fields outside Five Oaks to a faded pastel in which the yellow is now, at the beginning of July, beginning to be visible. The corn stalks are stunted, and each tree leaf has its own coating of dust. In the heat the sky is an ashy stagnant blue."

It's been so long since I admired the land, the sky. I wish I were up north at my mom's cabin, standing on the end of the dock, staring up into a pale evening sky. Sunset is my favorite time of day there. I love the feeling of hovering at the edge of dusk, when most of the lake is cast in shadow, but the sunlight is still held in the closed fists of thunderheads and in the trees along the south shore, the pines and ash glowing with intensity. I wish I could drive for hours across the flat expanse of the Midwest and lose myself in the changing sky ahead of me.

I jump when I notice Dr. Lanning walking toward me, and I shove the book into my purse. For some reason I don't want her to know I've been reading a novel instead of holding my sleeping daughter. I can imagine what the note in Stella's chart would say: "Mother prefers reading to kangarooing with her daughter."

I stand up and Dr. Lanning smiles. I don't. I'm ready to do battle with her. Donny and I talked about it this morning, and we agreed that we'd be adamant about Stella not getting any more bottles. Maybe in a week we'll have made up the ground that we've lost in the last two days.

"So," Dr. Lanning says, coming to a stop next to me. "I have the results of the brain scan."

Oh yes, I had forgotten that Stella had her brain scan yesterday.

She flips a page in Stella's chart, and I wait, expecting her to say that everything is fine, just as Stella's first scan was. Just as Joe's was.

"It showed," Dr. Lanning says quietly, "a Grade 1 intraventricular hemorrhage."

I stare at the doctor's pale hair, at the tortoiseshell rims of her glasses. The scan showed. She said *the scan showed*. Is she talking about Stella?

I turn to my daughter, who is sleeping, her eyelids fluttering.

"It's small," Dr. Lanning goes on. "The bleeding is confined to a very a small area of the ventricles."

Bleeding. Confined bleeding. Small area. Stella sucks on her green pacifier. This is impossible. I take a step back, lean against the wall.

"A hemorrhage," I say finally, turning to Dr. Lanning, who is watching me silently. "I don't understand."

Dr. Lanning pulls out a piece of paper and draws a picture of a brain. She draws two lima bean–shaped ventricles inside the brain. "It looks like this," she says, drawing a spot on one of the ventricles, a dark swirl of ink.

I look up, around the room. The girl baby by the door cries her thin pterodactyl cry, which sounds so lonely, muted by the quilt and the isolette. Her alarm flashes. I look at Stella's monitor. Her heart rate and oxygen—everything is fine.

Dr. Lanning says something else, but I don't understand. I turn to her. Her lips are moving, moving, but no sound is coming out. *I can't hear you. I can't hear you.*

Finally I say, "What does this mean?" It's a question I've asked myself a dozen times since Stella was born, but this is the first time I've said it aloud to a doctor. And now I need an answer. I need to know what this swirl of blood means for my daughter.

Dr. Lanning tilts her head. She says something about math-processing problems, ADHD. "Or," she says, "she could be totally fine." Her hand moves through the air. Her hand through the air as if she's showing me her garden, pointing out where the lavender will be planted, where the hostas will go.

"This is something you should put out of your head until she's in grade school. And then, if there seem to be problems, get her tested."

Put it out of my head. Out of my head.

In this moment, what I should have heard was that Stella is not in danger. What I should have heard is that this isn't a big deal. But the only thing I can hear is that my daughter has blood on her brain. I stare down at the swirl of ink on the ventricles in the brain in Dr. Lanning's hands. She should have drawn it in red. It should be red, not black.

"Okay," Dr. Lanning says then, and suddenly I hate her. I hate her drawing and her pale hair and her glasses. I hate her calm, even voice.

I don't know what else she says to me.

When she leaves, I sit back down in the rocker. The sunlight seeps in between the blinds—slats of light against the white wall. Stella is asleep. She's wearing a wool hat. She's in a bassinette. She looks fine. She has to be fine.

Pam comes over. "Are you okay?"

"A brain bleed," I say.

Pam nods, furrowing her brow. Then she touches Stella's head with her fingertips. Her fingers flutter over my daughter's wool cap. She's barely touching her, but it's as if there is power in her fingertips, some kind of healing energy. There has to be. She has magic in her hands, and she has stopped the bleeding in my daughter's brain.

Pam comes around and touches me next, and I let the warmth from her palm seep into my shoulder. My eyes begin to well with tears.

"You need to take care of yourself," she says quietly.

I probably look as if I'm going to fall apart.

"Fall apart" is an odd phrase, isn't it? As if big chunks of arm and shoulder could suddenly detach from my body and thunk to the floor. As if my rib cage could open, each rib snapping off and clattering around my feet. What the hell would they do with me then?

The air is suffocating. "I think I'm going to go," I say slowly.

Pam nods, smiling kindly. "I made an appointment for you to see the lactation consultant tomorrow at noon. She'll meet you here and help you with the nipple shield."

"Thank you," I say, grateful for Pam, for her hand on my shoulder, for her kind smile, for the fact that she believed me about the bottles when no one else did.

"Of course," Pam says. "Of course."

Twenty-five minutes later, I'm in a photo shop in St. Paul. I don't remember the drive; I'm just suddenly there, standing in line. When I step up to the counter, I tell the clerk my name and pull dollar bills from my wallet. He hands me an envelope of photos, and I walk out of the store. On the sidewalk, I open the envelope and flip through photos from the NICU: Stella with a tube of oxygen blowing in her face; Stella with adhesive on her temples; Stella in my arms, wrapped in fleece; Stella staring up at me, her arm stretching over the mound of my bare breast. In each photo, her cheeks are sunken, her eyes bulbous. In each photo, her skin is mottled. How could I have forgotten that she's a preemie? Now a preemie with a bleeding brain.

I slide the photos back into the envelope and look out at the parking lot, which is lined with cars. Women with large purses over their shoulders shepherd children into the grocery store. People file out of Bruegger's and Caribou with coffee and bags of bagels. I turn toward my car, but my legs are heavy, as if I'm walking through mud.

In the car I stretch the seatbelt across my lap and snap it into place as if it matters, as if that's the sort of thing that will keep me safe. And then I just sit there, staring at the car in front of me. It's a blue SUV, and its headlights, if on, would be beaming right into my face. Thank God it's not night, I think. The last thing I need is headlights in my face.

I start my car, but instead of driving home, I drive over the Ford Bridge toward Rachel's house.

I'm there in five minutes, and when she opens the door, she says, "Hey! I was just thinking about you. I want to try to see Stella today."

"I had to leave," I say, and that's when the tears come.

"Oh," she says, reaching for me. "Come in, come in."

And then I'm sitting on her couch, sobbing, choking through everything Dr. Lanning said: the blood on the ventricles, the drawing with that dark spot of ink, the ADHD, the math-processing problems.

"Oh, God," Rachel says.

"I mean, I don't know. I really don't know." Even though I've just repeated what I *do* know, I can't fully digest it. It still doesn't make sense, maybe because we're so close to getting her home. I had assumed her scan would be fine. Hadn't I learned my lesson yet? And this, coming on the tail of the sepsis, is too much. One of Rachel's fat cats jumps up on my lap and I absently rub its ears.

"Do you want something to eat?" Rachel asks.

I shake my head. I haven't even called Donny yet. But I hate calling him again at school with bad news.

But then I say, "I should call Donny."

Rachel hands me the phone, and I dial his classroom number. When he answers, I say, "More bad news."

He says, "What happened?"

And I repeat what I just told Rachel.

"Oh, no," he says. "I'll leave as soon as I can." I can't count the number of times we have had this exchange over the last month.

When I hang up, Rachel gives me another hug. "Do you want to stay here? Or I could go with you to your house."

"No, I'm okay," I say. I realize I need to get home to my computer. I've told Donny what I know, and now the researcher in me needs to double-check everything. I need to search out the information myself and see it on the screen. That's when it will feel real.

Rachel says she'll call later and gives me another hug.

At home, my basement is chilly, so I pull a blanket over my shoulders as our old computer boots up. Then I Google "intraventricular hemorrhage premature baby." A list of Web sites appears on the screen, and I begin the process of clicking on link after link.

One Web site states that extremely premature infants have a 50 percent chance of having an intraventricular hemorrhage (IVH), but that mildly premature infants only have a 15 percent chance of IVH. Stella wasn't extremely premature (born at less than twenty-eight weeks), but she wasn't mildly premature (born after thirty-four weeks) either. Her risk level is somewhere in between. I'm not sure why the statistics matter now anyway.

The shelves above the computer, which are lined with books, are also home to two wooden elephants—a mother and baby. They were given to us for our wedding by one of Donny's Thunder teammates. He and his wife, who were both from Eastern Europe, handed us the gift over the thumping of the DJ, shouting, "Elephants are lucky!"

I had put them on the shelf here in the basement because there wasn't a good place for them anywhere else in our house; they didn't match the large Costa Rican ceramic pieces that perched on other shelves and on top of our entertainment center in our living room. But now I regret that. I never should have snubbed luck.

I turn back to the computer and read that the blood vessels in a preemie brain are fragile, vulnerable to blood flow and oxygen levels. Fluctuations in flow and oxygen can cause them to rupture, leaking blood into the ventricles and surrounding tissue. Most IVH, one Web site says, occurs within a few days of birth. It's "very unlikely to occur again at a later date." But Stella's first scan, just after she was extubated, was clear. This bleed happened later.

The symptoms of IVH can include:

- breathing pauses (apnea)
- decreased muscle tone
- decreased reflexes
- excessive sleep
- lethargy
- weak suck

These are also the symptoms of sepsis. Stella has exhibited all of these in the last week, and I wonder if the bleed occurred before she developed sepsis. Or perhaps it was a result of it. I don't know if it's possible for sepsis to cause IVH. I also wonder if the IVH is one of the reasons that Stella is having so much trouble nursing now. I want to know the exact moment that the blood vessels in my daughter's brain ruptured, and I want to know why. I realize these questions can't be answered by a Web site, but I can't stop reading.

I learn that there are four grades of IVH:

- Grade 1 – bleeding occurs in the area of the ventricles
- Grade 2 – bleeding also occurs inside the ventricles
- Grade 3 – ventricles are enlarged by the blood
- Grade 4 – bleeding occurs in the brain tissue around the ventricles

I take a deep breath and read again that in a Grade 1 IVH, bleeding is on or near the ventricles but not inside them. Thank God. Maybe the elephants did their work from down here, hidden away on the top shelf. I read that a mild IVH is like a bruise; an infant's system will reabsorb the blood over several weeks. Could Stella's bleed have been worse than it appears now because she's already reabsorbed some of the blood?

Grade 3 and 4 bleeds can cause cerebral palsy and hydrocephalus, and sometimes a shunt needs to be placed in the baby's skull to drain the blood-tainted cerebral spinal fluid. Oh, God, like Noah. He had a shunt put in last week. Oh, Amy. My eyes fill with tears.

I'm suddenly overwhelmed with information, by the bleeding in my daughter's brain, and by the fact that I know she was lucky to have only a mild hemorrhage. Fear and gratitude seem to coexist for me in a way they never have before. Even when I'm terrified and aching with uncertainty, I feel the need to remind myself that it could be worse, much worse. This is exhausting.

I decide not to think about any of it until Donny gets home, and I walk upstairs to lie down. But as soon as I'm horizontal, the phone rings, and I answer it because I think it might be either Donny or the hospital. But it's Donny's mom, Patricia.

"Hi," she says in her gravelly smoker's voice. "I've been calling you. Why haven't you called me back?"

I sigh, wishing I had checked caller ID.

"I'm sorry, Patricia." Donny calls his mom every couple of days with updates, but she still leaves three or four messages a day, and I don't have the energy to return her calls. "I've been meaning to call," I lie.

"My friend Harry drove me by the hospital the other day," she says.

The image of Patricia and Harry rumbling down Chicago Avenue in Harry's rusty Cadillac makes my heart gallop. But it's not as if they could get into the Special Care Nursery, as if they could take Stella. I shake my head. It seems as though Harry genuinely cares for Patricia, and he wouldn't be convinced by any of her delusions—if she's having them—into doing anything crazy.

"I wanted to see my granddaughter, but Harry didn't think it was a good idea," Patricia says.

Thank God for Harry.

"I haven't even seen her, you know," she adds.

I do know this, of course. That's how Donny and I want it. I'm grateful that Harry seems to understand this, and I'm also grateful that the Special Care Nursery is locked. Patricia seems to be taking her medication (if she weren't, we'd be getting more than three calls a day), but Donny still thought it would be best to have her wait to meet Stella until we have her home.

Last spring when Patricia went off her medication, she sold (or gave away?) some of her furniture, packed four suitcases, and showed up on my dad's front step. She kept saying to my dad, "Well, I thought I could just live here. You don't need all this space, do you?" Dad called to let me know she was there and then made her breakfast. They were sitting at his kitchen table eating omelets and drinking coffee when I arrived.

I drove her back to her apartment, but she only stayed a week before taking off again, this time to California on a Greyhound bus. An uncle, whom none of us have met, called Donny's brother, Jim, to let him know where she was, and then he put her back on the bus. But when Jim went to meet her at the bus station, she never showed. Somewhere along the way she had changed her ticket, and she took the bus all the way to Manhattan. After more than a week, Jim got a call from Bellevue Hospital's locked ward.

I've wondered about those weeks she was wandering the streets. I hate the thought of her being alone or scared or in danger. I said this aloud to Donny once, and he said brusquely, "I don't want to think about it."

I'm sure it wasn't the first time she'd been on the streets, and I was sorry I'd brought it up. "I'm sorry, sweetie," I'd said, not able to imagine what it felt like to have your mother delusional and homeless. We never learned how Patricia ended up at Bellevue. But eventually, they, too, accompanied her to the bus station, and after another stint at a hospital in St. Paul, she's seemed stable. Still, I don't want her showing up at the hospital unannounced.

"I'm sorry I haven't called," I say again. "And I'm sorry you haven't met Stella yet, but she's been having a hard time, and she's not in the clear yet." I don't even know what this means.

"I'm free tonight. I can come tonight. Harry can drive me," Patricia says in a rush.

"Listen," I say carefully. "I just found out that Stella has had a brain hemorrhage. It's small, but you can't see her tonight. It's just too much to have visitors right now."

"Oh, no," Patricia says. "I'm sorry. I could help. I've been saying the rosary. I say it thirty times a day. Every day I pray for her."

My head is pounding, and all I want is to sleep.

"I know," I say softly. "I know you've been praying. Thank you."

"I say the rosary in the morning and then again at noon and before bed."

I picture Patricia alone in her smoke-filled apartment on bent knees, the rosary beads click clicking through her fingers, over and over again, praying for her granddaughter. I feel a pang of guilt. The least I could let her do is meet Stella. But then I imagine her loud voice booming across the Special Care Nursery. I imagine Stella breathing in the smoke on her clothes. "I'm sorry, Patricia," I say. "I promise that as soon as Stella comes home, you can come see her, okay? But today is not a good day."

"Okay," she says, and I know she's disappointed. "I love you."

"I love you, too," I say, and hang up. When I lie back down on the bed, I try to close my eyes, but I keep seeing Dr. Lanning's drawing of Stella's brain—the lima bean ventricles, the swirl of ink. I finally throw back the comforter and go downstairs to water the plants, which I've been neglecting. I don't even remember the last time I watered them.

I carry the orchids to the kitchen sink. Then I carefully spray the cattleya, which is still in bloom. I'm reassured by its fragrant, orange-yellow blossoms. When I spray its petals, the kitchen fills with its delicate sweetness. I inhale, close my eyes, and imagine being in a tropical forest somewhere—Brazil or Venezuela—surrounded by a thousand cattleyas clinging to tree trunks and craggy rocks. I imagine breathing in warm, humid air and being enveloped by lush green foliage and the caw of tropical birds. I imagine turning my head up to stare into a sliver of blue sky visible through a break in the canopy.

I'm not sure why this image calms me, but it does. I finish watering the plants and then begin to clean, throwing out the vases of dead flowers that line the hutch in the dining room. I vacuum the whole house and go through all of our mail, which had grown into a messy pile on our dining room table. My mother has always said that "cleaning is clarifying," and today at least this seems to be true. The bleed in Stella's brain hasn't changed the fact that I'm her mother, and it hasn't changed the fact that our goal is getting her home.

That night, when Donny and I are at the hospital, Stella is lethargic, and we can't keep her awake. Donny touches her cheek with his thumb, staring down at her as if he'll be able to see the blood on her ventricles if he just looks hard enough. Finally he says, "Do you think it happened when she got the infection?"

I had been wondering the same thing, of course, but I just say, "Do you think they're connected?"

"Could sepsis cause the bleeding?"

"Maybe when she went back on oxygen?"

We've taken to responding to each other's questions with more questions—some kind of Socratic method that we've inadvertently adopted in the face of all these unknowns. This should be annoying, but somehow it's not.

We take turns holding Stella, who seems especially small and vulnerable tonight. She refuses to latch on. She falls asleep as soon as we rouse her. It's not as if the day has been too much for her; she slept through the whole conversation with Dr. Lanning and wouldn't have understood the ramifications even if she'd been awake. But still, she seems so tired that it's easy to imagine she's overwhelmed.

Martha comes over to see how it's going.

"She's exhausted," I say. "This isn't normal for her."

"She's okay," Martha says, smiling, and for a moment I think I've been hasty in my judgment of her. But then she adds, "She was awake all afternoon. Nursing might have gone better if you'd been here for the three o'clock feeding."

I glare at her, and as she walks away, I can feel my dislike kindling into hatred, sharp and flinty in my chest.

After forty-five minutes, Donny and I leave the hospital and drive to a Chinese restaurant on Nicollet Avenue, where we're meeting my mom and Karl for dinner. As soon as I sit down, I order a glass of cabernet.

"How was Stella tonight?" my mom asks.

"Shitty day," I say. Then I blurt out everything I was told and everything I read about IVH. Mom and Karl are both looking back and forth between me and Donny with tears in their eyes.

I take a gulp of wine, which the waitress has put down next to me. It gives me the shivers, the tannins thick on my tongue. My mom wipes her eyes with her napkin, but I'm done crying for the day. I look past Mom and Karl to the fluorescent blue and yellow fish darting in and out of plastic castles in the huge fish tank behind our table. The light in the tank is the same color as a phototherapy light. I bet the fish hate it.

"What does this mean?" Mom asks.

"We don't know," Donny says.

We're all quiet then, and Karl finally asks Donny how school is going. I'm grateful that he's changed the subject.

My mom keeps watching me though, so I down my glass of wine and order another one before we've even received our appetizers. Soon I feel light-headed, and I eat and eat, suddenly famished. When we get home, I pump and pour my alcohol-rich milk down the bathtub drain. *Pump and dump. Bye-bye, milky.* I start to giggle as I lean over the edge of the bathtub, my thumb stuck in one of the plastic breast shields.

Donny comes in to brush his teeth. "Are you drunky skunky?"

"You're a skunk," I say and start giggling again. And I realize how easy it would be if this—drinking and giggling and not thinking of anything else—were my life.

28

THE NEXT MORNING, I HAVE A HEADACHE. DONNY comes in before he leaves and gives me a kiss. "How are you feeling?"

"Headache," I say. "What a lightweight."

"I'll say," he says, smiling.

I woke up thinking about the brain bleed and all the questions I still have, but the thought of going in and waiting for Dr. Lanning makes me feel heavy all over. "I might skip the morning feeding and go to book group instead," I say, feeling ashamed that I'm even contemplating this.

"You should," he says. "You don't have to meet the lactation person until noon, right?"

I nod, relieved that Donny approves of me playing hooky to go to book group. I missed the last two meetings. We meet the second Friday of each month, and the last meeting was just after I had been put on bed rest. That was the Friday that I spent lying down, waiting for Dr. Bradford to call. That was the Friday I went to the hospital, the Friday of high blood pressure and magnesium sulfate. It's hard to believe that was just a month ago.

I'm the youngest in my book group by ten years. My friend Margie, the one who invited me to join, is in her early forties and is the next youngest. Most of the other women are in their sixties, seventies, eighties, and even nineties. We only read women authors, and there is a complicated voting system that we undertake biannually to pick the books for the following six months. We also take turns hosting, and this month it's at Margie's house, so I know she'll have strong decaf coffee and my favorite cheese: Cotswold. I haven't read the book—Ursula LeGuin's *The Left Side of Darkness*—but I want nothing more than to sit with this group of women and listen to them talk about literature.

I drive to Margie's house in Northeast Minneapolis, and when I arrive, I'm greeted with hugs and questions: How is Stella? How are you? Toni, a former literature professor and the facilitator of our group, stands and hugs me tightly. "I've been praying," she says in my ear, which surprises me because I never took her for the praying kind. Janet, who is a nurse, has tears in her eyes, and starts asking me how Stella is feeding and whether she's still getting IV fluids.

"No IV, but she's had a brain bleed, and nursing isn't going well."

"Oh, Kate," she says, but I just shrug. Am I not talking about my own baby?

Toni calls everyone to sit down, so I quickly pour myself a cup of decaf with cream and sugar and heap my plate with fruit and bread and cheese. Then I sit in the corner of Margie's sunny living room, listening to the women in the group describe their reactions to LeGuin. Their words float around me and drift into the sunlight in the middle of the room like particles of dust. I try to grasp the meaning of their words, but it's futile. I can't make sense of them. I finally realize that it doesn't matter what they're saying; it only matters that I'm here, so I let myself relax into the cadence of their voices.

When it's my turn to talk, I admit that I didn't read the book, and I give an update on Stella for those who arrived after I did. "We're having a lot of trouble nursing," I say, as I look from face to concerned face. "And yesterday we found out that she's had a small bleed on the ventricles of her brain." My voice is flat, and I'm sure some of them are thinking I'm being cavalier, but this seems to be the only way I can describe the last month.

They nod, these women who have lived through so much more than I have. Some of them have lost children. I know one has had two children in the NICU and her son is severely disabled.

I shrug. "We'd love to have her home in a week or so."

Someone says, "I hope you're taking notes."

I shake my head. I've thought about it. I took notes when my grandmother Lucille was dying, jotting down details as soon as I got home from the hospital: the way the clear tape on her neck smoothed the wrinkles from her tissue-paper skin; the way her breath smelled like chocolate, sweet and sickly, as her organs began to shut down;

the way her ankles swelled and turned purple in the last days of her life. I thought remembering her death would be a way to somehow honor the long life she had lived. But I haven't been able to take notes with Stella in the hospital. It's as if committing the details of her very short life to paper would somehow release her from her obligations here. It would make it okay for her to die. And I won't do that. I won't make it easier for her to leave me.

"You should write about this," someone echoes.

"Someday," I say quietly.

When I leave Margie's house, I feel sad but full. I know these women don't know how much it meant to me to sit there and let the sound of their voices fill me up. It's as if I was thrown a buoy. And I understand that even when I can't absorb them, words and literature will always be something to which I can cling.

When I get to the Special Care Nursery, I'm relieved to see that Pam is working again. Stella's weight is down a little from yesterday, but Pam shrugs. "She's doing really well, Kate."

The lactation consultant, Anna, comes to Stella's bedside at noon. She smiles and speaks softly, telling me that decreased milk production can be a side effect of using a nipple shield. I actually have to sign a contract acknowledging that she explained this to me. But I don't have any other option. If Stella doesn't get the hang of nursing, it's going to do more than decrease my milk production; it's going to make me insane.

Anna dips the nipple shield in a cup of water and smooths it onto my breast much more gracefully than I did yesterday. Then she drips a little of my pumped milk onto the tip of the shield to entice Stella. And it works. Stella opens her mouth and laps up the milk with her tiny pink tongue, like a kitten.

"Okay," Anna says. "Let's get her to latch on and see what happens." My milk is letting down, and I can see it dribbling from my breast, filling up the nipple shield like a dispenser.

Stella latches on immediately and begins gulping my milk as if she's been starving.

"Bravo!" Anna says.

I stare at Stella—she's nursing!—and then look up at Anna. "Thank you so much," I say, not yet able to believe that this plastic shield might mean the end of Stella's nursing strike.

"I'll be back to check on you in a few minutes," Anna says.

Stella is taking such long drags of my milk that I can even hear her swallowing. She looks up at me with her eyes wide open. She seems to be thinking, "Finally. You got it. The problem was never with *me*."

"Don't patronize me," I whisper, smiling down at her. "You're a difficult girl, aren't you?"

Pam pops around the edge of the screen. "Well?"

"It works," I say, my eyes brimming with tears. But for once, I'm crying because I'm relieved. "It's already been four minutes!"

"I knew it," Pam says, and gives me the thumbs up.

Stella nurses steadily for fifteen minutes, and I feel like a superstar. When she finally pulls off, she flops into a milk coma in my arms as I've seen other babies—regular, full-term babies—do. I press her to my chest, rubbing her back. "Good girl."

I'm holding Stella, rocking her, when Pam walks over with Dr. Brown.

Dr. Brown is back! Thank God. I beam at both of them.

"I hear you're having success with the nipple shield," Dr. Brown says.

"Finally," I say. "She nursed."

"Wonderful!"

Pam nods. "I thought it would help."

Dr. Brown flips through Stella's chart. Then she says, "I see that her brain ultrasound showed a small bleed." She looks up at me.

I nod, immediately sober.

"I hope you're not worried about this."

"I told her you were upset yesterday," Pam adds, glancing from me to Dr. Brown.

"I *was* pretty upset," I admit, "and looking online didn't help."

"Oh, no," Dr. Brown says. "Never go online. You'll scare yourself to death."

"Too late," I say, although I was scared to death before I sat down at my computer. Looking online just didn't help. I touch Stella's forehead with my fingertips.

Dr. Brown tucks Stella's chart under her arm. "No, really. Don't worry about this. It's a very small amount of blood and it will reabsorb into her system, just like a bruise."

"I read that," I say.

"Listen," she says. "You could bring me ten grade-school kids who had bleeds like Stella's and ten who didn't, and I wouldn't be able to tell which ones had had the IVH."

"What about the ADHD and math-processing problems?" I look from Pam to Dr. Brown.

"I would say," Dr. Brown says slowly, "that there is no higher incidence of those issues in children who have had a mild hemorrhage than in children who have had no hemorrhage at all." She smiles then, and her whole face lights up. "Really, please don't worry about this."

I feel myself release the fear I've been clinging to, and I wonder why Dr. Lanning didn't say this to me. But it might not have mattered. I might not have heard her. Dr. Lanning was trying to reassure me yesterday with the drawing, and I couldn't take it in. I couldn't be reassured.

Pam smiles broadly, and I feel an urge to jump up and hug her.

"Thank you," I say. "Thank you both."

"And," Dr. Brown adds, nodding at Stella, "if her nursing continues to go well today and tonight, you might be able to take her home tomorrow."

"Tomorrow?" We get to take her home tomorrow?

I feel a flash of elation before my stomach lurches. This is the moment for which I've been waiting, but for some reason I thought we'd have a couple of days to prepare. I just nursed her for fifteen minutes for the first time, and I'm supposed to take her home? We don't even have a car seat!

"You should plan on staying the night," Dr. Brown says. "We'll have you nurse Stella through the day and night, and if everything goes well, you can take her home."

Pam is giving me the thumbs-up again. "I'll check on the overnight rooms and make sure one is available," she says. "This is wonderful!"

It *is* wonderful, of course. This has been our goal for the last month. I can't wait to spend all day with my daughter, to not have nurses peering over my shoulder. But it's also terrifying. What if we make a mistake? Who will tell us how to fix it? And it feels too sudden. This morning, I assumed she'd be here for another whole week. Now she may go home with us tomorrow? What about the car seat class we were going to take? What about the car seat we still need to buy?

"I'll see you tomorrow," Dr. Brown says, and I nod.

Pam is watching me, and she can probably tell that I'm totally freaked out. She smiles broadly. "It'll be just fine," she says. "Stella will sleep in the overnight room with you, but we'll be just down the hall. And then you'll get to take your baby home!"

"I can't believe it," I say.

When I call Donny from the lounge down the hall, he says the same thing: "I can't believe it. I can't believe it." We're like broken records.

"We don't even have a car seat," he says.

"I know. Can you stop and get one on your way home? And we'll need our toothbrushes and pajamas and clothes, I guess. And maybe someone could drop you off tonight so tomorrow we can ride home together?"

And just like that, it's settled.

Stella nurses well again at three o'clock, and as I hold her against my chest afterward, I rub my thumb over the patch of adhesive that still clings to her dark hair. "You might get to go home with us tomorrow," I whisper. "And then I can hold you all day."

She stirs, pressing her tiny fist into my breast, and I take this to mean she agrees with the plan.

"I'll take you to the coffee shop and you can sleep in your car seat while I read. And then we'll go home and rest on the couch. And when you nap, I'll write." And as I describe the contour of our lives, spreading it before my daughter like a map, I really believe this is how things will be. We'll be free of doctors, nurses, worry. And Stella will slide gracefully into the writing and thinking life I inhabited before she was born.

An hour later, Samantha, a nurse who will be helping us move

Stella into the overnight room, comes over with a stack of papers. "We need to go through this teaching," she says.

I must have a confused look on my face because Samantha says, "We need to make sure you're prepared to take your daughter home, so I'll walk you through some of these safety procedures."

This is the first time I've met Samantha, the first time I've even seen her, so it seems odd and a little uncomfortable that she is suddenly my "teacher." But I need this woman's approval in order to be given the go-ahead for the overnight room, so I pay close attention. She says never to let the baby sleep on her stomach. I nod. Never let the baby sleep in your bed. I nod again. She says we'll have to give Stella two bottles of formula-fortified breast milk and one bottle of iron-fortified breast milk every day.

I grimace and glance down at Stella, who is still asleep in my arms. "So much for getting rid of bottles, huh?"

Samantha gives me a stern look. "She needs those extra vitamins and minerals."

"Oh, I know," I say quickly.

"And, of course," Samantha says, "you'll have to keep Stella inside, away from people, because of RSV."

"RSV?"

"Oh," she says, looking surprised. "Hasn't anyone talked to you about this?"

I shake my head.

"RSV stands for respiratory syncytial virus. It's a virus that acts like a normal cold in adults. But in babies, especially premature babies who've been on ventilators, it can attack the lower respiratory system."

"Oh," I say. "What does that mean?"

Samantha looks irritated with me, her brows bunched together. She must think I'm a terribly dense student. "It means you can't take her out in public. You can't let anyone into your house who might have a cold."

"Oh," I say again. I can't take her out in public?

"Remember," says Samantha, "that a baby's immune system

develops in the last months of a pregnancy. Preemies miss those last weeks in utero, so they have immature immune systems."

I nod, although I don't remember ever learning this. Did I miss that section in the handbook? I must have. But how could I have missed it?

"RSV," says Samantha, "can land a preemie back in the hospital. It could kill her."

And there it is again: the fear like a rock in my belly. But there is also something else there: a dawning realization that even when we get home, Stella's infancy will not be a normal one. "How long inside?" I ask.

Samantha looks totally exasperated.

I'll do it, I want to tell her. Of course I'll do it. I just need to know how long.

"Until the end of the cold and flu season. Through March."

It's October 10. I tick through the months: October, November, December, January, February, March. Six months. No public places. No germs. *Oh, shit.*

I must look stricken because she says, "It's not that bad. People can visit, just not if they have a cold. No one who's sick. Everyone who comes into your house—even if they don't touch your baby—should wash their hands." Samantha looks as if she's about to take a ruler to the back of *my* hand, so I nod quickly. "I understand."

Samantha stares at me for a moment, and then, apparently satisfied that she's scared me into submission, she stands, hands me the folder of teaching material, and leaves. I adjust Stella in my arms, then lean back in the rocker and open the blinds. The sky is pink, and the brick buildings across the street have become fiery red with the last light of day. Just an hour ago I had filled myself with images of walking Stella along West River Parkway and sitting next to her in the coffee shop while I sipped a latte. I thought home would equal normal. Home would be an end to our worries.

How could I have been so stupid? With all of our hand washing and foam spraying over the last month, how could I have not realized that Stella would be quarantined from the world all winter?

Honestly, it hadn't even occurred to me. My focus had been on getting her home. *Make it through this, and you'll be okay.*

I brush the bangs from my eyes and realize that if I had known this from the beginning, I might not have made it through the last month. The daily challenges of navigating the NICU and Special Care Nursery would have paralyzed me. Now, at least I have the good news: Stella is going home. They've just tempered it with the bad: she will *stay* at home. She won't be able to leave, and neither will I.

When Donny gets to the hospital, it's almost seven o'clock. I tell him about the "teaching" and RSV.

He nods. "We'll have to be careful."

He doesn't seem at all surprised by the news, and I wonder if he's known about this all along. Did he read those pages in the handbook that I apparently missed? Or is he just taking this in stride the way he's taken everything else in stride? And why does this annoy me so much?

Samantha walks us down to the overnight room, which is attached to the family lounge. It overlooks western Minneapolis, which spreads before us like a blanket of light. People use this room to make calls during the day, but at night, the couch pulls out into a bed. It seems a little shabby, and I wish I had some bleach wipes so I could scrub everything down.

It's almost eight o'clock when we roll Stella's plastic bassinette out of the Special Care Nursery, past the elevators, and into the overnight room. She's sleeping, so Donny and I sit on the pulled-out bed and watch her. This is the first time since she was born that she's been unplugged. There is no monitor to tell us her heart rate or oxygen level. It's as if she's missing a limb.

I glance at Donny. "What if she stops breathing in the middle of the night?"

He looks scared, as well. "What if we fall asleep and something happens? Couldn't they have given us one of those little alarms? A portable monitor?"

"Right," I say. "And don't you think it's too cold in here?"

Donny nods, and then we sit silently side by side, staring at our daughter. She's wrapped in fleece blankets, sleeping, oblivious.

Finally, I get up and look over the chart on which we're supposed to record how frequently and for how long Stella nurses, and when she pees and poops. We have to save all of her dirty diapers in a plastic bag. They will be weighed in the morning to see if her "output" is normal. If she's peed enough, it means she's gotten enough milk. So the weighing is more than just weighing; it's a verdict. If she got enough milk, we get to take her home. If she didn't, we won't.

We don't sleep at all that night, of course. Each time Stella shifts or cries out, we both leap out of bed. I'm in and out of the bathroom a dozen times, washing my hands, wetting the nipple shield, trying to adhere it to my breast. Samantha said that I should nurse Stella "on demand," whenever she seems hungry. But we're not even sure what hungry looks like, so every time she fusses, pressing against her burrito wrap, I pick her up. I end up nursing her at 10:00 p.m, midnight, and 1:00 a.m.

"Do you think she's getting enough?" Donny asks from the bed, where his head is propped in his hand.

"I've no idea," I say. I'm exhausted but also wide awake in that sizzling, wired sort of way.

Stella finally settles back into her bassinette, but my breasts are aching with milk, so I walk down the hall to pump. Then I buzz the nursery and put the small jars of my labeled milk in the refrigerator. It's disorienting to be in the nursery without Stella. Wires hang down from the monitor into the gaping space where her bassinette should be as if she's gone missing.

I turn and hurry back to the overnight room, where Donny is dozing with Stella in the rocker. She's pressed to his bare chest, sleeping. His arms hold her tightly, but his head is thrown back, his mouth open.

I've walked in on the most intimate of scenes—a sleeping father holding his sleeping daughter—and I feel a swell of love for both of them. I realize that I've spent so much time worrying about when I would feel like a mother that I had forgotten to think of Donny as a father. But maybe that's because he slipped into the role effortlessly, transforming into a dad as soon as Stella was pulled from me.

I lean against the door frame and watch them sleep, and then I walk to the window and stare out at the city lights that stretch as far as I can see. It's the middle of the night, and here we are, alone with our daughter for the first time since she was born, four weeks ago. Tears catch in my throat. This month shouldn't have existed for Stella; she should still be inside me. And I can almost feel this time—these first weeks of her life—float up and vanish into the dark sky outside the window. I'm tempted to let them go. *This never happened.*

But when I look down at Donny, holding our daughter to his chest, I know I can't do that. These weeks *did* exist—for her, for us—and I can't pretend they didn't.

29

On Saturday morning, Stella weighs four pounds seven ounces, down an ounce. But apparently her diapers from the night before weighed enough, so Dr. Brown comes over with a smile and says, "Well, today is the day."

And then there is a rush to sign papers. A nurse walks out to the parking lot with Donny to make sure he installed the car seat base properly. Pam packs all the bottles of my pumped milk in a cardboard box. She fills plastic hospital bags with tiny diapers, miniature bottles, extra pacifiers, and the thermometers, salves, and lotions that they used on Stella over the last month.

"Are you sure?" I ask.

Pam laughs. "We can't reuse them, and you paid for everything anyway."

Or our insurance company did. Thank God for insurance. If we didn't have health insurance, we would owe upward of a hundred thousand dollars by now.

Pam gives me a tight hug, and when she pulls away, I say, "Thank you so much for everything. Thank you for believing me about the bottles, for the nipple shield." I know I'm not conveying the degree of my gratitude.

"You guys are going to do just fine," she says. "You're great parents."

Again, I'm not sure how she's decided this, so I just shrug. Donny goes to get the car, and I hug Pam again. Then I walk out of the nursery for the last time, carrying the car seat in which Stella has been wedged with rolled-up washcloths and receiving blankets. Car seats are made for babies who are at least six pounds, so Pam showed me how to add this reinforcement to keep Stella from sliding around and choking on the restraints.

A hospital aide pushes a cart overflowing with our stuff. Together we ride down the elevator, walk through the crowded hallways of the hospital, and wait at the entrance for Donny. I sit down on a bench and turn the car seat toward me, trying to shield Stella from the germs that I can almost see swirling around us.

And then Donny pulls our Honda Civic up to the hospital entrance, and we're rushing to the car in the rain. More thank-yous to the hospital aide, and then we are driving down Twenty-eighth Street, just as we have dozens of times over the last few weeks. But this time Stella is with us. She is twenty-eight days old, and she is coming home.

Rain pelts the windows, and the wipers hum over the windshield. I lean over her in the back seat, trying to loosen the seat straps, which I worry are too tight. We hit a pothole and she startles, her eyes opening and shutting again.

"Can't you drive more slowly?"

"I'm only going twenty-five," Donny says, exasperated.

"What if she stops breathing?"

"She'll be fine, Kate. She's fine." Donny rarely calls me Kate, so I know he's irritated. But honestly, can't he tell how bumpy it is?

Stella's face is mottled, and I'm worried she *has* stopped breathing, so I rub her cheek with my thumb until she opens her eyes. When she closes them again, I rub her cheek again. "Wake up, baby. Wake up." The poor thing is going to need to stay awake all the time so I know she's still alive.

At home, we crank the heat up and turn on all the lights downstairs so it's cozy for Stella, so she knows there is something other than fluorescent lights, white walls, and shiny floors in the world. Then we unstrap her from her car seat and walk her through the house: this is the kitchen, we say, this is the dining room, this is the living room. We walk upstairs, into our bedroom and then hers. "Here is your crib," I say, "and the chair where I'll nurse you and the changing table. Do you like it?" I ask, and she opens her eyes and stretches her tiny arm into the air.

"Me too," I say. "Your very own room."

"What now?" I ask Donny when we're back downstairs. We can do anything we want (so long as we stay in our house, away from people). No one is watching us or making notes in Stella's chart about what kind of parents we are.

"Let's take a nap," Donny says, and he leans back on the couch with Stella on his chest. He falls asleep instantly, but I just lie next to him, watching Stella's back rise and fall, rise and fall. I know this kind of vigilance will be difficult for me to abandon. I don't know why I thought I could leave that habit at the hospital.

At three o'clock Donny pulls on his sweats and a windbreaker to go coach a high school soccer game. It's still raining outside, and it seems ridiculous that he has to go out in that weather, especially when Stella is finally home, but he does, and I'm petrified when he shuts the door behind him.

The house is quiet except for the rain against the windows. I look down at Stella in my arms and run my finger down the slope of her tiny nose. This is how it's supposed to be: a mother and infant cuddled together inside a warm house. It should be the most natural thing in the world. All she needs is my milk, my arms holding her, my voice comforting her. But this is the first time I've been alone with her since she was born, and it doesn't feel at all natural. I have that fluttery, restless feeling I experience the first few days of every vacation. It always takes me a while to unwind. But motherhood isn't exactly a vacation, and I wonder if I'll ever feel at ease in this role.

Stella begins to cry, so I nurse her for seven minutes and record it on the chart. I change her diaper and record that on her chart, as well. Then I lie back down with her and try to sleep the way Donny slept with her, but I can't hold her and fall asleep. If I relax enough to let myself drift into dreams, I'm sure my arms will go slack and I'll drop her.

Finally I pull our borrowed Moses basket next to the couch, wrap Stella like a burrito, and lay her down. I close my eyes and fall asleep instantly, startle awake to check on Stella, sleep then wake, sleep and wake. Somehow after an hour of this I still feel more rested.

When Donny comes home, he's shivering, so we heat up the soup that my friend Leslie left on our porch. I nurse and pump, and we try to figure out where Stella should sleep. She could sleep in the Moses basket in our room, but if we put it on the floor, it will be too drafty. Her crib is far too big for her, so we could put the basket inside the crib in her room, but neither of us feels comfortable having her sleep so far away from us.

"I wish we had a hospital monitor," Donny says, and I'm relieved that I'm not the only one that craves this kind of reassurance.

"Just for a couple of weeks. Is that too much to ask?"

Finally, Donny suggests moving her crib into our room. Then she can sleep inside the basket inside the crib, and she'll be at the foot of our bed so we can keep an eye on her.

"Perfect," I say.

But when Donny tries to pull the crib into the hallway from Stella's room, it gets stuck in the doorway. "Shit," he says. "It won't fit." He ends up disassembling it and reassembling it in our room. I sit on our bed holding Stella, who sleeps through the hoopla.

When we finally get Stella situated in the basket inside the crib, it's eleven o'clock. Donny and I both fall into bed. But as soon as I turn off the light, Stella begins making gurgling sounds. I get out of bed again and lean over her, slipping the round hospital pacifier into her mouth. She sucks and sucks, her eyes closed, so I climb back into bed. Then she starts crying. I just fed her an hour ago, but I'm supposed to feed her whenever she's hungry. The sad thing is that I don't know which cries are hungry cries and which are uncomfortable or tired cries. All of her feedings at the hospital were timed and measured, and I miss that reliability.

I take her into her room, pluck the nipple shield from the nursing station, and wet it in the bathroom with Stella in my arms. Back in her room, I adhere the nipple shield and bring Stella to my breast. She nurses for three minutes before falling asleep. I rub her cheek and she begins nursing again, but only for a few seconds before she pulls off.

At this rate, we'll be up all night. But I can handle that. At least we're home. No one is telling me what to do or when to do it. I can say anything to Stella here. I can even sing to her without feeling self-conscious that the nurses are listening or worrying that I'm bothering another family.

When my sisters and I were little and Dad tucked us into bed, he would sing an old gospel song in a wavering voice that I still love. I haven't thought of that song for years, but it seems like just the thing for tonight, Stella's first night home.

"Brighten the corner where you are," I start, my own voice too high. I start again: "Brighten the corner where you are, someone far from harbor you may guide across the bar, brighten the corner where you are." These are the only lines I remember, so I sing them over and over. It's the middle of the night, and it's just she and I. I rub my thumb against her cheek, and when she opens her dark eyes and stares up at me, I feel almost dizzy with love. "It's me," I say. "It's your mama, and I love you."

When she closes her eyes again, I put her back in her crib and climb into bed. I fall asleep in less than a minute but then start awake when Stella cries out. Donny gets up and slips the pacifier into her mouth. In another half hour, she's crying, and I have her in my arms again, trying to get her to latch on.

The nurses said to make sure to feed her every two to three hours, "two to three hours from the start of one feeding to the start of the next." But if it takes Stella an hour and fifteen minutes to nurse—to actively nurse for fifteen minutes—I may have only forty-five minutes between the end of one feeding and the beginning of the next. So I'm like a marionette, up and down. I'm wetting and rewetting the nipple shield and holding my tiny baby with aching arms.

Finally, Donny gets up at five and takes Stella downstairs to give her one of the fortified bottles. And at eight we call my mom, who is at our door in a half hour. She washes her hands, and I pass Stella into her arms. This is the first time my mom has held Stella, and she's beaming, tears in her eyes. Donny and I stumble back upstairs. I sleep for an hour but jump up when I hear Stella's thin cries. "Where is the baby?" I say, desperate and disoriented, lurching from bed as if I've somehow misplaced her. I'm halfway downstairs before I remember that my mom is here holding her.

"I was just going to warm a bottle," Mom says, looking up.

"I can feed her," I say. "I can do it." But I feel light-headed, and I have to sit down on the stairs until it passes.

"You're exhausted," Mom says.

"This is how it's going to be, isn't it?"

My mom nods.

Sunday night, Stella is awake most of the night. She sleeps in my arms when I try to nurse her, but as soon as I put her down, she wakes up. How can this be? She seemed to sleep all the time at the hospital. She must understand that now that we're home and free from the strict schedule imposed by the nurses, she's the boss. I'm actually awake from one o'clock on, and when Donny leaves for work on Monday morning, I almost start to cry. When he closes the front door behind him, I have a sudden urge to pound on the window and yell, "Don't leave me! Please don't leave me!"

The day is a slow blur of pumping and nursing and crying and changing diapers. If I don't pump, my breasts become painfully hard. I know my body is supposed to adjust my milk production to meet Stella's needs, but since we must give her fortified bottles in addition to breastfeeding, I have to make sure I'm pumping and storing additional milk. But as soon as I put Stella down in the bassinette to pump, she begins to scream, and her angry, high-pitched wail seems to fill every corner of our tiny house. I fumble with the pump pieces, and it's difficult for me to catch my breath. I finally decide to wait to pump until Rachel comes over this afternoon after her class.

I walk Stella around the dining room table, I try to nurse her, and when she falls asleep in my arms, I stare down at her and marvel at the fact that she's my daughter. *I'm a mother,* I say to myself over and over again, wondering whether this feeling of disbelief will ever fade.

When Rachel arrives I pump and then wash the dishes while Rachel holds Stella. "Why don't you go take a nap?" she asks. "We're fine."

"I know," I say. But I don't want to be alone, so I just sit next to Rachel and she tells me about her day, her classes, and the other people in her program. She's doing research on an endangered minnow, the Topeka shiner, and ordinarily, details about the habitat of this minnow and the environmental incentives offered to farmers to help protect the streams (and thus the Topeka shiner) on their land would bore me, but today I'll listen to anything. I just want her to keep talking.

We were told to schedule a checkup with our pediatrician, Dr. Levine, within a week of Stella's discharge, but Dr. Levine is rounding at the hospital our first week home, so we schedule an appointment with one of his colleagues for Thursday.

Children's Clinic is in the same building as the NICU, and my heart begins to pound wildly as we drive down Twenty-sixth Street. *This is different,* I remind myself, looking down at Stella in her car seat. Luckily, Donny has two days off for teacher workshops, so he's going with us to the appointment, but I feel panicky when he drops me and Stella off at the hospital's main entrance. *We're not going to the NICU,* I whisper. *We're just going to the clinic.*

I walk with Stella through the wide glass doors into the hospital. But the smell—the disinfectant, the cafeteria food being consumed somewhere nearby, the worry, the worry, the worry—makes me feel dizzy. Years from now, I'll read an article in the *New York Times* about the high percentage of preemie parents who end up with symptoms of post-traumatic stress disorder as a result of weeks or months in the NICU, and I'll understand that the sinking in my stomach each time I drove down Twenty-sixth Street was probably a tinge of post-traumatic stress—not stress on the same level as a soldier returning from war, but stress nonetheless.

I carry the car seat into the elevator and, with the sleeve of my shirt pulled over my thumb, punch three instead of two. *This is totally different. It's just a doctor's appointment.* When I walk into the clinic, I tell the receptionist that Stella was a preemie. On the phone I had been told that all I had to do was utter these magic words and we would be led to a room right away so Stella wouldn't be exposed to the petri dish of the waiting room. But this receptionist seems to have missed the meeting in which Preemie Protocol was covered, and she says, "It'll just be a few minutes."

I scan the room for a chair as far away as possible from the other parents and children, but when I sit down in a chair at the end of the row with the car seat balanced on my knees, a man and a little girl come over and sit next to us. I shoot out of my seat before the girl has a chance to hack on us—she's coughing, coughing, coughing—and I end up with my back to the rest of the patients, the car seat balanced between my belly and the wall. I'm sure I look insane, but I don't care.

Donny finds me against the wall and raises his eyebrows, but I just shrug. Finally we're called into an examination room and Dr. Nelson, Dr. Levine's colleague, comes in. She's in her fifties and looks as if she had been a hippie in her younger days. She greets us with a warm smile. "So," she says, bending down to peer into the car seat, "this is Stella."

She holds up two sheets of paper. "Her chart hasn't been transferred yet, so I asked the NICU for a summary. I'll just read it aloud to make sure I'm not missing anything."

We nod, and she begins reading the summarized chart aloud: premature birth via cesarean due to preeclampsia. Yes. Oxygen needs at six hours of age. Respiratory distress at thirty-five hours of age. Yes. Transferred to the NICU and intubated, given two doses of Survanta. On ventilator for three days. Yes. Hyperbilirubinemia treated with phototherapy lights for seven days. Yes. Anemia. Never transfused, but needs a multivitamin with iron daily. Yes. Had apnea episodes with coagulase-negative staph sepsis on September 30. Sepsis treated with antibiotics. Yes. Grade 1 intraventricular hemorrhage on October 8 ultrasound. Yes. Discharged on October 11 at four weeks old.

"That's it," I say, amazed by how clinical Stella's first weeks sound when pared down to her medical needs and treatments with no mention of how it all *felt*.

"So," Dr. Nelson says, looking up at us. "You've had a rocky start."

Donny laughs. "You could say that."

Dr. Nelson smiles. "Well, let's take a look at this little darling."

The room is chilly, and after we undress Stella she curls into a little ball on the examining table. She definitely still looks fetal, but she's supposed to be inside me for another three weeks, so I guess that makes sense.

Dr. Nelson unrolls Stella, presses her abdomen, and runs her fingers over her skull. She listens to her heart and checks her ears and eyes. "She's small, of course," Dr. Nelson says. "She's only gained three ounces since Saturday. But she looks great." She recommends that we get monthly Synagis shots to help protect Stella from RSV. And she says she'll get us a referral to have a nurse come to our house twice a week to weigh Stella. "I want to keep an eye on how she's gaining, and this way you won't have to keep bringing her into this germ factory."

We nod and dress Stella, relieved for the extra protection against RSV.

I only begin to relax when we are back in the car, driving away from Children's. I realize that when I'm inside the hospital walls—even if we're just in the clinic—Stella somehow feels less like our baby, our daughter. As if a piece of her still belongs to the hospital. As if someone could stop us and take her back. *She'd be better off here. We'll just keep her for another week or so.* The thought makes me shudder.

On Friday, Donny insists that we go out on a date. "We need this," he says, and I have to agree. The last week at home has been harder on us than the previous weeks going back and forth to and from the hospital. We're both tired, which makes us snap at each other.

It seems horrible to leave Stella, who is barely four and a half pounds, while we go out for a glass of wine, but Rachel quickly volunteers to babysit. When she comes over, I go over the list on the table: give Stella a bottle with the iron supplement; another bottle, thirty ccs of straight breast milk, an hour later; keep her warm. I put the thermometer and a list of emergency phone numbers on the table, as well.

"We'll be fine," Rachel says when I pause at the front door, ready to call it off.

"We have the cell phone," I say for the third time.

"I know. I have the number, remember?" She's holding Stella in her arms. "We'll be just fine. Go."

"Okay," I say, and Donny pulls me out the door.

We start driving toward Lucia's Wine Bar in Uptown without having to discuss it. It's been our go-to spot since we started dating, the place we fell in love five years earlier. We would meet there a couple of nights a week after Donny's soccer practice and my shift at the café in St. Paul where I waited tables. We were in the early stage of our relationship, and those evenings were full of wine and crème brûlées and the sizzling spark of possibility. It's where we went the night we got engaged, tipsy and laughing, glasses of champagne shimmering between our fingertips. And now it's the place we'll go to try to unite us as parents.

When we get to Lucia's, it's packed. We hover at the bar until a table in the corner opens up, and we swoop in on it. We each order a glass of wine, and Donny puts the cell phone on the table between us so we can hear it ring if Rachel calls.

"Is it horrible that we're here?" I ask. "Do you think Rachel is okay?"

"She's fine," Donny says, covering my hand with his own. "We need this." Then he looks at me hard, as if he can glare me into being more laid-back.

"I know," I say. "But it feels weird. Don't you feel like an imposter?"

Donny shakes his head. "We still need to go out."

But I feel out of place, as if we're trying to inhabit a world to which we no longer belong, a world of restaurants and wine and new love. Not to mention the money, which we shouldn't be spending, especially since I won't be getting my teaching stipend after my six-week maternity leave ends. But I try not to think about that.

"Do you miss teaching?" Donny asks. Clearly, he is determined to make this a real date with real conversation, so I give myself a mental shake.

"I miss being *able* to teach," I say. "I'm not capable of standing up in front of students right now. My brain has been scrambled. I wouldn't make any sense."

"I know what you mean," Donny says. He has been leaving for work early and prepping five science lessons in the hour before school starts. I know having six grade levels rotate through his room every day isn't what he had in mind when he went into teaching. He's not with any of the students long enough to really connect with them.

"Maybe next year you'll have your own class."

He shrugs. "Maybe."

After an hour and a half at Lucia's, my breasts feel as if they'll explode, and I'm ready to go home. We hold hands as we walk into the crisp fall air.

"Do you want to walk a little?" Donny asks.

"I think we should go," I say, even though I know Donny is trying to extend the night. "I feel bad for leaving Stella so long. For leaving Rachel on her own."

"Okay," he says.

When we get home, Rachel is holding Stella, who is wrapped in three fleece blankets. They are both sweating profusely.

On Saturday afternoon, Jim brings Patricia over to meet Stella. They both wash their hands and then sit down on the loveseat. The scent of stale smoke settles in our living room, but I just shrug when Donny looks at me. It's not as if we can ask her to change. None of our clothes would fit her anyway. Besides, she's beaming. She's waited so long for this.

I pass Stella's swaddled body into her outstretched arms, and Patricia laughs an uncomfortable laugh. "Finally," she says. "I finally get to meet my granddaughter." There are tears in her eyes, and I reach for Donny's hand. I imagine that holding Stella brings back memories of holding her own four children. I imagine it also brings back everything that came later—her disappearance from their lives, all those years she missed.

I snap a photo. In it, Stella's sunken cheeks are still those of a preemie. She sucks on the big, green hospital pacifier. But she is looking up at her grandmother, and Patricia is smiling widely at the camera.

It's a relief to have Donny around for the long weekend. We pass Stella back and forth. We take turns sleeping. We float through the days in quiet exhaustion. But when the week starts again and Donny is gone all day teaching and coaching, I feel myself begin to unravel. And perhaps Stella senses the slow fraying of my nerves, and this is why she stops nursing. Or perhaps her nursing strike is the thing responsible for the unraveling. I can't figure out if one thing precipitates the other.

Sometimes she latches on right away. Other times she fusses and shakes her head and tries to squirm away. I try nursing her without the nipple shield, and she screams. I drag the bassinette into her room and place her in it so I can pump, and she becomes a coil of bright red fury, screaming screaming screaming. I fit the pump pieces together as fast as I can, flip the switch, and try to focus on the whoosh of the pump, which next to Stella's wails is barely audible, no more than the rustling of grass in the midst of a hurricane.

If it's the middle of the night, sometimes I'll call out for Donny, who could sleep through an earthquake at this point. I yell for him until my voice penetrates his dreams, and he comes in and rocks Stella in his arms as I pump. But if it's a weekday, I either grit my teeth and try to weather her wails or I pump until I have a few ounces of milk, then pour it into one of the tiny hospital bottles that Stella loves, and feed her the bottle with my left hand as I continue to pump my right breast.

She is clearly hungry, but nursing is becoming more and more difficult. When I complain to Donny about it, he says, "Well, stop it then."

This isn't what I want to hear, and I say, "I can't. Her immunity." It's the least I can do for her after leaving her in the hospital every night for a month, after everything she's been through. And how many times was I told in the hospital that preemies needed the nutrients in breast milk even more than full-term babies? If I stop now, I'll feel like less of a mother. I'll feel like a failure.

"And anyway," I add, "we can't afford formula. It's too expensive." There is no way we'd be able to afford the extra couple hundred dollars a month for preemie formula.

"She prefers bottles anyway," Donny says.

"She does not!" I snap, but I know he's right; Stella *sucks the bottles down in five minutes,* just as she had at the hospital. But the thought of pumping five times a day while she screams is unbearable.

I remember how condescending I was about breastfeeding before I tried it, before I was even pregnant. I have a friend who nursed her first baby for five or six weeks. When I asked her why she had stopped, she said it took too much time. "It was just too hard," she said.

She wasn't working outside the home, and I remember wondering what else she needed to do. *How could you not do what is best for your baby? That's your job.* I'm ashamed now that I thought this. How could I have been so superior? I hope she hadn't been able to read the disdain in my face.

Stella has been home a week and a half when we get our first visit from the home care nurse, Gloria. I'm annoyed when she arrives forty-five minutes late, but my irritation dissolves when I realize how relieved I am to have another adult in the house in the middle of the day. Gloria is tall and tidy-looking, wearing a blouse and a long, flowered skirt. As she washes her hands in the kitchen, I look around our cluttered living room and then down at my sweatpants, which are stained with spit-up. I look like hell.

But when Gloria comes back into the room, she just smiles and pulls a scale from her black briefcase.

I undress Stella and place her, squirming, on the scale.

"Four pounds twelve ounces," Gloria says.

"Oh, no," I say. "That's only two ounces since last week." Average weight gain for infants is four to seven ounces a week.

Gloria hands Stella back to me and rubs antibacterial gel into her hands. "How is she nursing?"

I bite my lip. "Not very well. She was given bottles in the hospital, and ever since then we've had problems. I try using a nipple shield, but it doesn't always work. And it takes an hour for her to actively nurse for fifteen minutes. So sometimes I pump and give her a bottle, but she cries whenever I put her down." I feel exhausted just telling Gloria about it.

Gloria smiles. "It takes so long to get in the swing of nursing, but she'll catch on."

"I hope so," I say.

"Do you have any other questions for me?" Gloria asks.

"I do, actually." I pull the paper from my pocket and look down at my list of questions:

My milk supply seems to be decreasing. What can I do?
Will my early milk (frozen while I was still in the hospital) have enough mag sulfate in it to affect Stella if she drinks it now?
Is there anything we can do for her gas?
How many ccs should she be getting at each bottle feeding?
I can't seem to burp her. Help!
Why does she scream so much?

I tick through my questions, and Gloria tries to answer each of them. She calls the pharmacist to ask about the mag sulfate, and he says my milk should be fine. She takes Stella from my arms, balances her on her knee with her hand cupping Stella's chest, and whacks her back until Stella lets out a small burp.

"That looks simple enough," I say, unclear now how I didn't figure that out.

Gloria siphons the snot from Stella's nose with a rubber bulb and mentions a few medications that might reduce Stella's gassy squirming. "And probably no more than forty ccs of milk per bottle feeding."

I jot notes on my sheet of paper, and Gloria starts packing up her things. She's already been here for an hour, but I'm not ready for her to go. I try to think of another question that will keep her here, delaying the long, lonely afternoon that stretches before me. But I've got nothing. "Well, thank you," I finally say.

She smiles and tilts her head. "Honey, when was the last time you left the house?"

"I don't know," I say slowly. Time has become indistinct. Every day runs into every other day. I don't even know when I last showered. "Maybe five days," I say.

Gloria rolls her eyes. "Honey, you need to get outside. No wonder you feel crazy. You bundle that baby up and put her in the stroller and walk around the block."

Did I say I felt crazy? Am I acting crazy? I look at the thermometer outside the living room window. It's only forty degrees. Didn't the nurse at the hospital say not to let her get a chill? Isn't forty degrees too cold for Stella?

"I'm fine," I say, glancing around the living room, taking in the piles of folded burp cloths and infant diapers. "Really."

Gloria walks over to me and puts a hand on each of my shoulders. I feel like I'm in grade school and I've just been sent to the principal's office (not that that ever happened).

"Honey," she says, "I'm not leaving until you promise me you'll take a walk."

I almost start to laugh because she just revealed the trick for keeping her here longer. *I don't have to promise anything,* I almost say, but then I really would seem crazy. So instead I nod. If she says it's safe, it must be safe, right? "Okay, yes. I guess some fresh air would be good."

"Girl, you need to get out of the house."

A half hour later, as I push a bundled-up Stella down the block toward the park in her covered stroller, the neighborhood is quiet, the sky gray, the air crisp. It doesn't feel like our neighborhood yet because I haven't spent any time exploring it. I think this is actually the first time I've really looked at the houses lining our street. They all seem deserted, their windows dark. The people who inhabit them must be off at work or school. At least there is no one to see me stop every few feet and peer into the darkness of the closed stroller to make sure Stella is still okay. I'm sure I look like a lunatic.

It takes me twenty minutes to walk around the block, but I do feel a little better for the fresh air. At home, I make myself some tea and turn on all the lights. "This isn't so bad, is it?" I say to Stella, who squirms in my arms.

I don't know how I'm functioning on as little sleep as I'm getting. Before—before pregnancy, before Stella—I used to get eight or nine hours a night, preferably nine. Now I sometimes get three or four, but these are broken into thirty- or forty-five-minute increments. Stella sleeps for the longest stretches if she's on my chest or Donny's chest, but whoever is holding her doesn't really sleep then. I know that Samantha, the nurse from our last night in the hospital, would have a conniption if she knew we were doing this, but what else can we do?

And even on the rare occasions when Stella is asleep in her bassinette and I could actually sleep deeply, I can't; I feel as though I'm always awake. I dream that she's stopped breathing. I dream that she's in our bed and that I've rolled over on her. I jolt up in bed, my arms swinging out, sweeping the bed. But I can't find her. I lunge at Donny. "Where is she? Where's Stella?"

"She's sleeping," he snaps, irritated that I've woken him as well.

Relief. She's in her bassinette. But it's not really relief, not yet. Because why isn't she crying, demanding I hold her? I slide from bed and stand above her. I lean down and put my ear close to her mouth and listen for her breath. I wait until I can feel her warm exhalations on my cheek before climbing back in bed. This happens a half dozen times a night. Up and down, up and down. I can't seem to squelch the fear that something else is going to happen to her. It feels as if we have her on borrowed time.

Gloria comes twice a week to weigh Stella, who is gaining slowly, and Rachel comes over a couple of days a week after her classes. She takes the bus straight from the university and holds Stella while I wash dishes. I don't know how she's getting all her homework and research done with all the time she's spending at our house, but she just shrugs when I ask. "I'm managing fine," she says, looking down at Stella. "And I'd rather be here." That she loves Stella so much makes me love her even more. And Stella seems calmer when Rachel is around. She cries less and sleeps more, as if Rachel is the antidote to me.

My dad stops by during the day sometimes, but he's still too nervous to hold Stella, and I spend most of my day topless and nursing, so it's a little awkward. And my friends Kate and Laura and Jess occasionally stop by, as well, so I *do* have visitors. But as soon as they leave, I am filled with loneliness.

On October 23, our fourth wedding anniversary, Donny has a late meeting at school. I want to do something special, something to nurture our relationship, but I'm incapable of cooking with Stella in my arms. Before I was pregnant I loved to cook. I would pour myself a glass of wine and chop and sauté as I listened to music. Partly, I loved to create, combining recipes and adjusting them depending on what ingredients we had in the cupboard. And partly, I loved making something for Donny because I knew how much he appreciated it. The first meal I made him, just after we started dating, was a chicken cacciatore from *Saveur* magazine, and he oohed and aahed over it.

"No one's ever cooked for me like this," he'd said. And this fact— the fact that he hadn't had a mother to cook for him growing up— made me want to cook for him even more. I had never had such an admiring subject.

But I wouldn't even know where to begin now. So I call my dad, and he goes to pick up Indian takeout and a nice bottle of wine for us. When Donny gets home, I pass Stella into his arms, go into the kitchen to arrange the khorma, chicken tikka masala, and fried poori on plates, and pour us each a glass of wine.

"Cheers," we say, holding up our glasses, but that's all we can muster. I am asleep by nine o'clock, then up with Stella from one to five.

Stella is almost seven weeks old when she begins to really gain weight. She is four pounds fourteen ounces, and five days later, she's five pounds seven ounces. "Good girl!" Gloria shouts, giving me a hug. Stella, who must sense the importance of breaking five pounds, pees all over the coffee table and floor, but I don't even care. Five pounds feels safe somehow, and I think this means I will relax and that nursing will get easier.

But nursing doesn't get easier, and I don't know what to do. I still spend hours and hours each day trying to get Stella to latch on and stay latched on. She's started the head-wagging thing again, and she screams and screams. I take the nipple shield on and off a dozen times a day, and I'm desperate to talk to someone about it.

Finally, I get Amy on the phone. We had exchanged a couple of voice-mail messages, but we haven't actually spoken since before Noah was discharged.

Amy sounds as tired as I am, but she's still upbeat. "Noah's doing really well," she says, "I can't believe what a difference the shunt has made. He has so much more energy. But nursing takes hours. He starts and stops, starts and falls asleep. I spend all day in this chair."

"Me too," I say, relieved that I'm not alone. "What are you going to do?" I'm hoping she'll say she's going to quit, because it would open the door for me to quit, as well.

"I've committed to giving him breast milk for a year," she says. "It's the least I can do."

I feel myself sink lower in my chair, my face flushing with shame.

"But I think I might give up on breastfeeding. I might just pump and give him bottles." She sighs. "I hate to do that, but he just hasn't gotten the hang of nursing. It's all we do."

"That's not giving up," I say, incredulous. Pumping and bottle-feeding is twice as much work as nursing.

"It will be easier than trying to breastfeed," she says.

I can tell she feels bad, as if she's somehow letting Noah down. "You're a superstar," I say. "Stella cries whenever I put her down, so pumping is almost impossible."

"Oh," she says. "Noah's pretty calm. He's been sleeping well. He's just a mellow little guy."

I almost tell Amy how lucky she is, but I catch myself. Is she lucky that her other son, Noah's twin, died? Is she lucky that Noah had a Grade 2 IVH and might have cerebral palsy? Do I really think she's lucky just because her baby doesn't cry? I give myself a mental shake. If Amy can pump for a year after everything she's been through, there is no way I can give up on nursing.

I juggle Stella in my arms, and she starts to cry. "I better go," I say.

"Me too," Amy says. "But let's talk soon."

"Okay," I say. When I hang up, I look down at Stella, who has fallen asleep in my arms again. I lift her up and press her against my bare chest; then I lean my head back against the chair. The light from the windows is gray and cold.

The truth is that I thought the hard part was over. I thought the hard part was the preeclampsia and mag sulfate and C-section. I thought it was Stella's respiratory distress, her sepsis, and her bleeding brain. But this, being home all alone, is much more challenging. I can't look around the room and see half a dozen other women in the same boat. I can't ask a nurse the questions that seem to race through my mind—about Stella's latch, the milk I pumped while I was still taking the Percocet, about why Stella is so fussy. I can't go home and sleep.

I also feel lost. At the hospital, the goal was to get Stella home alive and healthy. But now that she's home, it doesn't feel like I have a clear-cut goal. To get her to nurse well? To get her to continue gaining weight? To make it through the day without breaking down in tears? To keep the germs from the house? To get more sleep? All of the above?

30

THE TREES LINING OUR STREET CHANGE FROM green to yellow to red to brown—their color slowly draining away as the days become shorter. The maple tree in our backyard has been stripped bare. Sleet pelts the windows like a shower of pebbles. A rush of slushy water surges in the drainpipes. I have moved past exhaustion and into a state that feels otherworldly.

The days continue to be an endless blur of pumping and rocking and walking, and almost everything I do is now accompanied by my daughter's wails. I have no idea why she cries so much. I must be doing something wrong because it's getting worse.

Some days are better than others. Some days I feel I can be a mother to my fussy infant. Certainly many new mothers, even mothers of full-term babies, spend their days like this. So we walk and bounce. I pump and sing *Stella, Stella I love you* over and over again until it becomes a meditative, lulling chant. I make it through the crying by telling myself how lucky we are that she's alive and made it out of the NICU without serious complications.

Other days I feel desperate. Nothing I do—not nursing or bottle-feeding, not walking around and around the dining room table in endless laps—calms her. She arches her back and wails, squirming and furious. I take deep breaths. I try to sing, hum. I try to rock and dance. I turn up the music. I say, *listen listen listen*. I push her in the little swing, cranking the tinny lullabies as loud as they will go. I leave her there and walk into the kitchen. *Breathe, Kate, breathe.* I take her out of the swing and do deep lunges with her, feeling the burn in my quads. Nothing works. I look at the clock and count the hours until Donny will be home.

But when Donny *does* get home, I'm torn between loving him and being thankful that he's here and hating him for having been gone all day. It doesn't matter that he's spent his day with rowdy kids or that he's exhausted and never gets enough sleep either; he's been out in the world while I'm stuck at home with a screaming baby, and I'm filled with resentment.

It's worse if I've asked him to pick up something at the store on his way home, and he brings home the wrong thing, something that happens remarkably often. Today, the only thing I needed was hand soap. "Mrs. Meyers," I said. "You know, the kind we always get."

But when I open the plastic bag in the kitchen, I pull out the wrong kind of soap. It's Mrs. Meyers, true. But it's not lavender; it's lemon verbena. I unscrew the top and breathe in the astringent, bitter scent. I screw the top back on and try to convince myself that it's not a big deal. But it doesn't work. The real Kate—the one with interests and skills and patience—has been whittled down; what remains is a dazed, irritable version of myself.

I end up losing the battle to control my fury, and I walk into the living room with the soap in my hand. Donny is sitting on the couch with Stella. His head is tilted back, his eyes closed. *Is he sleeping?*

"I know I'm being crazy," I start.

Donny opens his eyes and lifts his head.

"But when—tell me when—we've ever bought lemon verbena hand soap." I hold up the evidence, brandish it at him. "It smells awful."

He continues to look at me, but no emotion registers on his face. Have I become mute? Is no sound coming from my mouth?

"Oh," he says.

"Oh? That's it?" And before I think about what I'm doing, I whip the bottle of soap into the living room.

He jolts up, clutching Stella. "What the hell?"

At least I got his attention.

"We use *lavender* soap." My arm slices through the air. "We've always used lavender soap. Do you even live in this house?"

Donny shakes his head, his eyes wide. "You need to relax." He looks horrified, as if he has no idea who I am.

I actually have no idea who I am. But instead of feeling scared by this, I'm even more furious. I spin around and stomp into the kitchen and pull out a pan and slam it onto the stove.

"I'll return it then," Donny calls out from the other room, but his voice is full of exasperation. And I don't want him to return it; I want him to get the right kind of hand soap on the first try. I want him to have to stay here all day with our screaming baby, and I'll go to work.

I pull a container of spaghetti sauce from the freezer and dump the frozen square into the pan. Then I move to the sink to fill another pot with water for the pasta. As it fills, I look up at my reflection in the window. The face staring back at me is gray, old looking. Suddenly all my anger drains out of me. How did this happen? How did I get from the hospital, from wanting nothing more than to be home with my daughter, to feeling so trapped at home with my daughter? I turn off the water and stand in front of the window, feeling lost.

I glance at the refrigerator, where the Rilke quote peeks from beneath a magnet. *Live the questions and perhaps without knowing it, you will live along some distant day into the answers.* But how long can you live the questions? My questions keep changing, and it doesn't seem as though I'll ever get the answers.

Donny comes into the kitchen with Stella cradled in his arms. "I'm sorry," he says, touching my shoulder. I turn to him and feel that familiar surge of love.

"I'm sorry, too," I say.

Donny folds me into a one-armed hug, and we stay like that for a long time.

I thought as Stella began to grow, I would worry less. I thought that once she hit five pounds we'd be in the clear, and I'd feel lighter. But at five pounds I still startle awake a dozen times a night to make sure she's breathing or to clutch her more tightly to my chest. At five and three-quarter pounds, the worrying intensifies: *What if I fall asleep while I'm nursing her and she slides from my lap onto the floor? What if I roll on top of her and suffocate her? What if I accidentally throw her down the stairs?*

I begin to worry that I might hurt her on purpose, like the mothers you read about in the news. And I wonder if some morning, while Stella was screaming and I'm trying to pump, I might just pick her up and throw her like a football—a perfect spiral against the bedroom wall.

When I was newly pregnant and teaching creative nonfiction to undergraduates at the University of Minnesota, I assigned the M. F. K. Fisher essay "Those Who Must Jump." In the essay, Fisher describes how once while she's crossing the Golden Gate Bridge she feels a force propelling her to the edge, urging her to jump. She writes that she doesn't *really* want to jump and, of course, she does not, but the possibility of it is almost unbearable for her.

The essay perplexed my students.

"Haven't any of you ever thought this while you're standing on a corner?" I asked. "How easy it would be to step into oncoming traffic? Or when you're climbing a tall flight of stairs? It's a force so magnetic that you feel as if you might jump?"

My students stared at me, their undergraduate eyes wide.

"Okay," I said, laughing a little, nervous by what I'd revealed about myself, and I abruptly moved on to the next essay. But I think of Fisher's essay often because I've felt the pull she describes. It's different from wanting to jump to kill yourself; it's more like a feeling (or fear) that your body will just do it, simply jump against your will.

And that's what I'm afraid will happen with Stella. It's not that I *want* to hurt her: I'm scared that I won't be able to stop myself. How easy it would be to drop her or punt her.

I worry about this for a week silently on my own, hoping the thoughts will dissipate. Instead, they grow stronger. *What if I drop her? What if I accidentally let her sail down the stairs in her Moses basket? What if I accidentally throw her? What if I can't help it?* Sometimes an hour goes by without worrying about hurting her, but often only minutes pass between each thought. Why am I thinking these things now when Stella is growing stronger? Is the constant crying shredding my nerves? Is it the lack of sleep? Is it being trapped inside with her all day, every day?

While I was still in the hospital, nurse after nurse warned me about postpartum depression. "With your history of depression," they said, "and a baby in the NICU, you're at high risk." But I don't actually feel depressed; it's more whacked-out, up-and-down, pulling-my-hair-out frustration. But perhaps this is the beginning of depression. It's as if I can sense that old gloom lurking on the outskirts of my consciousness, just far enough away that it doesn't reach me. But it's there, and I'm afraid of it. And this, the fear of depression, the fear of it returning, is something new for me.

Finally, I go through my hospital papers for the pamphlet on depression. It says that "1–20 percent of all women experience postpartum depression." I run through the list of symptoms:

nervousness, anxiety, or panic
sluggishness, fatigue, or exhaustion
sadness, depression, or hopelessness
appetite and sleep disturbances
poor concentration, confusion, or memory loss
overconcern for the baby
uncontrollable crying or irritability
exaggerated highs and lows
fear of harming baby or self

Some of the symptoms fit, but wouldn't a few be true for any and all new mothers? (I would like to meet a new mother whose sleep *wasn't* disturbed.) The symptom that most closely describes what I'm feeling, though, is the last one, fear of harming baby, and I wonder if this is serious. Do I need help? Do I need to be on medication? But the thought of calling the number on the pamphlet and admitting my fears to a stranger is terrifying. What if they think I'm crazy? What if they try to take Stella from me?

I shudder, but I know I need to tell someone, so that night, I confide in Donny. We're in Stella's room, and I'm rocking her in the thick yellow armchair.

"You don't think I'd hurt Stella, do you?"

"No," he says, looking up from the laundry he's folding, "of course not."

"But what if I accidentally drop her or . . ." I pause. "Or throw her like a football?"

"Like a football?" he asks, smiling. His hand cups an imaginary ball above his head and he whips it through the air.

"Don't laugh. I'm serious."

"I'm not laughing," he says, but he is. He has to struggle to look grave.

I glance down at Stella in my arms. She's sleeping, and right this minute, I can't imagine hurting her. But tomorrow could be different. Or the middle of the night, when the whole world is sleeping, when it's only me and the baby and the muffled clatter of the train passing nearby.

"I've read about this. It's a sign of postpartum depression," I say, handing him the pamphlet.

He takes it from me but doesn't even look at it. Instead, he comes over and kneels in front of me. He kisses my forehead, then presses his thumb between my eyebrows, trying to rub away the crease between my eyes. "You're not going to hurt our baby."

"But," I start.

"You need to trust yourself," he says.

"It's just that what if—"

"No. Kate, listen to me." He grabs my free hand. "You're not going to hurt our baby."

"But by accident, maybe?"

"No," he says, "not even by accident."

I felt slightly better after confessing my fears to Donny. If he trusts me to be alone with Stella all day, shouldn't I trust myself? These crazy thoughts are probably just a result of the trauma of the last months, the suddenness with which I became sick with pre-eclampsia, the loss of our perfectly planned birth. It's a result of those long hours sitting by her isolette, willing her to be okay. It's not being able to get out of the house with her. It's my constant worry about germs, the way I wipe down the bannisters and door-knobs with Clorox wipes every day, the way I ask friends and family to stay away if they have even the slightest cold. Could it be that all that worry and vigilance has somehow backfired and is now making me think *I* am capable of hurting my daughter?

Years later when I read the *New York Times* article about post-traumatic stress in preemie parents, I'll nod my head at the research. Four months after their children's birth, three of the eighteen preemie parents in one study had been diagnosed with PTSD, and seven were considered high risk. In another study, thirty parents were interviewed six months after their baby's due date and were scored on three post-traumatic stress symptoms: emotional avoidance, hyperarousal, and flashbacks or nightmares. "Of the 30 parents, 29 had two or three of the symptoms, and 16 had all three."

I didn't have any avoidance symptoms—I didn't avoid thinking of the NICU or try to block those memories. But I definitely had nightmares. And I would have scored high for hyperarousal, which is characterized by

> *having a difficult time falling or staying asleep*
> *feeling more irritable or having outbursts of anger*
> *having difficulty concentrating*
> *feeling constantly "on guard" or like danger is lurking around*
>   *every corner*
> *being "jumpy" or easily startled*

I wonder what I could have done differently, if there was any way I could have avoided the stress, somehow lessened my reaction to the NICU. I don't know what would have helped. While Stella was in the hospital, both the hospital staff's attention and my attention were focused on getting Stella out of the hospital alive and healthy. It never occurred to me how hard it would be to be isolated at home after she was discharged. It never occurred to me that the hardest part would come later.

At my postpartum checkup, two months after Stella was born, I don't mention my fear of hurting Stella, but I do tell Dr. Bradford that I sometimes feel a little crazy. I try to explain the way my craziness is different from my past depressions, but it's difficult for me to put into words. Instead, I admit that I've considered going back on antidepressants, but I'm concerned about the medication leaking into my breast milk. "I'm worried about the long-term effects," I say.

Dr. Bradford laughs a little and shakes her head. "This will sound bad," she starts.

I shrug. Every thought that crosses my mind *sounds bad*.

"Wouldn't it be worse for Stella if you threw yourself off a bridge or threw *her* off a bridge?"

She's right, of course, and I'm relieved that she's put my fears into words so I don't have to do it.

"You need to take care of yourself, and there are safe options. Zoloft is the one we'd start you on."

I nod, but I wonder how I'll know if I need it. I probably needed it three weeks ago. But maybe not. Maybe I don't need it yet, or ever. Finally I say, "I think I'll try it a little longer without them."

Dr. Bradford nods. "But don't hesitate if you feel like you're slipping," she says. "Someone is always on call."

"I know," I say, and I feel better, just knowing I can call if I really need to.

Dr. Bradford examines my incision, does a pelvic exam, and announces that I can have intercourse again.

"Great," I say flatly. Having sex is the last thing I want to do. I crave the heat of Donny's body. I crave the intimacy, but I'd be happy never to have sex again. The thought that I could get pregnant and have to go through this all over again terrifies me.

"You'll be ready sometime," Dr. Bradford says.

"I doubt it," I say, and Dr. Bradford laughs. I love this woman. I love her dry sense of humor. I love that she knows me even though we've only spent a total of a few hours together, if that, over the last months.

Before she leaves I say, "Thank you. For catching the preeclampsia, for sending me to the hospital when you did. For saving our lives."

"It was my pleasure," she says, smiling.

31

It's early November and Stella is two months old, but things aren't getting easier. She still cries most of the time she's awake, and nursing is still a struggle. Everything I've read about breastfeeding claims that most babies get the hang of nursing after six weeks. But of course they're referring to full-term babies. Even though Stella is eight weeks old, gestationally she is only a few days old. Does that mean I need to wait another six weeks until things get easier? I can't hold out that long. No fucking way.

To make matters worse, Stella has developed diarrhea. She poops everywhere, but it's not poop; it's liquid shit. It leaks from the sides of her diapers. It squirts up her back. What doesn't soak immediately into her diapers remains in oily clumps on her bare butt, and she's developing a killer rash. When I call the clinic, the nurse reminds me that breastfed babies have runny stools.

"This is different," I say. "It's like pee."

I'm ready to insist on an appointment—my motherly instinct must finally be kicking in—but I don't need to insist. The nurse agrees that Stella should be seen, so later that day Rachel accompanies us to the clinic. I need reinforcements whenever I step through the hospital doors.

When we check in, I ask to be put in a room right away. The receptionist gives me an irritated look, but this time I'm determined not to spend a minute longer than necessary in the waiting room, where kids are hacking away and wiping their runny noses with the backs of their hands. "She was a preemie, and it's cold and flu season." I'm polite, but firm.

The receptionist nods then, and we're led to an examining room.

Rachel and I sit down, and I unbuckle Stella from her car seat. When Dr. Levine comes in, he smiles and shakes our hands. I explain her continued fussiness, the challenges getting her to nurse, and the diarrhea.

"Can you describe her stools?"

"I can show you," I say. "I'm sure there's some in there."

I unfasten Stella's diaper to reveal oily clumps on her butt. The rest of her stool has already been absorbed into her diaper. Her poor little butt is covered in bright red bumps.

"I'd like to test her for malabsorption," Dr. Levine says. He says something about her body having trouble absorbing certain vitamins, fats, or proteins.

I don't really understand.

"It's not severe or she wouldn't be gaining weight as well as she is, but let's test her stools. You may need to supplement your breast milk with a different kind of formula."

Dr. Levine tells us to come back in two days, then leaves, and a nurse comes in to help us collect the stool sample. Stella has been pooping almost constantly over the last few days, so this should be an easy task, but now that we *want* her to poop, she refuses.

The nurse slides a thermometer into her rectum to try to provoke a geyser. Rachel opens her eyes wide and raises her eyebrows at me. "Yikes," she mouths.

I hold Stella's squirming body, and Rachel stands next to me, smoothing down the paper on the exam table. The nurse tries the thermometer again with no results.

In a fake English accent, Rachel says, "A watched bum never craps."

I start giggling, and the nurse furrows her brow.

Finally, the nurse says she has to take care of other patients and leaves.

"She's got a great sense of humor," Rachel says. "No, really. I love that."

We start laughing harder then, because what else is there to do? We are standing above my naked squirming baby, waiting for her to poop.

But today Stella practices amazing bowel control, so eventually we're sent home with a few plastic cups and some wooden popsicle sticks, and I spend the rest of the afternoon trying to get a large enough sample for the test. But even when I rush her upstairs just after an explosion, most of the diarrhea has disappeared into the ultra-absorbent diaper by the time I get her undressed.

Finally I'm able to scrape enough poop from her diaper for a testable dollop, and as soon as Donny gets home from work, I jump in the car and drive it over to the lab at Children's. I'm driving a cup of human poop across town, and I'm not even disgusted by this fact; I'm just relieved to be out of the house by myself. I slip Dinosaur Jr. into the stereo, turn up the volume, and scream my way down Twenty-sixth Street.

Two days later, Donny and I take Stella back to see Dr. Levine. It turns out that Stella *does* have a malabsorption problem. Her intestines are not absorbing as many nutrients as they should. I'm not sure if this has anything to do with her prematurity or the digestion problems she had while she was in the hospital, whether it is a problem with *my* milk, or whether it's from the formula we're using to supplement her daily bottles. Regardless, it feels like another mark against me as a mother.

I probably look as though I'm going to cry because Dr. Levine says, "No, don't worry about this. It's a mild case—Stella is still absorbing enough nutrients to gain weight." But explosive diarrhea isn't exactly good, so he suggests we use a special kind of formula when we give her the fortified bottles of my breast milk.

Donny and I stop at the drugstore on our way home, and I run in while he waits in the car. All the baby formula is kept behind the counter because, the pharmacist tells me, it's the number one stolen item in the store. That parents have to steal food for their babies is horrifying. I thought there were programs that provided formula to low-income families. I don't realize that we would probably qualify for these programs. I just open my eyes wide when the pharmacist tells me that a sixteen-ounce can of Pregestimil costs twenty-seven dollars. Luckily we only have to use a small amount of it each day, but still, I have to put it on my Visa. There is no way we'd be able to afford exclusively feeding this formula to Stella; we'd max out our credit cards.

The next day I receive a bill from the university for twelve hundred dollars. It takes me a moment to realize it means *I* owe *them* twelve hundred dollars. I'm holding Stella at the dining room table, and as I read it over, I'm convinced it must be a mistake. But when I call the number listed on the bill, a young man tells me that I do, indeed, owe them money because I didn't actually drop my thesis credits and I'm not getting paid because of my leave of absence.

"What do I do?" I ask the guy.

"You're going to need to file an appeal, but you have to come to campus to do it."

"Okay," I say. When I hang up, I look down at Stella sleeping in my arms and then put my head down on the table. Finally I call Rachel, who agrees to come over in the afternoon so I can drive to campus.

I end up running from office to office at the university, explaining the birth of my premature daughter. I start to cry in an official's office as she watches me impassively. I realize, as I stand in front of her weeping, that I have no control over this situation either. I'm totally at her mercy.

"Please," I finally say. "I don't know what to do."

She sends me to another office, and I finally discover that as long as I'm taking a one-credit class this semester, I will retain my status as a teaching assistant and I'll retain my health insurance, even though I'll have to pay for it out-of-pocket. There is no alternative, so I thank this woman and go talk to the director of creative writing, who agrees to do a one-credit independent study with me, for which she'll give me an incomplete this semester. "You can do the work in the spring, when things are a little easier."

I stand and give her a hug. "Thank you so much."

Then I'm back and forth from office to office getting the necessary signatures and filing the necessary petitions. By the time I'm finished, milk is leaking through my breast pads, my heavy-duty nursing bra, and the front of my shirt. But it's settled: I no longer owe the university money, and I'm no longer an active graduate student.

I'm relieved about the money, but being officially removed from my thesis credits makes me want to cry, as if the last thread connecting me to that old version of myself—Kate the student, Kate the writer—has been severed.

I wish I could go home and fall into bed, but when I walk through the door, Rachel looks exhausted. "She's been really fussy," she says. "Screaming and farting and diarrhea. I changed her clothes four times. The poop keeps shooting straight up her back."

"I'm sorry," I say, though a part of me is relieved that Rachel looks as tired as I usually feel.

I'm ready to throw in the towel with nursing, but I can't stand that I would fail at the one thing that is supposed to be so natural, the one thing that my body was made to do for my daughter. Finally, I call my friend Laura, and she suggests I call La Leche League. "They were helpful when I was having some problems nursing Desi."

I check out their Web site and read that their mission is "to help mothers worldwide to breastfeed through mother-to-mother support, encouragement, information, and education, and to promote a better understanding of breastfeeding as an important element in the healthy development of the baby and mother." Okay, I think, and I submit one of their help forms, explaining Stella's prematurity, her trouble staying latched on, her preference for bottles. I don't know if my desperation comes through in the message, but that evening, a volunteer from the national La Leche office calls me while I'm pumping.

"Tell me how things are going," she says, her voice gentle.

"Well," I say, taking a breath, "it's not going well." I repeat what I wrote in my message and tell her about the Pregestimil-fortified bottles. I tell her about the way Stella fusses and wags her head after she's latched on.

"Hmm," she says. "Maybe it's a problem with milk protein. Have you tried to give up dairy?"

I hate the thought of giving up cheese and vanilla lattes (which I always request when I know someone is coming for a visit) and chocolate ice cream, but I'll do anything at this point, so I agree to try it.

"And can you stop giving her bottles?"

"I can't," I say. "She needs the extra calories and vitamins in the Pregestimil."

"Have you tried a supplemental nursing system?" she asks.

I hadn't, but I'd read about it. It sounded complicated, involving tubes and a pouch of formula hanging around your neck. The last thing I want to do at this point is add more equipment to our nursing gig. "I'll think about it," I say slowly, turning off my breast pump.

"You might also want to call your local La Leche group and see if they can offer you more support." I can hear her riffling through papers and then she rattles off a number, which I scribble on the back of my hand.

"Thank you," I say. "I'll call."

I'm grateful for the woman's kind voice on the phone, and I'm hoping I'll find the same support from the local person, so the next day, I call the smudged number on my hand, and a woman answers. She sounds a little annoyed when I explain that I was given her number by someone in the national group, but maybe she's just tired.

As I recount what now feels like a nursing saga, I can hear a child in the background—*Mama! Mama!*—and I think that maybe I've called at a bad time, but the woman—I'll call her Sally—doesn't say it's a bad time, so I continue cataloging our challenges at the breast.

When I'm finished she says, "Well, you shouldn't be giving her bottles at all, not when she's that young." I know that ideally babies shouldn't be given bottles until they're at least four weeks old (corrected age), but there is nothing I can do about this; she's been getting bottles for weeks now and the damage is done.

"There *are* alternatives," Sally says. "You could try supplementing with tubes."

"She's been getting bottles since she was in the hospital," I say, trying to control the anger that's suddenly awake and pulsing in my belly. "And frankly, giving her bottles is the only thing that allows me to get out of the house once in a while and to get a little sleep." I don't mention that I spend hours each day convincing myself that I won't accidentally hurt my daughter and that I need—I desperately need—time away from her, even an hour to go to the grocery store.

"She probably has nipple confusion," Sally says. The superiority is thick in her voice, and I resist the urge to tell her to fuck off.

Finally Sally says, almost reluctantly, "Well, you could come to one of our meetings."

Maybe it would help. At least I would be getting out of the house. "I guess I could get someone to watch Stella," I say.

"Oh," Sally says.

She clearly still doesn't understand. "Remember," I say, "that I can't take her out in public. I can't have her around a bunch of people who might have colds."

"Well," she says, hesitating. "I *guess* you could come without her."

Apparently a baby latched onto your breast is the ticket into this secret society. Without the baby, you don't get in. Or you have to cajole your way in. An image of a circle of women with bare chests, flowing skirts, and beaded bracelets in a room thick with patchouli flashes through my mind.

I don't ask Sally when they meet. I don't ask for her to call and check in on me (if this is even an option). I have decided that her particular La Leche group is the last place I want to be. I just thank her for her time and hang up. Then I stare at the phone in my hand and say, "Thanks a fucking lot." And even though I realize I'm being unfair, I let the first, very supportive La Leche volunteer be eclipsed by Sally, and I end up judging them all the way Sally seemed to be judging me. "Breastfeeding Nazis," I say, and I slam the phone into its cradle.

32

THE NEXT DAY, STELLA CRIES ALL MORNING. As soon as I get her to latch on and start nursing, she pulls back as if she's in pain. I grit my teeth. I take deep breaths and try to get her to latch on again. Nothing works. Finally, I pump and give her a bottle, and she sucks that down, but she doesn't fall asleep. She's still distraught, squirming and wailing and spitting up all over the couch.

Finally I start doing my laps around the dining room table—*Stella, Stella, I love you. Stella, Stella, I love you.* But I don't feel full of love for my daughter. I'm desperate for her to stop crying. *I'll be a better mother if she stops crying. What if I accidentally drop her? What if I accidentally throw her?* I shake the thoughts from my mind.

After twenty laps, Stella quiets a little, but as soon as I stop walking, she starts crying. So I have to keep going—around and around and around—and as I do my laps, I witness one of my orchids bloom.

It's a phalaenopsis, and over the last week its buds have become heavy, tumescent. I always forget the exact hue of an orchid's blossoms over the year that the plant is dormant, so each time one blooms, the brilliance of the color always surprises me. And that's what I need now: a forgotten flare of color to brighten the dining room.

It seems that each time I lap the table, the buds have opened a little more, loosening like a fist, fingers relaxing outward. I have an urge to call Mimi and describe how it feels to watch the petals open like this, millimeter by millimeter. Everything else in the world recedes; it's just Stella and me and this prehistoric-looking plant, which is nothing special most of the year, but which now—at this moment, at this second—is on the brink of resplendence. Mimi would be delighted if I called her, if I described it like this, but her hearing is so bad that it's difficult for her to understand me on the phone unless I yell, and I can't risk waking Stella, who is finally asleep.

At noon, Gloria arrives to weigh Stella, and I undress Stella and place her on Gloria's scale. "Seven pounds!" Gloria exclaims, holding Stella's squirming body in the air. "You did it!"

With all of Stella's diarrhea and spitting up, I'm surprised that she's still gaining so quickly. I should be thrilled about this, but I just feel flat.

"This is wonderful," Gloria says.

I nod. "Yes, it is."

"Well, this is it," she says then, smiling. "Stella is gaining. You don't need me."

I must look terrified, because Gloria puts down the scale and comes over and gives me a pat on the shoulder. "You're doing great," she says softly.

But of course I'm not doing great. I'm taking care of my daughter; I'm feeding her and bouncing her and making sure she's safe at home with me. But I definitely do not feel great. I feel wobbly, desperate, lonely.

Gloria packs up her scale and hand sanitizer and begins filling out her paperwork. I put Stella back into her sleeper. "It's okay, sweetie," I say when she fusses. "It's okay."

Then Gloria gives me a hug and touches Stella on the cheek with her fingertip. "You take care of yourself, now," she says. "Don't forget to get out of the house."

"Okay," I say, and I stand at the door and watch her get into her beige sedan and pull away from the curb. Then I sit down on the couch and try to get Stella to latch on. She nurses for a minute and pulls away, crying.

The afternoon is more pumping and crying, more walking around the table. I stand and stare at the orchid, which *is* brilliant, its petals now open wide, like the wings of a moth. The lip of each blossom is deep fuchsia, which fades to a lighter shade of pink at the edge of the petals. The possibility of this kind of color in my small midwestern house as we teeter at the edge of winter astounds me, and I wish I could lose myself in it. But I can only stop walking for a few minutes before Stella starts squirming in my arms.

When I finally get Stella to fall asleep again, I sit on the edge of the couch and stare out the window at the gray sky, the leafless trees, the empty street. I look around our cluttered living room, taking in the landscape of my life: burp cloths, diapers, dirty dishes on the coffee table. This is my world. It's claustrophobic.

I remember how, almost a decade ago, shortly after I arrived in San Vicente, I climbed up into the mountains behind the village. I wanted to see where the townspeople dug for *curiol,* the powdery white and red clay that they use as slip paints for their ceramic art.

My host-sister, Sara, and I left at five o'clock in the morning, starting out in the dark to avoid having to climb back down the mountain in the midday heat. Regardless, an hour into the climb, sweat dripped down my neck and the backs of my legs. At eight o'clock, when we made it to the top, I was drenched. But the view was worth it. Sara and I stood there, our feet dusted in fine, white clay, as we looked out over all of Guanacaste: burned pastures spotted with the dark-green canopies of matapalo trees. In the far distance, we could see the hazy peaks of the Guanacaste Cordillera, the volcanic range that stretches north toward Nicaragua. And what I couldn't see, I could imagine: the neck of Central America twisting up toward Mexico, the curve of Mexico where it meets the Gulf, the flatness of the Midwest, the pocked blue of Minnesota's fifteen thousand lakes. I felt so free, and I wished I could float down over it all.

I can't imagine feeling that kind of freedom ever again. My current world exists within the walls of this house; it is nursing and pumping and walking this fussy baby around and around. It is disinfecting doorknobs and the banister. It is constant worry.

I jump when the phone rings. It's Rachel, and she says she's free this afternoon. "Do you want me to come over?"

"Oh, my God, would you?"

"Of course. I'll be there in a half hour."

When she opens the door twenty-five minutes later, I start to cry.

"What is it?" she asks. "What's the matter?"

"I hate this," I manage between sobs. "I hate what I've become."

She quickly washes her hands and then gives me a hug. "Give me that baby," she says. "Why don't you go out for a little while?"

I shake my head. "No, I'm okay," I say.

"Really," she says. "Why don't you go somewhere and have a glass of wine and read."

"Really?"

"Go," she says. "I'm fine. I'll stay here until Donny gets home. We'll be fine."

There it is, escape. So I quickly shower and change into a loose skirt, and I practically run from the house. And I do as Rachel says. I drive to a trendy neighborhood in St. Paul and park in front of a bookstore.

In a recent e-mail, one of my MFA professors had recommended Sharon Olds's *Satan Says,* so I walk through the store until I find the poetry section. They don't have *Satan Says,* but they do have *The Dead and the Living,* so I buy it and walk across the street to a wine bar. I feel decadent and guilty when I order a glass of pinot grigio and a salad. A book and dinner out are more than I can afford. But I understand that I need something to both bring me back to life and ground me.

I take a sip of wine and hold the tart crispness in my mouth as I open the book. I read a few poems in part 1 of the collection, "Poems for the Dead," and I let Olds's words—powerful and disturbing—sink into my mind. But I don't want to think about death or abuse, so I flip to part 2, "Poems for the Living," and stop at the section titled "The Children." I read one poem after another. Her words pulse with energy and also with violence and the unreliability of life. I flip quickly past the poem about a child on a burn unit, and I settle on "Relinquishment":

> *On a black night in early March,*
> *the fire hot, my daughter says*
> Wrap me in something. *I get the old*
> *grey quilt, gleaming like a sloughed*
> *insect casing, and wrap it around and*
> *around her narrow nine-year-old body,*
> *hollow and flexible.* Cover my face,
> *she hisses in excitement. I cover her face*
> *and fall back from the narrow, silver*
> *shape on the carpet.*

How finally
she is getting away—an Egyptian child
bound in gauze, set in a boat
on a black night in early March
and pushed out on the water, given
over to the gods of the next world
who will find her
or not find her.

I look up and around the restaurant, which is almost empty because it's not yet five o'clock. Outside, the sky is already dark. I have tears in my eyes, but I'm not sure why. I cannot imagine my daughter as anything other than a fussy infant. I cannot imagine that someday she will be old enough to talk, to say *wrap me in something, cover my face*. But she *will* do these things, won't she? Isn't this poem proof that my baby will not always be a baby, that she will grow into a little girl hissing in excitement? I want to be able to count on that.

I finish my salad and wine and read a few more poems. When my breasts begin to ache, I know it's time to go home, and I'm ready. I drive slowly down Summit Avenue, across the Lake Street bridge, and then along West River Parkway, passing one glowing mansion after the other. I'm still tired, but I feel refreshed, and when I stop in front of our house, I feel thankful for Donny, for my parents and sister, and for Stella, for the fact that I get to go home to her, even if she'll be crying when I walk in the door.

When the next day begins with more crying, more fussing at the breast, I call the clinic and see if I can get an appointment for Stella to be seen. I'm not willing to struggle on my own again. I won't remember the magic words that get me in right away; I just know that Dr. Nelson has an opening. I bundle Stella up and drive her to the clinic right away.

Dr. Nelson, whom we haven't seen since that first appointment, says Stella looks great.

"She just cries so much," I say. "And the breast-feeding is still so hard. She nurses for a minute then pulls back, screaming."

Dr. Nelson is holding Stella. "Hi, darling," she says. Then she looks at me, her eyes gentle.

"You know," she says. "You can stop nursing. You can put her on formula if you want. You've already done amazing things for her."

I start to cry. A doctor telling me I can quit? That it's okay?

"You got her off to a great start. Some breast milk is better than no breast milk. And you need to take care of yourself. If this is too stressful—and breast-feeding can be very stressful—it's not worth it." She smiles at me. "But if you want, I can have the lactation consultant come in and observe you. Maybe she'll be able to help."

As I wipe my tears on the back of my sleeve, I realize that I *do* want to see the lactation consultant. I *do* want to try to continue nursing. I want to try to make this connection work. I know it's partly societal pressure to nurse, but I realize that it is something that I want as well. I want to nurse my daughter. I just needed to hear that it was okay for me to stop. Oddly, having that endorsement from a doctor gives me the strength to keep trying. It's the same way I felt when Dr. Bradford said I could go on antidepressants; just knowing that they were an option made me feel as though I could handle life a little longer without them.

"Yes," I say. "I'd like to see the lactation consultant."

Ten minutes later, Marisol, the lactation consultant, watches as Stella nurses. She adjusts Stella's latch a little, and then she steps back. Stella actually nurses for four minutes.

"It looks good," Marisol says.

"I know," I say. "This is unusual." I'm embarrassed. Marisol probably thinks I made it all up.

When Stella pulls off, Marisol burps her, and then we try the other breast. Stella latches on okay, but then pulls back, wagging her head. I'm relieved. I would have felt crazy if she had transformed into a rock-star nurser as soon as she had an educated audience.

"See," I say.

Marisol nods. "It looks as though she's really uncomfortable," she says. "She might have acid reflux. It's common in preemies."

She calls Dr. Nelson back in and Dr. Nelson agrees that we can try Stella on Prilosec and see if it makes a difference. Dr. Levine had mentioned that we could try this as well, but at that point I wasn't feeling as desperate as I am now, and I was hesitant to put any more medication into Stella's body, so we didn't take him up on the prescription. But now I know that if nursing doesn't improve, my determination will crumble and I'll stop, so I agree to try it.

33

When I research acid reflux on the Internet, I learn that it's common in preemies because the muscle that separates the stomach from the esophagus, the lower esophageal sphincter, is often underdeveloped. It's not strong enough to stay closed, so stomach acid sloshes up into the esophagus. One Web site says, "As the acid irritates the tissue inside the esophagus, it becomes inflamed and reddened. This condition is called esophagitis. Esophagitis is painful, similar to the pain of heartburn. This is why an infant will refuse to eat or stop eating—she is protecting herself from the pain of the acid touching the damaged tissue."

Poor Stella. No wonder she's pulling back. No wonder I can't put her down. She's been in pain. I think of the ways over the last two months that I have pulled back emotionally to protect myself from pain, and I feel as if I could cry when I think of my daughter's physical pain, her esophagus burning with stomach acid. After all this time, how could I not be in tune enough with my daughter to realize when she's hurting?

We're religious about the Prilosec—1.25 milliliters twice a day—and after two weeks, it seems to make a difference. Stella cries a little less and nurses a little better, and I don't have to do my constant laps around the table to keep her wailing at bay. And when I don't have to listen to my daughter cry all day, I also feel calmer. I still can't put her down, but she sleeps more, and as she lies in my arms, I lean down and kiss the top of her head. I brush my lips against the fuzz of her hair, realizing that she finally smells like a real baby, like shampoo and spit-up and baby lotion. I run my finger over her forehead and the silky skin at her temple, and I pick at the bits of adhesive that still cling to her hair even after all this time. I finally manage to pull apart the matted strands of hair with my fingernails until her hair is free from the remnants of the NICU.

I still startle awake a dozen times a night to check on Stella. I still struggle with the hours that she cries each day. But there are moments each day when I can just sit and stare at her, when I feel full of gratitude.

Over Thanksgiving, we make sure no one in either of our families has a cold. We spend the afternoon with Donny's family, and Stella does well, even nursing twice in a darkened bedroom. But when we arrive at my mom's house for our second turkey dinner, Stella transforms into a monster. Her cries are ear-splitting, and she refuses to nurse. I only have the manual pump with me, so I spend forty-five minutes pumping one side and then the other with aching arms. My sister Sara is in town, and she and my mom and Rachel pass Stella back and forth, rocking her and dancing with her, but Stella will have none of them. She will only stop crying if Donny holds her. She wants nothing to do with me, which is devastating at the same time it's a huge relief.

We spend the night at my mom's house. The next day, when we arrive back home, our house feels especially dark and small. Stella is miraculously asleep in her car seat, and Donny and I sit on the couch, staring into the middle of the living room. "I feel so depressed," I finally say.

"You want to go back to your mom's, don't you?"

I didn't want to admit this to him because it felt like admitting that our house, our small family, isn't enough. But it's true; I want to go back to my mom and Karl's large suburban house. I want to be surrounded by people, by my own mother, who will not only take care of me but will help us take care of Stella.

"Is that okay with you?" I say.

"Sure," he says. He looks exhausted.

"Thank you," I say, and lean into his arms.

We spend the rest of the weekend at my mom's, and when we arrive back home on Sunday night, I feel refreshed and rested and also a little melancholy, as I'd feel if we had just returned from vacation.

The next few weeks are more of the same—long and lonely days and wakeful nights—but just before Christmas, Stella has a day of nursing well, all day. She is three months old and she finally seems to get it. Or maybe I do, though I'm not doing anything differently.

In the late afternoon, Stella smiles up at me, her lips dripping with milk, and I almost burst into crazed laughter. "You did it!" I say. "You nursed five times today!" Could it be that things will get easier now?

Stella lifts her fist in the air and turns her head to stare up at the corners of the window.

"We should throw a party," I say, laughing. "But of course we wouldn't be able to invite anyone."

Christmas is exhausting—we're at Donny's dad's house and my mom's house on Christmas Eve, and then we spend Christmas Day with my dad. I have to keep reminding everyone to wash their hands before they touch Stella. I'm sure Donny's family is irritated that I keep asking whether anyone has a cold, but I don't care. Things are finally getting a little easier, and I don't want to jeopardize our progress with a cold or something worse.

Over New Year's we drive up to my mom's cabin in northern Minnesota. Mom and Karl and Sara and Rachel and Josh are all there as well, and I spend more time laughing than I have in months. Stella is up a lot at night, but I can nap during the day, which feels luxurious.

There is a foot of snow on the ground, and it's perfect for cross-country skiing. On New Year's Eve, my mom agrees to hold Stella so Donny and I can go out together with Sara. We ski down the snow-covered road and turn onto the forest path marked by a red flag. Snow collects on our hats and melts on our cheeks, and I take breath after deep breath, unable to believe how alive I feel.

Donny leads the way, forging a path in the snow, and we ski and ski, making a series of loops among the leafless trees. I glide through the snow, my left leg pushing forward with my right arm, right leg following with left arm. I'm amazed that my body remembers how to do this: push, glide, push, glide. At the top of a small hill I stop and feel my heart pounding beneath my jacket. Sara and Donny are a hundred yards ahead of me. I stare up into the sky, watching the snowflakes drift between the naked branches. There is no breeze, and it's so quiet that you can actually hear the snow hitting the ground and the trees; it sounds like the air is fizzing.

The more I ski, the more I feel my body straightening. It's as if I'm shaking off those countless hours hunched in the chair in Stella's room, trying to get her to nurse. I'm shaking off the bend that I've been walking with ever since my C-section. And oddly, my C-section scar doesn't hurt the way I thought it might. Instead, I feel a burn in the back of my arms, in my hips—muscles I haven't thought about in months.

On our last run, Donny stops at the top of a ridge and waves Sara and me up. "I'll wait for you."

Sara makes it up the hill without a problem, but the tip of one of my skis catches on a branch and I fall forward into the snow. When I try to get up, I fall again and start to laugh. Wet snow is down my pants and up my sweater. Donny sidesteps back down the hill to me.

"Did that branch get in your way?"

"Are you calling me a klutz?"

He reaches down and grabs my elbow, pulling me up. "Why would I do that?"

I make a face at him, and he smiles broadly.

"I love you," he says, leaning forward to kiss me.

"I love you, too," I say, and I pull off my mitten and rest my palm against his cold cheek. His eyes are bright and smiling, and I realize that he looks happier than I've seen him in a long time.

"Give me another kiss," I say, and we lean together on our skis.

"Come on, you guys," Sara finally says, so we make our way back up the hill. When we get to the top, it's no longer snowing, but the sky ahead of us is dark. God, I love it here. I love this quiet and this air that makes my lungs sting with cold.

Donny pushes himself off, screeching as he flies down the hill. Sara goes next, letting out a whoop as she makes it over the bump in the middle of the run. Before I push myself off, I look up at the sky one more time and take another deep breath, and I have a sense that things will get easier now. "Good-bye 2003," I whisper aloud. "I'm so done with you." And I fly down the hill as well, cold air on my face, laughing when I make it to the bottom without falling.

34

Things *do* feel easier in January because I know there are only a few more months of quarantine. Minutes and hours and days continue on their inevitable march, and soon it will be spring. There is light at the end of the tunnel. Stella continues to grow, and though breast-feeding is still sometimes a struggle, she usually has at least two or three good nursing sessions a day, and they take a half hour rather than an hour and a half. And in mid-January, when Stella is four months old, she finally begins to nap without being held. One afternoon, I put her down next to me on the couch, and miraculously, she falls asleep. She just closes her eyes and falls asleep. I watch her for a moment, thinking she'll wake with a cry, but she doesn't. I stand and stretch. She stays asleep, so I go into the kitchen and wash a few dishes. And then I go back into the living room and sit down next to her, watching the way her eyelids flutter and her lips, which are now full baby lips, pucker as she dreams. I have been holding this baby for months, and I don't know what to do with my free arms.

Stella is still fussy in the evenings when Donny gets home—*she's just a fussy baby,* he says—so he doesn't reap the benefits of her solo daytime naps. He's still exhausted, and he's withdrawn as well. When I ask him what's going on, he just says, "This time of year is hard." It's true that we're in the depth of winter. The temperature has been hovering around zero, and the days are short and dark. But there is something else going on with him.

I know he's worried about money, about the debt we're racking up on our credit cards as we charge groceries and formula and diapers. I also know that teaching science was not what he envisioned. He's always scrambling to get to school early enough to prepare his lessons. He's ordinarily not much of a drinker, but now in the evenings, he pours himself a Jack and Coke, and if we can get Stella to fall asleep in her crib, we watch a movie that Donny has picked up at the library on his way home from work. Then we fall into bed.

I don't push him into talking, and maybe this is because I finally feel lighter and I'm scared that I'll be pulled back down if I let in even a little bit of someone else's darkness. I justify our distance with the fact that since Stella was born, Donny and I have experienced the same events in such different ways. Why should that change now?

Through January, I still spend much of each day holding Stella, but she takes an occasional nap in her crib, and at night she now sleeps for a couple of hours at a time in her crib. I still startle awake, suddenly terrified that she is suffocating in our bed, but these night-mares, like my worries of hurting her, are slowly fading.

I feel so much more relaxed, which I'm sure is one of the reasons that Stella is more relaxed. Sometimes I buckle her into the bouncy chair for a few minutes while I go to the bathroom or get something to eat, and instead of filling the house with ear-splitting wails, she just bounces and gnaws on the scrunchy, crinkly elephant bracelet my mom gave her.

I've even begun to read again. I'm slowly making my way through Naomi Shihab Nye's *19 Varieties of Gazelle: Poems of the Middle East* for my book group. I love it, and if I read one poem a day, I feel I have accomplished something.

In the introduction, Shihab Nye writes, "We need poetry for nourishment and for noticing, for the way language and imagery reach comfortably into experience, holding and connecting it." Shihab Nye's poems are full of details outside my experience—olive trees and shriveled garlic and the aftermath of war—but still, I feel connected to her words, which create snapshots of another world. A word or image from her poems stays with me long after I have put her collection down. They seem to be slowly pulling me back toward a writing and reading life.

I usually turn to writing to help me make sense of the life I'm liv-ing, but since Stella's birth, I haven't been interested in, or capable of, writing. But now that familiar urge has begun to bubble inside me. I'm also craving other people's words—the words of other preemie parents who have made it through the NICU, through the long and lonely months following discharge. I want to see some of what we've experienced reflected in other mothers' stories.

So with Stella asleep in the curve of my arm, I turn to the computer and read everything I can find about prematurity. I scroll through photos of premature babies, my breath catching in my throat at the photos of one-pound premature twins. I learn that half a million babies are born prematurely in the United States every year. I learn that if a baby is born between twenty-four and twenty-eight weeks, it has a 20 to 30 percent chance of having a severe disability. Many preemies never "catch up," and for those that do, it often takes longer than the two years cited by so many doctors and nurses and well-meaning friends. I learn that no one really knows how an extended stay in the NICU affects the smallest preemies. I think about all the plastic tubing and drugs and overstimulation in the hospital. I feel sick to my stomach with the knowledge that things could have been much different for us and a tightening in my chest when I realize that if we ever try to have another child, we might not be so lucky.

I read through parent stories on the Internet and recognize myself both in their desperation and in the matter-of-fact descriptions of the early days of their babies' lives, as if the only way to get the details of those days onto the page is to strip all the emotion from their words. I recognize the long paragraphs, the run-on sentences, the apparent need to describe what happened over and over again. I do this as well.

When I get out of the house now, I recount the story of Stella's birth and first months to anyone who will listen. I can't stop myself. I tell my dental hygienist, the woman at the coffee shop who happened to be sitting next to me, the mother of the toddler at Target. A strange urgency takes hold of me, and I can't control myself. Afterward, I'm as embarrassed as if I had just vomited into a stranger's lap. Still, I can't stop, and I'm not sure why. Stella is okay. We're okay. But maybe that's why I'm doing it: now it feels safe to begin to look back, to tell this story.

One evening when I'm at my friend Linda's house for a small cocktail party, I'm introduced to a woman whose daughter, Becky, was born at thirty-one weeks, nine years ago. I know my eyes light up when I hear this, and I sit down next to her. I ask her about Becky's birth, and she recounts the shock of the early labor, those hard first weeks in the hospital.

"How is she doing now?" I ask.

Janet smiles. "She's great. She's still small, but she's doing great."

I smile. "When did she start being just 'Becky' and not 'Becky who was born nine weeks early'?"

"Hmm," she says, tilting her head. "That's a really good question. I can't remember."

I've just met this woman, and she seems ready to move on to another topic, but I press her. "Do you remember what age she was when it didn't matter anymore?" I want to explain that I can't imagine *not* telling the story of Stella's birth—every gory detail—to anyone who asks and even those who don't. Maybe this is because our lives are still ruled by the fact that Stella was born two months early: we still don't take her out in public; we still patrol visitors for colds; I still wipe down doorknobs and faucets and phones with Clorox wipes every week. Stella is over four months old, and she has never been to a grocery store, a bank, or to baby story time at the library. I rarely kiss her on the face, just to be safe. And every month, a nurse still comes to our house to give Stella a Synagis shot to protect her from RSV.

"Well, she was actually pretty old, I guess, probably four. But Becky was tiny; she weighed less than twelve pounds when she was six months old. It took her a long time to start growing. It was probably after my second was born. Maybe even after my third."

Oh, my God. She had more children. I want to ask her how she made it through a second pregnancy and whether she knew what her chances of having another preemie would be. But another friend of hers comes over and starts talking about their upcoming move out of state, so I get up to get a plate of food. My questions will have to wait.

Later that week, at the end of January, Amy brings Noah over for lunch. This is the first time we have seen each other since before Noah was discharged from the hospital, almost four months ago, and Amy and I give each other tight hugs when they come in from the cold.

We eat salad and crusty bread. Amy puts Noah on a blanket on the floor at her feet, but I have to hold Stella or she'll start crying. Amy tells me about Noah being in day care for a while, which didn't work because he kept getting sick. They've decided to hire a personal-care attendant to take care of him at home. But Amy is as optimistic as ever, not complaining about all the work she's had to miss because of Noah's illnesses.

"How are you guys doing?" she asks then.

"Things are getting easier," I say, trying to match her tone.

After lunch, we prop up Stella and Noah on the couch next to each other and snap photos. Stella is bald and round-faced with old-man jowls. Noah is much bigger, with a head full of hair that hides the bump on his skull where the shunt rests under his skin.

A few days later, we move Stella's crib into her own room. On the nights we can get her to fall asleep in her crib, Donny and I watch television or episode after episode of *The Sopranos,* which Donny checks out from the library. One evening we're flipping through channels, and I stop when I realize that *ER* is on. The episode title is "NICU," and I know we should turn it off right away, but we don't. It's as if we need to see it. We need to know if the babies survive. But as the story unfolds, it's clear that one of the babies will die. Donny and I keep looking at each other and saying, *Oh, no. Oh, my God. Oh, no.*

When Abby hands the dying infant to his mother, Donny and I both start to cry.

"Why are we watching this?" I say. "What's our problem?"

"We're so lucky," Donny says.

"I feel sick to my stomach," I say. It's all there before us, how this could have ended differently. I wonder what our lives would look like now if it had. How would we be able to breathe or eat or smile? How does anyone do that?

"Let's go check on her," Donny says.

Upstairs, we lean over her crib.

"She's so precious," he says.

"She is," I say. Then I lean over to feel her warm breath on my hand.

35

At the beginning of February, I sign up for a four-week class at the Loft Literary Center. It's a class for advanced writers taught by local author Barrie Jean Borich, from whom I'd taken a course at the university a few years ago prior to entering the MFA program. I need to start writing again because I'm scheduled to reenter my graduate program in September, and if I don't get started, I know I'll never finish my thesis.

I'm still planning to return to my book about San Vicente, about Sara and Betty and Tirza, the three generations of women I had been writing about before Stella was born. But a few days before the Loft class begins, I go to the coffee shop near my house, and what comes out when I put pen to paper is this: Stella in the NICU, yellow and mottled, goggles covering her eyes, a ventilator tube taped to her mouth. And as I write, image after image comes back to me, a slow collision of memories on the page. I can feel my heart beating fast, my eyes filling with tears again and again. I keep my head bent over my notebook, not wanting the other people in the coffee shop to see me cry. I'm exhausted when I get home, but I also feel lighter than I have in months.

In Barrie's class, I write about watching Stella on the television in my hospital room. I write about her looking like a baby squirrel, about how I felt that she could not possibly be my baby. And when I read my paragraph aloud to the class, a woman sitting at the corner of the large square table suggests that I write more about the amazing bonding that happens between mother and infant. She says she'd like to hear more about that connection. "After all," she adds, "you are your baby's first lover."

I stare at her for a moment and try to control my anger. I grit my teeth and imagine what it would feel like to lunge across the table and grab her by the jugular. What would these other nice women think of me then?

I want to explain to her that that's exactly the point: I didn't feel connected to my daughter when I first saw her. Hell, I didn't even want to love her because I was so afraid I'd lose her. I felt guilty about this, like a failure. And it's people like her, perpetuating the myths of motherhood—*You'll fall instantly in love! Everything will be perfect!*—who make it harder for those of us who don't experience that to reconcile myth with reality. I want to explain all of this to her, but we're already on to the next person.

I'm quiet for the remainder of class, but as I drive home that evening, snowflakes melting on my windshield, I feel a spark of determination. What we usually hear about motherhood is exactly what this woman was spouting in class: bonding and connection, instant love between mother and child. *You are your child's first lover.* Gross, by the way.

Where are the other versions of that story? The fear and disappointment, the hours and hours spent each day trying to get your baby to stop crying? Where are the stories about what to do if you're afraid you're going to hurt your baby? Those stories need to be told, too, don't they?

Soon, I've arranged to have my dad come over one morning a week so I can go to the coffee shop near our house and write. Dad is now totally comfortable with Stella; he's head over heels for her. He bounces her on his knees, and when she stares into his face, he laughs and laughs. "She's giving me *the look,*" he says, so proud of his chubby granddaughter and, I think, of himself as well.

The two hours of writing one morning a week are heavenly. There is none of the old procrastination that plagued me before Stella was born, none of the worrying about the purpose of my writing. I just sit in front of my laptop with a cup of decaf and let the words spill out. There is no chronology; I simply vomit image after image onto my computer: the photos that line the hallway leading to the NICU; sepsis, Stella's limp body with an IV jutting from her head.

The more I get down, the more grounded and less alone I feel. It has always seemed strange to me that the solitary act of writing makes me feel more connected to the world, but it does. So I write and write, a new sense of urgency pulling me back to my computer again and again. And as the pages start adding up on my computer, I begin to feel more human.

March is still cold in Minnesota, and it's still technically cold and flu season, but on March 13, when Stella is exactly six months old, she is introduced to society. Our friends Laura and Mike host a baby book shower for us—Stella's debut. It feels like a coming-out ball, so Donny and I dress her in tights and a pink plaid dress. Our friends gather at Mike and Laura's, and we laugh and pass Stella around. I refrain from asking everyone to wash their hands before they hold her. Stella is chubby and bald and the belle of the ball.

The next week, we decide to drive out to Boulder, Colorado, to visit my friend Emily and her husband, Pete, for Donny's spring break. We can't afford to do this, but Donny and I need some kind of reward for making it through the winter, and it's a little warmer in Boulder, so we'll be able to take Stella out, go for walks, breathe fresh air.

We pack up the car with everything—the baby bath, the stroller, the breast pump, the formula, baby clothes, and the pureed baby food that Stella has just started eating. I sit in the back seat with Stella, who cries for four hours, until we're well into Iowa. But even this is not enough to dampen my spirits; all that matters is that we're getting the hell out of Dodge.

Driving across the open plains of Nebraska and eastern Colorado the next day, Donny and I are mesmerized by the way the wind whips the sea of pale yellow grass on either side of the freeway into a frenzy of waves. We're drunk with sky and open land and with the fact that we're not stuck in our house. When Stella falls asleep, I climb into the front seat and rest my hand on the back of Donny's neck. He looks tired but relaxed.

"What are you thinking about?" I ask, ready to pick apart the layers of quiet and distance that have grown between us over the last months of handing our crying baby back and forth, months of not having sex, months of not even thinking about it.

He shrugs and glances at me.

"What?"

"I'm just thinking about soccer," he says.

"You miss it, don't you?"

"Yeah, of course," he says, and I can hear the tension in his voice. I rub the back of his neck with my fingertips.

"This is the first spring that I'm not getting ready for the season. I keep thinking about the team, about the fact that they're at spring training." He shrugs again. "I knew this first year would be hard."

"I'm sorry, babe," I say, suddenly understanding how hard this transition has been on him. I'd been so absorbed in my reality that I hadn't given much thought to the ways Donny's life had been transformed. Years later, he'll admit that he was probably depressed that winter because of all the changes: his first year teaching, his first year not playing, his rocky first year as a father.

"I'm glad we're doing this," he says, nodding at the open freeway ahead of us. In the distance we can see the hazy peaks of the Rockies. "I love this land," he says, and we fall back into silence, but it's a different kind of silence; it's full of calm and awe and understanding.

Our week in Colorado is a week of firsts for Stella. It's her first time out in public with people who haven't been vetted for illness; her first time in a restaurant; her first time hiking into the mountains; her first time eating peas and carrots. And it's somehow much easier to be away from home as we forge out into the world. If we had been in Minnesota, I think it would have been more difficult for me to shake off our quarantine. The trip offers a clean break, and when we get back home, we'll be out, free.

Emily has a couple of days off work, so we walk around the parks near Boulder with Stella kicking and laughing in the Baby Björn, and we take naps and make dinners in Emily and Pete's huge, open kitchen.

One evening as Emily and I are making a salad, she asks whether we're going to have any more kids.

My stomach clenches at the question, and I glance into their backyard, where Pete and Donny are standing by the grill, beers in hand. Stella is strapped to Donny's chest, waving her arms as if she's participating in their conversation. "I don't know," I say slowly. "We always talked about having two." I turn to Emily, who is chopping carrots next to me. "But honestly, I can't imagine having to go through all this again. The thought is terrifying."

"But Stella's fine." Emily looks out the window. "She's great."

"I know," I say. "We're incredibly lucky. But I could get sick again and not make it to thirty-two weeks. There is so much that could go wrong."

"But maybe nothing will go wrong. Maybe everything will be just fine."

"Maybe," I say. But *maybe* doesn't feel like enough. I'm still craving a guarantee even though I know I won't get one.

One day while Emily and Pete are both at work, Donny and I decide to drive up to Rocky Mountain National Park for the day. It's gorgeous—sixty-five and sunny—and the sky is huge and blue. We drive through the resort town and into the park, where we stare up at the steep, craggy cliffs and the fields of antelope. We pull the car over and ask strangers to take pictures of us, smiling and squinting into the sun.

We climb up a trail, and it feels as though we could hike forever. I fill my lungs with the scent of pine and dirt. Stella seems fascinated by everything, looking left and right and then straight up, as if she's thinking *so this is what I've been missing.*

You and me both, babe. You and me both.

We stop at an opening in the trees and stare down at a deep ravine. The sun burns pink across the rocks, and I am almost giddy with how big the world feels. These rocks and trees and the deep blue of the sky are all reminders that the earth has been around for billions of years. But instead of feeling small and insignificant, I feel myself swell with life. I can't believe that we made it through the last six months. I can't believe I didn't accidentally punt my daughter down the stairs. I can't believe that Donny and I still love each other. I keep saying, "This is so amazing."

Donny laughs. "I love it out here."

Stella smiles, bobbing her head, and before we turn around to head back down to the car, Donny and I kiss, squashing a laughing Stella between us.

36

With Stella out of quarantine, our lives develop a new rhythm. I continue to write one day a week, trying to get as much down as possible. But now Stella and I also spend as much time as possible outside. We go for long walks along West River Parkway under budding trees. I push her for hours, staring up at the pale green that is transforming the craggy trees into something fresh and lush. While we walk, Stella pulls off her socks and tries to get her feet into her mouth. She smiles up at me and tries to mimic everything I do: if I cough, she coughs; if I laugh, she laughs. Stella still nurses at night, but while we were in Boulder I decided to stop pumping and exclusively feed Stella formula during the day. The first few days I felt the familiar tug of guilt trying to take root in my stomach, but I shrugged it off. I did the best I could, and it's time to move on.

When Donny gets home from work, I hand Stella to him and head into the kitchen, which once again calls to me. She has finally stopped her evening crying jags, and these have been replaced by an hour of Donny and Stella on the floor, rolling around and laughing. I listen to their giggles from the kitchen, where I flip through the most recent *Bon Appétit* magazine, searching for something to make for dinner.

I never follow the recipes exactly; that would require a more extensive herb collection and a more fully stocked pantry than we possess. So I adapt and modify and substitute ingredients and just see what happens. This is strangely out of character for me, but somehow it works. The rule follower is subjugated, at least for an hour, by the scent of garlic on my fingertips. And I am transformed by the weight of a good knife in my hand and the lulling action of chopping.

In April we sign up for an early childhood education class for preemies, which we heard about while Stella was in the hospital. It's the first time we've been around a group of preemie parents since leaving the NICU, and I feel an immediate sense of affinity with them. We don't have to explain about colds or hand washing. Everyone knows the rules, and we all understand at least a little bit of what the others have experienced.

Two of the five babies at the first class are now chubby like Stella, but the other two still look very much like preemies: bulbous eyes, scrawny bodies. And I'm struck, again, with knowledge that every premature baby and his or her parents have their own story, their own journey, their own struggles. Anything can happen, anything at all.

When we walk into the room for the second class meeting, Joe's parents are sitting on the floor on the mat. I stop, and even though I'm not sure they recognize us, we smile at each other. For me, it's as if no time has passed at all. I see them walking by me in the NICU, going to their son's isolette. I see the deep set of Joe's mother's mouth, and I hear the low murmur of their voices from behind the privacy screen. I would have recognized them anywhere.

Today they are the same, but different. Joe's mother is smiling. "I'm Andrea," she says. "And this is Brian." Brian smiles and says, "Hey, how's it going?" He's holding Joe, who is bigger than he was six months ago, but who still looks very much like a preemie with a large head and underdeveloped body.

Andrea and Brian have no idea how often I eavesdropped on their conversations with doctors and nurses, and I'm a little embarrassed by how much I know about them. But I also feel totally invested in the welfare of their son, and I want to tell them how often I've thought about them. What I'd love to do is sit down and go over every detail of Andrea's pregnancy and Joe's health. I want to know everything that went wrong and how they've made it through. Unfortunately, they have colds the following week, and we have colds after that and can't go to class, so we end up seeing them only that one time.

When I'm out at the park with Stella or at the grocery store, I still tell people the story of her birth, and they tell me stories in return. I hear about a woman's niece, born at twenty-eight weeks, seventeen years ago. She's now the captain of her high-school soccer team, and she's trying to decide where she wants to go to college. I hear about a friend's child, born at twenty-nine weeks. She's five now, still small, but "totally fine." But then I hear the story of a nephew, born at thirty-two weeks, who is sixteen months old and still doesn't crawl. He can't stand to be touched or held, and he sits only when propped up with pillows. His mother is having a nervous break-down. I hear the story of a neighbor's daughter, who was born at twenty-five weeks and is now five years old and has autism and sensory problems. With each story, I want to hear all the details: What caused the premature birth? How long was the baby in the hospital? What did it feel like? How did and do the parents make it through?

I realize that everyone must tell their stories, the ones they and their loved ones have lived. And I can feel it, the desperation in each of these narratives, no matter how different its outcome. I understand the need to tell and retell, to make sense of how their lives have changed.

It's a chilly evening in May. Stella is asleep, and Donny and I are sitting on our front porch, cuddling under a blanket, when he says, "I still wonder if it was my fault."

"If what was your fault?"

"When Stella's IV line came out."

"What?" I say. "What are you talking about?" I stare at my husband's face, which is becoming tan again from afternoons at the park pushing Stella in the swing. His eyes are worried.

"I was holding her the night before it happened," he says. He's looking straight ahead now, staring at the window, as if he can see that evening reflecting back at him in the glass. "What if I knocked the IV from her vein when I lifted her from the isolette? What if I held her too tightly or something? What if it was my fault?"

I know Donny better than anyone else does, yet I'm often surprised by what he doesn't tell me. I had no idea that he was harboring those worries all these months. Why hadn't he said anything?

"Of course you didn't do it," I say.

"But I might have."

I run my finger down his temple and along his jaw. "No, sweetie," I say. "And anyway, it doesn't matter now. She's okay." But I wonder what else he keeps tight inside, not willing to share with me. What other burdens does he nurse?

He turns to me and kisses me gently. When he pulls back, he smiles tenderly. "She is okay, isn't she?"

I can hear the steady rhythm of Stella's breath through the static of the baby monitor, and I smile. "She is. She's okay."

37

On Stella's first birthday, I wake to sunlight pouring in our window and look at the clock. It's 6:30, and I think, yes, one year ago this is when I jolted from the hospital bed, the magnesium sulfate thick in my veins. And later in the day, as we prepare for Stella's birthday party, as I run to Target for the forgotten paper plates, I look at the clock and think, yes, this is when Dr. Anderson hooked me up to the rice bag, this is when, this is when, this is when. As if I need to relive every detail now that I know how it turned out, now that I know the answers to the questions that ran through my head that day.

I let it be a day of contrasts. I stare at my beautiful, one-year-old daughter as she toddles around our packed house, holding onto Donny's fingers for support, and I wonder: is this the same child as that skinny three-pound baby I delivered? Is this the same child I hovered over for all those weeks in the NICU? I try to hug her, to squeeze her tightly, and she wiggles away. I just want her to know how much I love her.

When Rachel and Josh are ready to leave the party, I start to cry. "Thank you for everything you did this year, for being there with me at the hospital the night before Stella was born—" The words catch in my throat. I know I've thanked Rachel for all the visits, for not letting me sink into depression in the depths of winter, but I'm not sure if she understands how far my gratitude reaches.

"Of course," she says, hugging me. "Oh, don't cry. Of course. Of course."

That evening, after everyone has left and Stella is asleep and Donny and I have cleaned up the remains of the party, I go through the house closing the curtains. In the dining room, I pause over the table of orchids and bend down to breathe in the sweetness of the cattleya. This orchid blooms annually, so I shouldn't have been surprised when it stretched its orangey yellow blossoms into the room two days ago, but I was. It was as if it had unfurled its sweetness for Stella, in honor of her birthday. As if it understood that this anniversary needed to be honored. I run my index finger lightly over its silky petals and smile as I pull the curtains closed against the darkness outside.

The following week, when I take Stella in for her one-year checkup, Dr. Levine says she's on track with her development. She weighs twenty-two pounds, can crawl up stairs and point at noses and pull herself up and clap and wave bye-bye. She still has reflux, so we agree to continue to give her the Prilosec but not increase her dosage. "She should outgrow it," Dr. Levine says.

I thank Dr. Levine for never making me feel like a bother despite our multiple visits last year, and he says, "I love to see you guys!"

When we leave the clinic, instead of taking the elevator to the ground floor, I get off on the second with Stella in my arms. And then I carry Stella down the long hallway to the NICU, staring at the photos on the wall. "This is where we came every day to see you," I say quietly, and when we come to the poster at the end of the hall, Amanda in her graduation gown, I say, "This is what you're going do someday, little one." Stella reaches out her hand and points at Amanda as an infant and says, "Baba!"

Then we turn to the receptionist at the welcome desk and I tell her that Stella is a NICU graduate. "We'd love to say hi to Kally or—" I pause and realize that the person I really want to see is Kris, even though Kris wasn't Stella's primary nurse. "Or Kris," I add.

She dials the NICU, and a few minutes later, Kris walks through the wide metal doors, riding on the sweet antiseptic smell of the NICU. I smile widely. She looks exactly the same, her blond hair pulled into a ponytail, and she smiles as soon as she sees us. I'm impressed that she remembers us at all, but she says, "Of course!" And then she gives us hugs and takes a picture for the bulletin board in the NICU. "I can't believe it," she says. "She's just beautiful."

My eyes fill with tears, and I smile. It feels as if I'm finally saying good-bye to the NICU, finally letting it go. "Thank you," I say. "When Stella got sepsis, you knew. You seemed to know what I needed."

"Oh, sweetie," she says, and gives me another hug. "I'm so glad you stopped by."

Then I hitch Stella up higher on my hip and watch as the NICU doors close behind Kris.

The next months are consumed with writing and teaching—I get my dream class back at the university. I'm more relaxed about school and teaching than I have ever been in my life. I don't get involved in the politics of the English department, reminding myself what is really important—my family, writing, words.

I spend four mornings of each week writing, and by December I have one hundred pages of my new thesis written. We pay Rachel to watch Stella two full days a week while I'm at the university, and she and Stella are as close as ever.

Donny has his own class this year—fourth grade—and he seems relaxed and happy. He still misses soccer, but he's finding a place in his school, with kids who depend on him and look up to him.

And maybe it's the fact that we are both settled again that we start talking about the possibility of having another child. "God," Donny says. "I can't imagine."

"I can't either," I say. And when Stella starts going to a day care center in January and develops respiratory infections that require a nebulizer and oral steroids whenever she gets a cold, the thought of another child—another preemie who could have much more serious complications—is pushed further into the future.

Stella is a year and a half old when I drive her out to Amy and Mark's house for brunch one Sunday. Amy and I have stayed in touch, but it's been difficult to coordinate a playdate between colds and schedules, so this is the first time we have seen them since Amy brought Noah over to our house for lunch over a year ago. When Amy opens the door and I see Noah standing behind her, I can't believe how big he is. He towers over Stella.

The two of them survey each other warily before each taking off in different directions. When Noah walks off, I can tell that his gait is slightly uneven, but other than that, there is no physical evidence of his brain bleed.

I sit in the kitchen as Amy pours me a cup of coffee and Mark stands at the stove, making frittatas. Amy tells me about their year, about Noah's infections and a surgery to replace his shunt.

"Wow," I say. "You've had a rough year."

"It's been a great year," Amy says, and she and Mark smile at each other.

Again I'm struck by how positive and united they are. But look at how well Noah is doing, even after a Grade 2 bilateral IVH. He probably has mild cerebral palsy, but other than that he's totally fine—delightful and happy and incredibly verbal.

After breakfast, we walk downstairs to their playroom, which is lined with shelves of toys. Stella and Noah do okay until Stella yanks an Elmo doll from Noah and pushes him down. He falls backward, and I'm up, holding Stella's hands in my own.

"No pushing," I say firmly. "That hurts Noah." And then I hand her a different toy.

"Sorry," I say to Amy. "She's always been feisty—even in the NICU—but this is a new development." I roll my eyes.

When Stella and Noah are settled with their toys on opposite sides of the room, I sit back down and watch our now-huge preemies exploring their world, picking up toys and putting them in their mouths, dropping them, and moving on to the next thing.

"Have you guys thought of having another baby?" I finally ask, looking over at Amy, who is sitting by the window, gray light streaming in around her. "We're terrified at the thought of another preemie."

"Us too," Amy says, "but we'd really like Noah to have a sibling." She ruffles Noah's curly hair then, and Noah points to the Sesame Street characters on the little couch and begins naming them: "Elmo. Big Bird. Grover."

"I just can't imagine doing it again," I say, meaning the NICU. "Do you know what your chances are?"

"Pretty low, actually," Amy says. "Since I had twin-to-twin transfusion syndrome, the likelihood of us becoming pregnant with twins *and* getting twin-to-twin again is very slim."

"Oh, right," I say. I hadn't thought of how different our illnesses were. Stella pulls a bucket of toys from the shelf, and I watch her for a moment, wishing my chances of getting preeclampsia again were just as slim.

"What about you guys?" Amy asks.

From where I'm sitting on the floor amid a rainbow of plastic toys, I look up at Amy. "Well, preeclampsia is a distinct possibility," I say. "Having it in a previous pregnancy is the largest risk factor for getting it again, but no one can tell me exactly what the odds are. The statistic I keep reading is anywhere between 5 and 80 percent."

"That's helpful," Amy says, shaking her head.

"I *know.*"

Amy holds a rattle toy out for Noah, and he grabs it.

"Sometimes," I say, "I get frustrated with other parents. I know a woman who has three kids and she talks about wanting a fourth, and I just want to shake her. Three healthy full-term babies and she wants more? It's as if she's taking it all for granted. She assumes her next birth will be the same, and she's probably right."

Amy tilts her head and watches me for a moment. "I think," she says, "that God knows what we can handle. Your friend might not have been able to handle more than perfect births and healthy children. God knows who is strong enough."

Outside the ground is still covered with March snow, and Amy looks beautiful, sitting there at the windowsill, filled with grace.

I give myself a mental shake and nod. "I guess." But I don't really believe that there is a divine force that's testing us, making us show our mettle. If there *is* a God, I don't believe He is meddling in our day-to-day lives.

Nonetheless, Amy's words rumble around in my head for weeks after our visit.

When Stella was in the hospital, and even the day she developed sepsis, I didn't pray to God. I sent my thoughts up, out into the universe, but I didn't really believe they would be answered; it was a reflex, something to make me feel as though I was doing everything I could do to save my daughter. I didn't believe there was a God looking down on us, waiting to either grant my wish or not. And maybe that's why I was so angry at that woman in the NICU lounge who asked my dad if he believed in Jesus. As if believing in Jesus, praying, begging, would be enough. As if it would keep my daughter alive.

I know another preemie mom whose son was born at thirty-two weeks. He developed sepsis like Stella, but then he developed necrotizing enterocolitis and had to have a portion of his intestines removed. After his surgery he seemed fine, and his mother thought their prayers had been answered. But when she took her son home, he died suddenly from complications of the surgery. The woman told me that she often used to say things like "We've been blessed."

"But after my son died, I realized how awful it sounded," she said. "When you say 'I've been blessed,' it implies that God chose you, blessed you. But what about the other people? What if you lose your child? What if you prayed and prayed and God decides against you? Does that mean you didn't pray hard enough? Or that He decided to bless a different baby, just for kicks? No, there's no God meddling in our lives, not like that. And I refuse to ever use that term again."

I agree with this woman, so why then do Amy's words keep ringing in my ears? Maybe because there is something about them that reminds me of the Rilke quote.

A few weeks after my visit with Amy, when I am at my old college library working on my thesis, I wander over to one of the catalog computers and type in Rilke, *Letters to a Young Poet*. Then I scribble down the call number and walk up two flights of stairs and into the stacks, running my finger over the spines of books until I find that thin collection of letters.

I settle in a corner by the window, curl my legs under me, and open the book, which is a collection of letters written by Ranier Maria Rilke to the young poet Franz Xaver Kappus between 1902 and 1908. The correspondence is one-sided, consisting only of

Rilke's letters to Kappus, but I gather from Rilke's tone that the young man is struggling. I skim the book, searching for the quote that Leni e-mailed to me just after Stella was born. Finally, I find it, and though the translation is somewhat different, the sentiment is the same: "Have patience with everything that remains unsolved in your heart. Try to cherish the questions themselves. . . . Live the questions now. Perhaps you will then gradually, without noticing it, one distant day live right into the answer."

Cherish the questions, have patience. I look out the window, over the college campus spread below me: the dark red of old brick, the green, newly cut lawn, the old elm trees, which are full of the pale green of spring, of new life.

I know I will always have questions. I will probably always be a worrier. But as I sit in the quiet of the library, surrounded by the words of thousands of writers, I realize that's okay.

I think back over the month that Stella was in the hospital and the long winter that followed, and I know, too, that my strength doesn't come, nor will it probably ever come, from God. It comes from stories, from other people's words. It comes from Sharon Olds and Naomi Shihab Nye and regular people who take the time to e-mail me or hand me a photo and tell me their stories. There is something in this realization that fills me with strength. I stare out at the bright green campus lawn and the buds on the huge trees, and I understand that Amy is right: I *am* strong enough. Strong enough to make it through whatever another pregnancy might bring, whatever our lives may bring. As long as I have words, I'll be strong enough.

Epilogue

I VOLUNTEER IN THE NICU NOW, WHICH HAS
been entirely remodeled, providing a private room for each baby. I
knock quietly on doors and spray foam onto my hands and explain
that I'm a former preemie parent. Then I sit and listen to parents and
grandparents describe the texture of their days as they sit next to their
tiny babies, willing them to be okay. I recognize the same look in the
faces of mother after mother—the fear, the not-knowing, the worry,
the pure exhaustion. I never know which babies will make it out of
the NICU or what challenges they will face, so I'm careful what I say.
I ask questions and I listen. "I see you," I want to say. "I understand."

Sometimes they ask me about my daughter, and I tell them that
Stella is nine and that she has a little sister who is four. I tell them that
Stella is a third-grader who loves soccer and dance, who spends hours
at the dining room table with her head bent over beads and sequins, a
bottle of glue in hand. And next to her, wanting to see, is her gregari-
ous little sister, Zoë, pestering, wanting to be involved in everything.

When I tell these parents about my daughters, I think of the
winemaker at my friend Scott's restaurant, the man who handed me
the photo of *his* girls and told me that Stella would be okay. So I
describe my feisty daughter to these preemie parents, and sometimes
in their faces I see a rush of hope.

When I walk away from the NICU at the end of the night, I
feel heavy and elated all at once. I get in my car, turn onto Twenty-
eighth Street, and drive the road I've driven a hundred times. And as
I make my way home to my girls, who are waiting up for me, I think
of Stella, and I think of my pregnancy with Zoë, which *was* full of
worry, as I expected it would be.

When I was fourteen weeks pregnant with Zoë, I developed a
blood clot and woke in the middle of the night with my pajamas

covered in blood. There were ultrasounds, and I was put on partial bed rest. But she was okay. I napped every day, stayed off my feet as much as possible, and worked part-time, mostly from home. I worried and I counted the weeks, the days.

When we were contemplating a second pregnancy, I thought that the twenty-fourth through twenty-eighth weeks of the pregnancy would be the most difficult for me. A baby born earlier than twenty-three weeks has virtually no chance of survival, but twenty-four-weekers have a 25 percent chance of survival after four or five months in intensive care, after months on ventilators, after umbilical catheters and IVs in their heads and arms, after feeding tubes taped to their faces, after complications that you only learn about if you are forced to live through them. So I thought I'd be terrified when I reached this point in the pregnancy. But strangely, I wasn't. Oh, I was careful, watching myself for swelling and trying to rest as much as possible. But I actually breathed a sigh of relief when I woke up and knew I was carrying a viable fetus. And then I held my breath and counted more.

And suddenly I was thirty-three weeks and more pregnant than I had ever been, and it was as if it were my first pregnancy. Donny and I would watch our little bugger roll and flip in my belly in the evenings and say *This is incredible!*

At thirty-nine weeks and four days, I was wheeled into the operating room for a C-section. Everything was completely different from the first time. There was no vomiting, no dizziness, no whisking my baby away, no team of neonatologists waiting in the wings. Zoë cried as soon as she was pulled from me, and I was able to touch her right away.

I nursed her in the recovery room, and she latched on immediately. It felt so fabulously normal at the same time it was all new to us. There were no isolettes, no ventilators, no umbilical catheters, no IVs taped to her arms or her skull. Stella, who was four and a half and had become—at some point, without me knowing when—just "Stella" and not "Stella who was born at thirty-two weeks," was able to hold Zoë as soon as we were moved to a postpartum room. She sat patiently in the rocking chair, her legs dangling above the floor, and when Donny passed Zoë into her arms, she smiled down at her baby sister with pride and cooed in a high voice, "Hi, sweetheart. I'm your big sister." Then she looked up at me and said, "Isn't she the most precious baby ever?"

And I smiled at her through tears in my eyes. "Yes," I said. "She's just as precious as you were, sweetie. Just as precious as you."

I'm a teacher now. I help other women write the stories they need to write. Just last week I sat in a semicircle in a sunlit room, surrounded by women, mothers. Each had a pad of paper or a laptop open in front of her, and the sound of fingers tapping on keyboards and pens scratching across paper filled the room. Outside, a single crow cawed loudly, and leaves rustled in the breeze.

When I asked the women why they had come to the writing workshop, some said they wanted to record their birth stories and those moments with their children they didn't want to forget. Others were writing to make sense of incomprehensible losses and realities for which it had been impossible to plan. Some arrived with a desperate need to connect.

One after another they shared their writing, and with each hopeful and sometimes heartbreaking rush of words, with each mother's fear given voice, I felt the circle of my life expand.

"Your stories matter," I said. "Putting them down on paper and crafting them matters." That I know for sure.

Acknowledgments

I AM GRATEFUL TO MANY PEOPLE WHO INSPIRED and supported me in writing this book.

First, thank you to the University of Minnesota Creative Writing faculty, especially Charles Baxter, Julie Schumacher, and Patricia Hampl. Thank you to Charles Sugnet for feedback on an early draft of my manuscript. I'm grateful to my MFA colleagues for their support and careful reading—in particular, Marge Barrett, Bryan Bradford, Kevin Fenton, Amanda Fields, Sari Fordham, Kate Freeborn, Cheri Johnson, Laurie Lindeen, Rob McGinley Myers, Amy Shearn, Francine Marie Tolf, and Andria Williams.

I am indebted to my wonderful agent, Amy Burkhardt of Kimberley Cameron and Associates, for her editorial eye, her unflagging support, and her steadfast belief in this book. Thank you!

Many others provided support and encouragement during the writing of this book. Thank you to Diane Brown, Erin Erickson, Marti Erickson, Claire Haiman, Jess Hopeman, Kay Krhin, Laura and Mike LaFave, Kristine Miller, Paige Parranto, Bonnie Rough, Emily Sellergren, Margie Siegel, and Linda and Brian Siverson-Hall, as well as to Marilyn Bousquin, Jill Christman, Sonya Huber, and Caroline Grant and the *Literary Mama* family.

For financial support, I'm grateful to the Minnesota State Arts Board and to the Sustainable Arts Foundation for seeing the value in telling this story. Thank you to Lisa Belkin, formerly of the *New York Times,* and to the editors of *MotherVerse,* where portions of this book were initially published.

To the doctors and nurses who cared for us during the events of this book, I'm grateful for your knowledge, your skills, and your heart.

To Amy and Mark Spencer, thank you for your hope and optimism and for allowing me to tell some of your story here. This book is for you, too.

To my students, who, through telling their motherhood stories, helped me find the heart of my own. Thank you for your bravery.

A huge thank-you to Rob McGinley Myers and Rhena Tantisunthorn Refsland for helping to shape this book. It wouldn't be what it is without you. Thank you to Mary Mahoney and Laura LaFave for reading portions of my manuscript with their medical sensibilities.

I'm immensely grateful to Todd Orjala at the University of Minnesota Press for understanding my vision for this book. And thank you to the entire team at the University of Minnesota Press for helping to get it out into the world.

I couldn't have written this book or survived the events described here without my family. Thank you to my dad, David Hopper, and to my mom and step-dad, Nancy and Karl Olson. I know how lucky I am to have such loving and supportive parents. And to my in-laws, especially Dave and Armelita Gramenz, thank you for welcoming me into your family. I'm grateful to my sisters, Rachel Hopper and Sara Hopper, for their friendship and laughter and for being such an important part of my life. To my grandpa, Spencer Nelson, my aunt, Julia Colman, and my friends Mimi Davidson and Juanita Garciagodoy: you continue to inspire me and live on in my heart.

Finally, Donny: thank you for your love and support, your generosity in allowing me to write about our lives, and for your belief in this book when I questioned it. To our daughters, Stella and Zoë: thank you for your daily gift of laughter and love. I am grateful for you every day. This story is for you.

Kate Hopper teaches writing online and at the Loft Literary Center in Minneapolis, where she lives with her husband and two daughters. She is the author of *Use Your Words: A Writing Guide for Mothers* and an editor at *Literary Mama*. For more information about her writing and classes, visit http://www.katehopper.com.